Western Trout Fly Tying Manual Volume II

By Jack H. Dennis, Jr.

Photographs and Cover by Dan Abrams
Illustrations by Mike Stidham

Editorial Assistance and
Production Management
By Bruce E. James

Production by Riddell PhotoGraphics
Typesetting by Jones Boys/Printers
Printing
By Sun Lithographing Company
Salt Lake City, Utah U.S.A.

Snake River Books
Jackson Hole, Wyoming

ISBN 0-937-556-00-9

Dedicated to the Fly Fishermen
Who Have Made This Book Possible

Dan Bailey

Mary and Don Martinez

Bud Lilly

Pat and Sig Barnes

Son, God made this valley for us. Never abuse its beauty nor its wildlife, love it and it will always take care of you. Remember, men will come and men will go, but the streams and mountains go on forever!

Bob Carmichael to his son shortly before his death.

Bob Carmichael

Jim Poor

ACKNOWLEDGEMENTS

Deep appreciation to the following:

to my family: my wife, Sandy; my children, Brian, Amy and Ann, for their many hours of patience.

to Dan Abrams, whose photos and editing made the book possible.

to Bruce James, as production manager, whose patience and persistance kept me writing and somewhat organized.

to Mike Stidham, whose artistic talent graces this book and was always there with the right drawing.

to Ed and Lee Riddell — graphics and design — without their efforts I would have been lost.

to Felix Buchenroth, my fishing banker, who believed in my book.

to Blaine Hall, my printer, whose technical knowledge and friendship has been invaluable.

to all of my fishing friends, whose encouragement made it all possible.

CONTENTS

PREFACE

After the success of **Jack Dennis' Western Fly Tying Manual,** Volume I, it became apparent that our many friends wanted a follow up book. During the past four years, I have taken the time to gather some interesting information about a selection of new and successful fly patterns which I hope will be useful to the reader. The imitations represented in this book are the contributions of many experts and amateurs who are developing new, exciting patterns for our western fishing.

In Volume One, I remarked that the West didn't seem to get the notice it richly deserved. Now things are different! The lure of the great streams — the Madison, the Yellowstone, the Snake, the Deschutes and the Big Hole — brings anglers from all around the world to cast to the trout of these fabled waters. Whether they flock to the frenzied stonefly hatches of fast waters or to catch the famous green drake hatch on the Henry's Fork, all have something in common...they are seeking a respite from the routine and the pressures upon their lives by spending a little time on a special piece of this planet that God has created for the pleasure of fishing.

The West has been blessed with some wide open spaces, high craggy peaks, clear rushing rivers, cold deep lakes, wide flowing springs and an abundance of trout. With the hopes and prayers of the fly fishing fraternity, we hope that new regulations designed to enhance our wild trout fisheries, along with a growing desire to protect what is free and beautiful, will continue.

We, as fly fishermen, owe it to ourselves to make sure that our wonderful western streams are preserved, and that anglers in the generations to come will enjoy them as much as I have for the past thirty years.

Come and share some special moments in our West...the time when the sun drops behind the mountains, and the fish are biting almost as well as the mosquitos! Or those precious moments in the morning when the awakening sun first breaks across the quiet, gray mountains and you are shivering, not so much because of the cold, but rather in anticipation of a large trout.

Or maybe it's a bright, hot, mid-afternoon when nothing seems to be working and you decide to rest along the cool grassy bank. You try to forget how lousy you felt that morning after a night drinking West Yellowstone dry, while you tried to convince your friend how big that brown you released really was. Or the time on a bleak, chilly opening day of the season when the guides of your line freeze and you do too, but the hope of catching that first trout keeps you standing and shivering in 30 degree weather.

The West means a lot to all of us. To some it means fishing all day long and not seeing another person. To others it's the remembrance of the time you chased that ornery old bull moose out of the middle of your favorite fishing hole, but, instead, you ended up high in a pine tree. To a few it is recalling the time you were drifting down your favorite river at the peak of the best hatch, only to find out your friend had never rowed a boat, and you were stuck at the oars.

The memory that I think really symbolizes the West is that particular evening when the crickets are chirping and the sun drifts slowly behind the snowcapped mountains. Several Northern Canadian honkers glide overhead playing their own special Sound of Music. The pesky mosquitos are darting and buzzing by your ears. Coyotes have begun their evening song on a distant hill. Suddenly in the distance you hear a trout rise and there is a slow whirl in the velvet-smooth spring creek. As you sneak gently along the reed covered bank, two green headed mallards land in front of you. As they quack loudly a few yards away, you think to yourself, "They never do that during hunting season".

Suddenly, it happens! With a whip of immense tail, a loud slurp and a giant ring on the water, there he is — the lord of the stream — your trophy! There is the challenge — you and the fish. These are our memories.

Please come and join me! This book is for you, my friends, the fly fishermen who join in a common admiration for fly fishing and for our favorite place, the West.

NOTES TO MY FRIENDS

I have always claimed to be a practical man, and believe in a simplified approach to my fishing. In the upcoming chapters, you will find a concise and straight forward approach to the flies shown in the manual. I tried to bring you some new and exciting patterns, but also we have quite a few of the older, standardized western patterns we did not include in our first book.

With today's emphasis on matching the imitation to the natural, we offer a practical approach to this representative school of fly tying. I believe entomology to be an important and valuable tool for the enterprising fly tyer and fly fisherman, but it isn't essential to have a biology degree and know every insect by its Latin name. A good basic working knowledge of mayflies, stoneflies, caddis, and others will be important to you and help you enjoy the spirit of fly fishing.

This book isn't a study in entomology, but you will learn some working basics and the relationship of the natural to the imitation you tie. However, to learn more about insects, and why trout react the way they do, let me suggest a couple of fine books. One book, **Nymphs** by Ernie Schwiebert is the bible for learning about those mysterious underwater little creatures. **Selective Trout** by Doug Schwisher and Carl Richards is an instructive, classic study of the relationship of fly tying to stream entomology. Another book by Ernie Schwiebert is **Matching the Hatch**. It was one of the first guides to learning the basics of streamside entomology. Another excellent book is Al Caucci and Bob Nastiasi's **Hatches**, which outlines times, cycles and theories of insect hatches.

These books will help you to wade through the somewhat difficult task of learning all about the strange little insects that frequent our fishing waters. The more you learn about the important insects of the streams you fish, the better your success will be in taking larger fish. Be practical in your approach. Gather the information that you feel necessary and apply it to your fishing.

FLY MATERIALS, TOOLS AND OTHER GOODIES

Feathers Hair and Fur

By Frank Johnson and Rich Anderson

When not busy inventing flies, Frank Johnson can be found with his partner Rich Anderson at Streamside Anglers, their business in Missoula, Montana. There, they offer a guide service as well as selling quality flies and fly fishing paraphernalia to dealers and the public at large.

The most significant change in fly tying and fly fishing over the past twenty or so years is that there are so many more of us doing it. This is not all bad — there is strength in numbers. Another good aspect of this incredible increase in fly tying is that we are discovering exciting new tyers who are developing new patterns, tying techniques, materials and generally adding to our knowledge of fly tying and fishing.

On the other hand, however, the increase in tying and fishing has created a very competitive situation both for the tyer and fisherman. As tyers we are faced with actual and apparent shortages of the tying materials we covet so. Many of our favorite materials have become virtually impossible to obtain. The disappearence of materials has been caused by several factors: Laws and regulations have been enacted to protect (and rightfully so) many animals and birds that were formerly used in fly tying; changes in poultry growing technology have eliminated many of the feathers we like to use, and last but not least, many of our domestic plucking and processing operations have gone out of business because it is no longer profitable to cater to the fly tyers of the world. Europe and Japan and other countries are putting pressure on material supplies because of increasing activity there.

The apparent shortage of materials is due partly to the increase in tying activity outstripping the current supplies of materials. Throughout the world new sources of materials are being developed to keep up with the increasing demand. Another, and perhaps the most significant, reason for our materials shortage is the fact that today's tyers demand much higher quality fly tying materials than did the tyers of a quarter of a century ago. Today's fly tyers are much better educated in our art. The mass eruption of fly tying and fly fishing literature over the past decade has, at least in theory, made experts of all of us. Because we now know more about the fish and his eating habits we are now dressing better imitations of the fishes natural food. Our imitations of today are much more sophisticated than they used to be.

The knowledgeable fly fisherman of today demands ultra quality flies. He is not interested in a pretty fly that looks 'fishy'. He is interested in a fly that imitates a specific species of mayfly or caddis. We must admit that we sometimes get a little carried away with our exact imitations. There are times when the fish just don't care — but we do. In our effort to catch a trout on a fly we often give a one pound fish credit for having a two pound brain.

At any rate we have established the fact that there are more fly fishermen and fly tyers than ever before tying more and better flies than ever, and that there may not be enough feathers and furs for everyone. What do we do about these problems? We learn to more fully utilize those materials that are available and discover new materials and substitutes for those that are gone.

Hackle

The hackle feather of the dry fly seems to be the key to good fly tying. Dry fly hackle quality is the standard by which we judge tackle shops and feather merchants. The hackle on the dry fly is that part which represents the legs of the insect and causes the dry fly to float. Hackle feathers from both the neck and saddle area of roosters are used for tying flies. Most hackles used for fly tying come from India, China, The Philippines or the U.S.

The quality of foreign necks seems to be deteriorating from year to year. This is probably due to overharvest and the taking of immature birds. Nearly all imported necks are a by-product of the food industry so we have little or no control as to quality. This apparent degradation of quality is also in part due to the great increase in demand for fly tying necks — we are using every neck we can find. On the other hand, our domestic hackle producers have made monumental strides. The Metz Hatchery is producing outstanding hackle — Henry Hoffman, the father of the "Super Grizzly" produces capes of incredible quality. Hackle quality, length and feather count on these outstanding domestic capes makes them worth every penny of the cost. It is such a delight to tie from these capes. Unfortunately these capes are neither available or affordable to all tyers.

Super Grizzly Neck

Selection of Hackle

When selecting necks a tyer has several decisions to make even before looking at necks. It is of primary importance for a tyer to select a neck exactly for his needs — in other words, if a tyer uses primarily size 12 hackle don't purchase a neck with a preponderence of size 16 hackle. If a tyer uses mostly size eight and ten hackle, don't buy a neck at all — use saddle hackle. All necks are different; when selecting necks in a fly shop one should look at all necks possible before making your selection. Nearly all dealers are more than willing to let their customers examine the capes. The tyer must have an equal amount of respect for the dealer and handle the necks with care. DO NOT BEND THE NECK SKINS. If it breaks, buy it! Some capes are very soft and flexible and some are very brittle. Dyed necks are invariably brittle and will break easily. To examine a neck hold the neck in one hand and pick up a few feathers with the other. A complete examination can thus be accomplished in this fashion without fear of embarrasment to you or the person selling the necks.

Quality Factors

Regardless of the color of the cape the following quality factors should be considered in the selection of necks.

GLOSS OR SHEEN: A shiny neck usually indicates good quality and maturity of the feathers. Sometimes, however, the decontamination process that all capes imported into the U.S. must go thru will tend to dull the feathers without causing any real damage.

WEB: For tying top quality dry flies it is necessary to use hackle that is as web free as possible. It is acceptable to use hackle that is webby for one third the length of the individual hackle fibre or barbule. Recent years have given us such new dry fly floatants as Dab, Gink, Free Float, and Dilly Wax that it is not as important as it once was that the hackle float the fly. These new preparations should nearly float a Mepps spinner.

FEATHER LENGTH: It is rare to find an imported neck with long enough feathers to tie a good western dry fly using only one hackle feather. In recent years an imported neck with an honest size 18 hackle long enough for four or five wraps is indeed rare. Such a neck should be considered to be a "AA", No. 1 neck and should be immediately purchased.

FEATHER SHAPE: Although it is not always a true indicator most hackles with sharply pointed tips turn out to be of very good quality. Immature hackles tend to be rounded on the tips. Close examination of expanded hackle feathers will show that on some necks the hackles are very tapered and on others the individual hackle fibres are much more uniform in length.

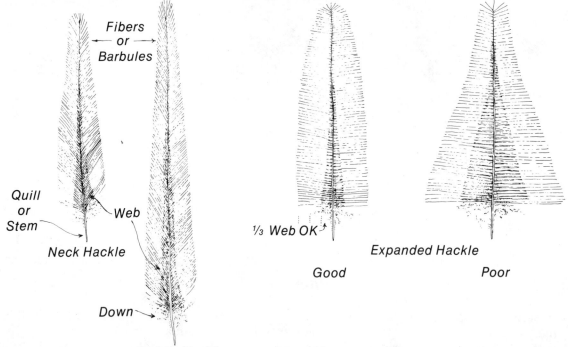

NECK HACKLE OR SADDLE HACKLE? Whenever possible a tyer should use saddle hackle. Unfortunately it is seldom that we can find saddle hackle any smaller than size ten. In the case of grizzly saddle it is unusual to find a size ten at all except on the very finest saddle capes. Saddle hackle is desirable for several reasons. First it is normally much longer than neck hackle. Secondly saddle is much more web free. Thirdly the barbules are of much more uniform length. Saddle has a much finer stem or rib which makes wrapping the hackle much easier and allows the wraps of hackle to be closer together, allowing heavier hackling of flies. Last but not least; saddle hackle is much less expensive than neck hackle.

Hackle Color

Natural hackle colors range from white or cream to brown and from grey to black with nearly conceivable combination of these colors. Those colors that don't occur in nature are easily made by any of several dyeing process.

Within the spectrum of natural hackle colors there are certain genetic hackle quality characteristics that go along with each color. Along with the color descriptions that follow are comments regarding quality characteristics of most of the colors. These comments apply to imported necks rather than the domestic necks. Our fine domestic necks are of superb feather quality regardless of color.

WHITE OR CREAM: A pure white neck is very rare. Most necks that we call white are actually cream or off-white. White hackle is normally very poor quality, and cream is only slightly better. These necks are generally soft and the web extends quite far up the feather.

GINGER: This elusive color name fills the color spectrum from cream to light brown. The most popular and sought after shade is the color of straw. This straw or light ginger color is very rare. In one thousand necks imported from India we find only five or ten that are of good quality. The Metz Hatchery is producing some very beautiful light ginger necks and hopefully there will soon be enough to go around. Hackle quality in ginger varies much from neck to neck but usually is better and even good in the darker shades of ginger.

BADGER: Badger hackle color is from white to dark ginger with a dark brown to black center. It is difficult to find badger hackles in the very small sizes (18 and smaller). Although there are not a great number of dry fly patterns that require badger, the feathers are very popular for use on streamer patterns. When dyed these necks make excellent dun or olive. Badger hackle quality is usually excellent.

BROWN: Probably the most used of all hackle colors (and the most common color found in nature). For our purposes as fly tyers brown means any shade from cinnamon (Light Brown) to the color of cocoa (Dark Brown). Brown hackle quality ranges from good to excellent.

COACHMAN BROWN: Coachman is the darkest of the bown colors. It is a deep rich brown much like well aged and oiled leather. The general feather quality of coachman hackle is not as good as brown. Often the hackle barbules are somewhat curved and of a very fine texture which makes them appear to be soft.

FURNACE: These feathers are brown or coachman brown with a black center. As with badger it is rather unusual to find very small furnace feathers that are well marked. Fortunately there are few small flies that require furnace hackle. Furnace hackle is usually good quality but it should be noted that the black center in both furnace and badger is web.

BLACK: Natural black neck hackle from imported necks is usually of very poor hackle quality. For this reason it is best to use dyed necks for your black flies. Also, most natural black necks are not really as black as dyed black. A look at the underside of the feathers will reveal that they are grey.

GRIZZLY: This hackle color variously known as barred rock or Plymouth rock is recognizable as being a combination of black and white. Each feather has either straight or "V" shaped striped of black and white perpendicular to the stem of the feather. Feather quality in grizzly is highly variable because the birds (all domestic) are bred from many different crosses. Usually in any given lot of grizzly necks the darker necks will be the best feather quality.

BLUE DUN: Dun is a very hard color to describe because there are so many variations and shades. The basic dun color ranges from that of the light bluish-grey of cigarette smoke to the dark grey of the underside of a thunder cloud. When dealing with the dun colors it seems that each experienced tyer and feather dyer has a different idea of what a dark or medium dun should look like. We have put many names on the various shaded of dun. A medium dun to one tyer will be a dark dun to another. The same applies to the bronze dun and rusty dun. In many cases it is possible to use a dun color a little lighter or darker than desired with very satisfactory results. The reason for this is that the back side of most feathers is much lighter than the front or top and the hackle on the fly will appear to be lighter than the hackle on the neck. Also, hackle tends to assume the color of the body of the fly.

Dyed duns are made from either cream, badger, or very light variant necks. As a result, the hackle quality is that of the color from which it was dyed. The better hackle quality is that of the color from which it was dyed. The better hackle quality in dyed duns will be found in those necks that contain a little color.

The imported natural duns are rarely of good quality—they tend to reflect the worst qualities of both black and white. This is not the case with the fine domestic duns that are available today.
IRON BLUE DUN: Almost Black—very dark dun.
RUSTY BLUE DUN: A medium dun with flecks of brown or ginger.
VARIANTS: Multi-colored necks not fitting into any specific color catagory are called variants. Nearly half of all imported necks are variants. Almost all are of excellent feather quality. Most feather importers try to dye as many as possible to salvage as many as possible, but sad to say many really outstanding necks go to waste because tyers are not adventurous enough to use them.
CREE Tri color necks consisting of white, brown and black barring are a real aid to the tyer. Many of these hackles can be used on any of the many western patterns that require both grizzly and brown hackle (Adams, Joe's Hopper, Humpy, etc.). These necks are usually fairly inexpensive and by using them a tyer can save his valuable grizzly hackle. Feather quality of Cree hackle is almost always good.
GINGER VARIANT: Sometimes called ginger grizzly. Barred much like grizzly with cream or light ginger and brown stripes. Some of these necks are very light and can be used effectively as a ginger substitute — the darker ones can be mixed with grizzly very effectively. Ginger Variant hackle is of excellent quality.

There are many other variants of almost any imaginable color combination. As tyers we should examine these necks whenever possible and evaluate them in reference to their usefulness in tying. Most suppliers offer variants at bargain prices. Many of our most outstanding professional and amateur tyers seek out these necks. The hackle quality is so good and the break-up of the color pattern creates a very buggy effect when properly applied.

Hair

Of all the changes that have taken place in fly tying in recent years, the most logical and practical change has been the increase in the use of hollow animal hairs. Deer, elk, moose, antelope, and caribou are the most popular. These hairs are readily available and inexpensive. Natural colors range from pure white to pure black — with all the browns and greys in between. Texture ranges can be found from very soft, straight and silky to very coarse, stiff and kinky. The incorporation of more hair into fly tying has opened new vistas to the fly tyer. The Troth Elk Hair Caddis is a fine example of the utilization of hair. Fluttering Stones, Goddard Caddis, Elk Hair Humpies and extended bodied drakes are samples of just a few of the very diverse applications that we can find for hollow hair.

Selection of hollow hair should be keyed to the particular fly that is being tied. For a size 10 Humpy the hair can come from the middle of the back of a deer or elk. For a size 18 Humpy the hair should come from the foreleg of the same animal or from the coastal deer which has very short fine hair.

When tying tails and wings, elk hair or moose hair are more desirable than deer because they have less tendency to flare and are more durable than deer. Deer hair, however is still our favorite for spinning bodies and muddler type heads. Antelope and caribou are both good materials for spinning because they are ultra hollow. Sometimes it is difficult to find these in consistent quality — they sometimes tend to be rather brittle and will break under thread pressure.

Moose body hair has become popular over the past few years for tying tails on dry flies and wing cases and legs on nymphs. This material can also be used for wings on dry flies. Close examination of most moose hides will reveal that the legs have areas of very fine silver grey hair. This hair makes beautiful wings and tails and is virtually indestructable.

When selecting hair — whether it be deer, elk or moose — look for straight, clean hair with even tips and a minimum of the fine fuzzy underfur that causes us so much trouble. If the hair is to be used for wings and tails examine the tips to insure that they are as even as possible and that the color pattern of the barring is consistent. Mule deer is usually not as good as whitetail or coastal deer for this purpose.

Tanned hide rather than cured hide is most desirable. The tanning process cleans the hair and makes it easier to work with. It also helps to eliminate the potential of insect infestation. (All fly tying feathers, furs and hairs should be stored in plastic bags or other closed containers with some moth balls or crystals.)

If untanned hide is used it can be made much more workable if it is washed in hot water and laundry detergent. It should then be pressed flat or tacked out and allowed to dry thoroughly. A little trick that will make the hollow hairs easier to handle is to sprinkle them with a small amount of baby powder. This baby powder, besides smelling good, does several things to make tying easier: it eliminates static electricity, it makes the under fur slick and thus easier to remove, and it allows the hairs to slide into the hair evener much better.

If the opportunity to select hair from a complete hide presents itself a complete selection of hair types can be taken from a 3" to 6" strip from the middle of the hide, and by taking a leg or two. By taking a strip from the middle of the hide you get an amount of the white belly hair, a selection of the long straight side hair for spinning, and from the middle of the back you get the finest, darkest most distinctly barred hair for wings and tails. If it is necessary to mail order your materials you will do better if you specify to the supplier the type of hair you want or the purpose for which you are buying the hair. A good selection of hollow hair types should be as important to a fly tyer as having a good selection of necks. Suppliers of materials are beginning to understand that there is, in fact, more than one type of hair and are more than willing to work with tyers in finding the hair for the job.

Furs and Dubbing Materials

Many tyers still utilize natural furs for all of their dubbing materials. Traditional materials such as muskrat, mink, beaver, rabbit and others are still very popular. Many tyers feel that the natural color, sheen and buoyancy characteristics of natural fur exceed those of synthetics. There are, however, new synthetic dubbing materials available that in many respects are much better than the natural furs. Many professional and top amateur tyers are very enthusiastic and vocal about these new materials. Fly-Rite poly dubbing, Spectrum dubbing, and Seal-Ex are just a few.

The synthetics are available in an extremely wide range of colors selected and blended specifically to imitate natural fur or to imitate the more popular insect colors. When selecting synthetic dubbing a tyer should try to find a material with the texture that is easiest for him to use. Some of these materials are rather difficult to use. A variety of these materials that can be mixed and blended will form a nucleus for an almost limitless selection of colors.

VANISHING MATERIALS

By Frank Johnson and Rich Anderson

Over the years, a large number of feathers and furs have become unavailable. Generally these materials are obtained from animals that are endangered or nearly extinct and thus protected by the U. S. or other governments. The list of these animals and birds grows each year and as it does, tyers can expect to suffer more shortages.

In order to overcome the effects of these disappearing materials we must find and develop suitable substitutes for the materials that are no longer available. As conservationists, we tyers and fishermen would be more than foolish if we would knowingly support or contribute to the further disappearance of our birds and animals today. There are hardly any materials for which we can't find suitable substitutes.

Jungle Cock Feather

JUNGLE COCK   This beautiful eyed feather from India has been protected for quite a number of years now. So far, the best substitute has been the plastic eyes which are painted on. We use them but no one likes them.

At this time *Streamside Anglers* is working with several firms in India in an effort to duplicate the real Jungle Cock feather with a chicken feather painted by hand. These painted feathers will no doubt be expensive, but they will be hard to tell from the original. To most trout fly tyers the loss of Jungle Cock feathers is no great loss, but those of us who appreciate the classic beauty of a full-dress salmon fly or brilliant steelhead fly sorely miss these beautiful feathers.

PARTRIDGE HACKLE   For a number of years demand declined along with supply but now with the upsurge of flies like soft hackles, we again have a real need for partridge hackle. For many years the major portion of our supply of partridge feathers were imported from Europe, but that practice is now prohibited.

Today tyers who are also bird hunters are supplying themselves and their friends with this type of feather from a number of species of partridge and grouse.

For the rest of us, hen chicken body plumage and saddle hackle are serving as a suitable substitutes.

Not only does the hen chicken feather serve as partridge hackle, but it is available in a wide range of colors which are inviting new applications. Imagine the most common and available feathers on earth finally discovered by fly tyers.

MOTTLED OAK TURKEY   Where these feathers came from and why they are no longer available is something of a mystery. Other than in occasional small quantities, these feathers are seldom available today. Most western tyers are now using bleached barred turkey pointers for our hoppers. For our Muddlers we are using either bleached barred turkey feathers or turkey tail feathers. Neither of these substitutes is exactly like the original but they do a good job — sometimes fooling the fishermen and almost always fooling the fish.

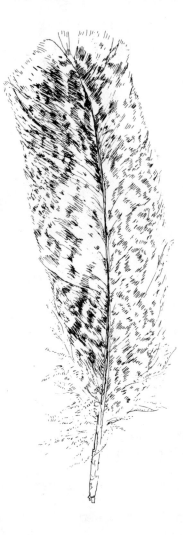

Mottled Oak Turkey   *Turkey Tail Feather*

At this time it appears that there is no great new source for mottled oak turkey, but our substitutes are adequate and in good supply. There are a number of producers making an effort toward again producing oak turkey but so far they all seem to be either too light, too dark, or too small.

CONDOR A material which, sad to say, most of todays tyers have never seen. In years past condor was used for feelers, tails, and bodies and was highly prized for its durability. Today we are using the leading edge from goose and turkey primaries. Both of these materials provide excellent substitutes.

SEAL FUR Our substitutes for baby seal fur do not yet duplicate the natural sheen and texture of seal but Poul Jorgensen's Seal-Ex (R) is so close as to be nearly ideal. Mr. Jorgensen's knowledge of tying and materials has allowed him to create a very good substitute.

POLAR BEAR Some steelhead fly tyers lost their most important materials when we ran out of it. This material has been for many years the principal winging material on the most popular steelhead patterns. Many steelhead fishermen still feel their flies aren't as effective without the gloss and translucence of polar bear.

Today, steelheaders are using calf tail, bucktail, Rocky Mountain Goat hair and various synthetic hairs. The calf tail has emerged as the most popular polar bear substitute. Some tyers go so far as to wash and iron their calf tails to make the hair as straight as possible — this is a good practice for trout fly tyers, because calf hair that is as straight as possible is much easier to work with.

DYEING FLY TYING MATERIALS FOR THE HOBBIEST

By Mike Wilkerson

Mike Wilkerson is the wholesale manager for "Streamside Anglers" in Missoula, Montana. This position requires that he dyes a lot of fly tying materials. He is also a professional fly tyer, which helps him to understand the needs of his customers.

It seems that sooner or later many fly tyers decide to dye their own feathers and furs. Unfortunately, the majority have little knowledge of the processes which are basic for successful dyeing, and their attempts end in frustration and failure. Valuable materials are often needlessly wasted and would-be dyers give up in disgust.

Actually, the dyeing of most fly tying materials, at least on a small scale, is uncomplicated and easy to manage if a person follows a few basic steps.

The equipment needed for dyeing materials is minimal and need not be expensive. Aside from the dyes and acetic acid, you need only a couple of containers, a pair of tongs and some device for stirring.

Porcelain and stainless steel pans are best for the dye bath, but if you don't have one, don't despair. Aluminum works and even coffee cans are adequate for small jobs.

You will use one of the pans for the dye bath and the other for a cold water rinse to set the dye. The tongs are helpful in handling the materials and a stick or spoon is used to mix the dyes and to stir the feathers and hair while they are in the dye.

Most of the dyes you use are acid dyes. These can be obtained from fly tying material outlets, and although relatively expensive, a little usually goes a long way.

Household dyes such as RIT are also useful, less expensive and generally easier to get. In fact, for a few colors, RIT is my first choice. Acetic acid, which is used in the dye as a catalyst to set the colors, can be obtained from photography shops or from the local grocery store in the form of white vinegar. Both work well, however, with the full strength acid you will need only about a teaspoon with each dye bath, and with the vinegar you may use a half a cup or more.

The first important step in successful dyeing is the preparation of the materials. Hair and feathers, especially those from water fowl, contain oils and grease which resist dyes. Materials must first be washed and soaked for at least an hour before they go into the dye.

A mixture of hot water and dishwashing detergent such as Dawn does an excellent job. This is followed by rinsing with hot or warm water until all the soap is gone. Then squeeze out the water and the dyeing process is ready to begin.

While you are rinsing the materials to be dyed, you should also be heating the water for the dye bath. When it is hot, but not boiling, add the dye. Generally it takes more RIT than acid dyes to get the same results, but in either case put in only small amounts, since additional dye can always be added later.

When the dye has dissolved in the water, put in your materials. Agitate them frequently and after they have been in the dye for a few minutes add the acetic acid.

Sitting next to the dye bath is your second pan, which contains cold water. This will stop the action of the dye and when the dyed materials are placed in cold water, you will have a better idea of the true colors. This process may be repeated several times until the desired color and shade is obtained.

Keep in mind that wet materials appear darker than when they are dry, so periodically pick a feather or piece of hair from the dye, dry it as quickly as possible to examine its true color. When you are satisfied with the color, remove the materials and rinse again in cold water. Rinse them as dry as possible and then prepare them for the final drying.

Small pieces of hair and fur, as well as individual feathers, may be placed on paper to air dry. Necks and saddle patches should be lightly brushed and laid flat between layers of newspaper with enough weight on top to keep them from curling. Change the papers when they become damp, and in a few days your necks and saddles should be dry.

Large sections of hair with the hide attached should be tacked to a board with the hair side down until they are dry.

If you want to use a dye bath for more than one operation, it's fine as long as the dye is clean. Avoid, however, dyeing hair first and then using the same bath for feathers. Grease from the hair will gum up the feather fibers and create an unwanted mess.

Now that we've gone through the dyeing processes, let's examine some of the common colors you may wish to dye and any special requirements connected with them.

WOOD DUCK Due to the scarcity and high price of real wood duck, most fly tyers today use dyed mallard as a substitute. This is an easy color to dye and normally takes just a short time in the bath.

Many of the acid wood duck dyes that we have used recently seem too brown, so we mix it with yellow at a ratio of 15 parts yellow to one part wood duck. The result is a color which is almost identical to the real thing. Incidently, wood duck dye can be used on hair to dye various shades of tan.

OLIVE One of most popular colors for the tyer, olive is also easy to dye. Because many of the acid dyes labeled olive tend towards a yellow-brown, we prefer to use RIT avocado. It works well with both feathers and hair and dyes quickly. If the RIT avocado is a bit too green for your taste, add some yellow until you get the shade of olive you desire.

YELLOW, RED, ORANGE I have lumped these three colors together because they are very easy to dye and no special preparations or mixtures are necessary for good results.

BROWN Here again, RIT is the preferred dye for this color. Chestnut and cocoa work well and I use them for practically all of our brown dyeing.

Used in a straight form these colors have a reddish cast. You can eliminate this by:
1.   Put a piece of material in the dye bath to absorb the red out of the dye before you put in the materials you wish to dye.
2.   Add a small amount of yellow. (about a teaspoon)
   To darken brown RIT, add a little black.
   Very good brown can also be achieved with hair by using black acid dyes and removing the hair from the bath and setting the color before it turns black.

GINGER   A much sought after color, this one is, unfortunately rare in quality necks. A good substitiue can be made by dyeing white necks with an equal amount of gold and tan RIT. The result is a straw color which is very like a genuine light ginger. This dye takes very quickly, and the dyer should inspect the feathers every few moments. If they stay in the dye too long, they will turn out dark.

BLACK   This is by far the hardest of all colors to dye. It takes longer, as much as three or four days, and the dye bath needs to be hotter. The trick is to get the bath hot enough so that the dye penetrates the materials without burning them.

One technique which works well in dyeing feathers black is to bring the dye bath to a full boil, and then remove it from the heat. When the bubbles have subsided, then put in the feathers and about 15 minutes later add the acetic acid. Let it set overnight, and the next day check out the color. If it isn't black enough heat the bath again (don't boil) and add more dye. Let it set overnight again and it should be black.

CONCLUSION   Since many of the colors you wish to dye require mixing, it is good idea to keep records. By doing this you will be able to get more succcessful results as well as eliminate previous mistakes.

Always proceed slowly, and never assume that particular dyes or combinations of dyes will always react the same on different materials.

Various types of feathers and hair will absorb colors at different rates with the result that your dyed materials may not turn out as you had expected.

If you follow procedures outlined in the beginning of this article, you should achieve good results with your dyeing and you will certainly add a new and interesting dimension to your fly tying experiences.

ABOUT VISES

From Left to Right Price Vise, HMH Standard, Thompson Mod. A

By Jim Chestney

We thank Jim Chestney for writing the following article for us. Jim is a very talented professional fly tyer from Palatine, Illinois. Aside from his fly tying talents, Jim is also chairman of the advisory board to Thompson Tool Co. for product development.

There are a great many styles of vises available to today's fly tyer, each one supposedly having some special feature according to the manufacturer, which gives it a decided advantage over all others. Frankly, few if any of them have any apparent advantage, other than the quality of workmanship and the reliability of the manufacturer. So, when buying a vise the purchaser should rely chiefly upon the above criteria, because these are the features that will render the most satisfaction in the long run.

There are several methods that vise makers have adopted to close the jaws of their vises but one method is by far the most prevalent and has stood the test of time far longer than all others. The one being referred to is the tapered collet (jaw) and sleeve type such as the THOMPSON Model A. This cam operated type closes the jaws by drawing the tapered neck of the jaws into a tapered cone neck of the sleeve. The constricting pressures generated by this action closes the jaws and provides a very rigid support for the hook. The fact that the THOMPSON A vise has been the most copied vise in the annals of fly tying speaks overwhelmingly in favor of its overall design and functional capabilities. However, vises with other methods of jaw closure such as the side cam and thrust screw are still being produced to some degree.

A really first rate vise will have relatively smooth and unobstructed surfaces. Jaws should be highly polished externally and have flat and smooth jaw surfaces internally, which effectively hold a hook because of the friction created between the jaw and hook surfaces. Cutting serrations or teeth into the internal surfaces of the jaws does not necessarily improve the holding qualities of the vise. In fact, many manufacturers actually believe serrated jaws are less efficient because the serrations act as bearing surfaces thereby reducing the actual metal to metal contact between the jaws and the hook. Also, there is some likelihood that the serrations could score the hook surface thereby increasing the chances of breakage.

Jaw shape or external design is another point of contention which has been around and discussed for years. Quite frankly, the shape of the jaws has very little affect on the holding capacity of the vise. Rather, the shape will have a more definite effect on the user's ability to gain access to the hook for the various tying procedures. Jaw size, on the other hand, will have a direct relation to the holding capabilities of the vise. If you are only tying flies ranging in sizes from 16 up to 2, you can easily get by with the standard jaws furnished by the manufacturer. But, if your tying runs the gamut from midges to the salt water monsters, you may want a special set of midge jaws and you definitely will require a more massive set of jaws, which provide greater frictional surfaces, for the salt water ties. Thus, it becomes apparent that a vise with interchangeable jaws is a realistic approach to consider.

Knowing how to use and care for your vise is a topic that has been noticeably absent from the many works on fly tying. This is a point that I find rather disturbing because the tyer's ability to dress a really top quality fly is directly contingent upon getting the utmost efficiency from the vise being used. Regardless of the make or style vise that one may own, they all are equipped with jaws that will have improved holding capabilities if the hook is inserted in the jaws properly. In other words, there is a right way and a wrong way of inserting a hook in a vise despite what some writers would have you believe.

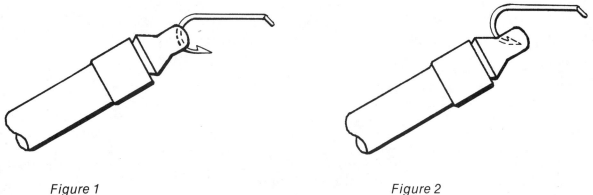

Figure 1   *Figure 2*

Illustration by B. Montwid

FIGURE 1 shows the correct hook placement in the vise jaws. In this position the maximum friction is being achieved because a parallel portion of the hook is in direct contact with the greatest mass area of the jaw tips. Even greater holding qualities could be gained if the hook were inserted more deeply into the jaws, but this would have the affect of largely restricting or prohibiting some tying operations. Naturally, this method of hook placement will require the tyer learn how to tie around the exposed hook point but with practice this is an easy task to accomplish.

FIGURE 2 shows an incorrect hook placement. With the hook in this position, the vise jaws are being asked to gain a rigid supporting hold on a tapered portion (point) of the hook. This prohibits maximum contact between the jaws and hook and results in vastly reduced holding power. Many tyers have approached me over the years with a problem of repeated hook slippage and I found in almost every instance they were inserting the hook in this fashion. After showing them the much better way of inserting the hook (figure 1), their problems vanished.

Finally, here are five points which, if remembered and followed, will make your tying hours more enjoyable and trouble free.

1... Don't attempt to get by with an inexpensive vise. Instead, choose a medium priced model by a reputable manufacturer. This will prove to be your best buy over the long haul.

2... Keep your vise correctly adjusted for the size hook being used. Collet type vises have a threaded adjustment bushing which is extremely easy to operate so if you are going to use a hook three (3) sizes larger or smaller than the one to which the vise had been previously adjusted ---- READJUST!!

3... Your vise is a fine precision instrument. Treat it accordingly. A periodic drop of high grade machine oil to the bearing surfaces (cam and sleeve cone) will prolong its life and make it work more efficiently. CAUTION: Wipe away any excess oil as it plays havoc with fur and feathers.

4... An occasional light coating of furniture or auto wax to all plated or oxide finished surfaces of your vise will keep it looking new and help prevent rust, chipping, and wear.

5... Never leave a hook inserted in your vise for prolonged periods of time. When not in use your vise's jaws should be free and unrestricted.

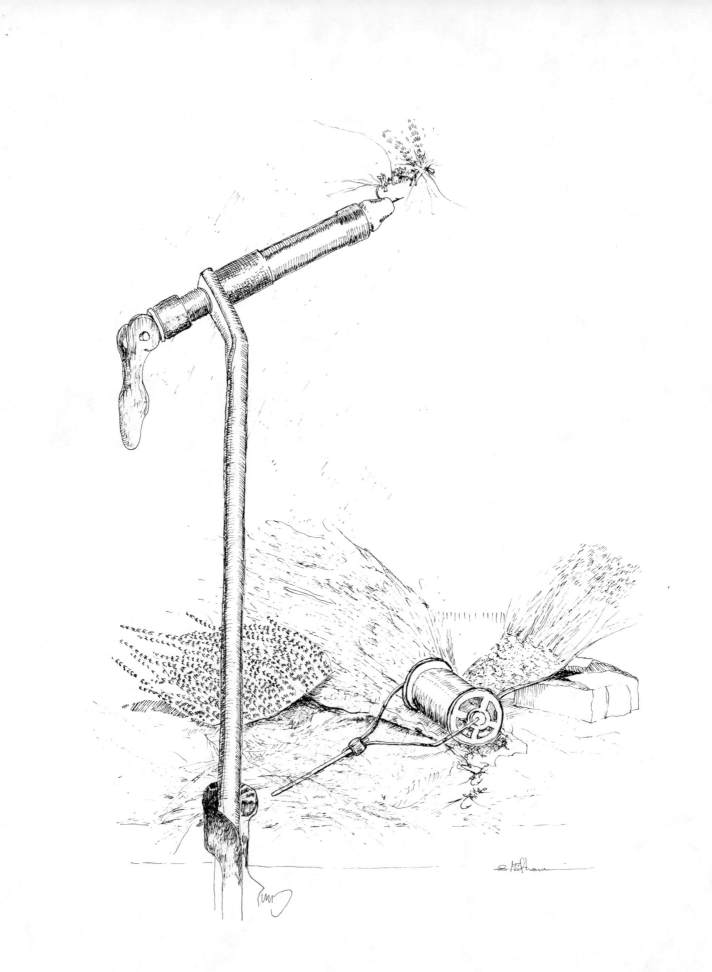

HAIR — THE FLY TYER'S NEMESIS

When fly tyers think about the first fly they ever tied, they think about a Wooly Worm, Brown Hackle, or a similar simple fly. My first venture into fly tying was not one of these patterns, but one of the most dreaded patterns for the fly tyer's vise — the Irresistible.

It all started as a youngster of 11 years, when I received a package in the mail from Norm Thompson Outfitters in Portland, Oregon. This first-class mail order shop had sent me a copy of a tantalizing catalog which, in addition to a good selection of hats, fine cane rods, and wispy gut leaders, featured a very interesting new fly pattern.

I sent an order and, in a few days, the mailman delivered a package containing four of the "floatinest fools" to ever crawl out of a fly box. In examining the Irresistible (as the new fly was named), I found a beautiful pattern, featuring a finely clipped deer hair body and a buggy-looking profile. A magnificent creature!

Looking at the Irresistible there in my hand, I knew what my immediate goal in life would be. I had to learn to tie that fly!

To the dismay of my mother and the delight of my father, I proceeded to buy a big share of a local sporting good store's inventory of furs, feathers, and fly tying tools. Then, armed with a pad of paper, I marched down to the Denver City Library, and there, I leafed through every fly tying book I could find in an effort to learn about fly tying and especially how to tie the Irresistible.

That evening, I dashed home and attempted to translate my notes and sketches into reality on my new Thompson Model A vise. It was a classic struggle of man against material and man against deer hair, and I found there was a lot more to fly tying than clipping deer hair and twirling thread.

After several months of struggles, failures, and some successes, I learned to tie flies. But I just couldn't master that ornery little critter, the Irresistible. The more I tried, the worse it got, and the more frustrated I became. I threw things, jumped up and down, cut thread, broke thread, and when I got it just right, the body twisted off. Nothing went right! I learned to tie the Adams, Wooly Worm, Royal Coachman, but still after a year, I hadn't mastered the Irresistible.

A year later, my new Norm Thompson catalog arrived, with its delectable offerings of fly tying and fly fishing goodies. Again, I thumbed through the fly section and looked at my archnemesis, the Irresistible. This time, appearing alongside the picture and description of the Irresistible, was a notice stating, "We need fly tyers — send us your samples — we pay cash for quality tied flies."

I thought, "This might be a chance for me to make money to buy some more materials." Since my father and grandfather had encouraged me about the good quality of the efforts from my tying vise, I decided to send a few samples to the folks at Norm Thompson's.

I asked my father to rummage through my fly box and pick out what he thought were my best patterns. Well, my father selected the flies, wrapped them carefully, and sent them off, accompanied by a neatly typed letter to the General Manager, Mr. Peter Alport. I never had a chance to see the letter, nor did I even know which fly patterns he picked from my box.

About two weeks later, a nicely engraved envelope addressed to "Mr. Jack Dennis, Jr." appeared in our mail box. I hurriedly tore it open and the letter stated, "Dear Mr. Dennis: We were quite impressed with the flies you sent us, especially the Irresistible. We would like to submit the following order to you for the flies we have listed. Enclosed you will find your samples returned with an order for each that we would like."

"Irresistible?" I thought. "I didn't send them any Irresistible!" I then looked at the next page, which was a purchase order for 144 dozen Irresistibles, plus some Adams, and several other patterns which had been sent. There, staring at me, was an order for 144 dozen Irresistibles. That was 1,728 hard-to-tie flies they expected from me. The initial excitement of the order was lost as I tried to figure out what had gone wrong. Finally, it dawned on me what had happened. The Irresistible I had originally bought from Norm Thompson had been in the fly box from which my father had chosen the samples. When I looked through the box, I saw that pattern was missing. My father didn't know that I didn't tie Irresistibles and he thought that particular fly in my vest was nicely done, so he had submitted it to them. Boy, was I in trouble! I didn't know what to do.

After recovering from shock, I decided the only way to get out of this tight spot I found myself in would be to master the Irresistible. I had to find out what I was doing wrong, and then learn to do it right.

The Denver Sports Show was being held that week, and one of booths at the Sports Show was a fly tying booth provided by Hank Roberts of Boulder, Colorado. I always liked to hang around Hank's booth and watch some of the fly tyers as they demonstrated their skills.

There were a couple of fly tyers who were whipping out a variety of patterns. One little, oriental girl was tying some Royal Wulffs. I mustered my courage and walked up to her and nonchalantly asked her if she could tie an Irresistible for me. She threw up her hands, exclaiming, "No, no, I don't tie that fly!" Mr. Roberts had overheard my question to the tyer and walked up and asked me if he could help me. Thus began a long friendship that has gone on for many years.

The Hank Roberts Fly Company was the main supplier of most of the flies in the Colorado area at that time, and he had employed several girls who tied some very good Adam's Irresistibles. I explained my problem to Hank to see if he could help me. He asked to see some of my patterns, which I just happened to have in my back pocket. I'll never forget as he grabbed hold of one of my neatly tied wonders. A quick flip of the hand revealed that the body was not tied on tight enough as it quickly slipped off the hook and into Hank's hands. He looked down at me and said, "Young man, if you are going to be a commercial fly tyer, one of the first things you must learn is a fly must be durable. It must be able to catch fish after fish and hold together. No matter how well it's tied, if it isn't durable it is not a good fly. Durability is the key to fly tying, and this quality is the key to constructing a good hair fly."

Hank then revealed to me the first secret in tying the Irresistible — you must have soft, coarse hair from either a soft, tanned deer hide or, preferably, a caribou hide — a short, dense, coarse hair. Caribou hair! The thought had never occured to me. Hank further explained that caribou hair flared much easier and it was much simpler to learn to tie the fly with that material. After getting the hang of it, deer hair could be used if a darker color was needed.

After a quick, urgent search, I found a source for caribou hair. It came in small, tanned strips, and was very easy to work with. The caribou hair packed tightly and readily flared as I wrapped it to the hook. I soon mastered the knack of getting the hair tied tightly to the body. I found that a base of thread wrapped along the shank of the hook helped to securely anchor the hair as well as enhancing the amount of flare I was after. After hours of practice, I had mastered this spinning and flaring operation, and now I was ready to tackle the art of the body of this fly.

I leaned that after the hair had been flared on the hook, that it was better to half-hitch and trim the body before the hackle and wing were put on. Trimming from the head to the tail in a tapered manner formed a nice bullet-like body which was essential to the balance of the fly.

It was a long summer, but I finished that one hundred and forty-four dozen Irresistibles. I had learned a lot about hair bodies during that time, especially about the importance of learning to select proper hair. From that point, I leaned to tie more Irresistibles with hair wings, Wulffs, Humpies, and a variety of other hair flies. As I became more and more proficient as a professional tyer, I became more and more interested in hair flies, and as it turned out, my reputation as a professional fly tyer was established through the tying of hair flies.

WORKING WITH HAIR

Many western patterns incorporate the use of hair for wings, bodies, and tails. Beginners often find hair difficult to work with and I'm constantly asked for helpful hints. I hope the following paragraphs will offer some assistance when working with hair.

The length and texture of hair will usually vary according to the part of the hide from which the hair was taken. The hair is generally long along the back and becomes shorter along the legs, thighs, and belly of the animal. The texture and density also varies with location on the hide. If at all possible, examine a full hide at a taxidermist's shop. This will allow you to examine the various textures at one time.

Of primary importance when working with any type of hair is to get a hide that has been completely dried or tanned. If the hide hasn't been tanned, be sure there is no flesh or decay on it. This is a very good breeding ground for worms that will soon destroy your precious fly tying materials.

Once you have obtained a hide, or part of a hide, be sure it is clean. This is especially important if you are allergic to the various pollens and dust that are often present in hides. A good, stiff brush, such as a dog brush, or wire comb is excellent for cleaning a hide. After brushing it, if you still find yourself sneezing, wash the hide in a bucket of water and dry it thoroughly. Usually, a tanned hide is fairly clean and also easier to work with than a stiff untanned hide.

After working with hair for a long period of time, your hands can become dry and rough. Baby lotion will prevent this from happening and will keep the hair from sticking to your fingers.

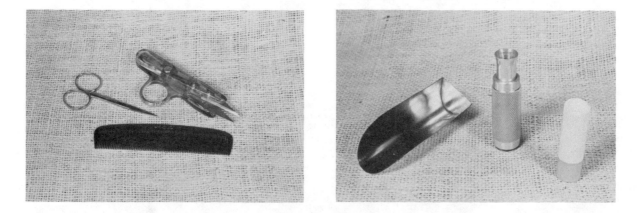

I am often asked what scissor is best for working with hair. This is a hard question to answer because hair wears out scissors faster than any other material. I like a pair of heavy-duty scissors for trimming the hair off the hide and fine-pointed scissors, such as the German Solingen scissor, for trimming hair flies such as Irresistible bodies. D. H. Thompson, Inc. makes an excellent scissor for working with hair called the Thompson Adjustable. It is an extra heavy-duty scissor with a nice fine point. The holes are covered with hard rubber, keeping them from digging into your fingers and large enough to easily put your thumb through. I am constantly amazed at all of the fly tying scissors with holes too small for the average set of fingers.

Another very popular scissor is the Wiss Quick Clips, which a lot of tyers are finding to be an inexpensive but durable scissor. These work on a principle similar to the Thompson Adjustable, but have replaceable blades and fit the hand very well.

A fly looks much neater, and is easier to tie, when all of the hair tips are even. This is easily accomplished with a hair stacker. There are several good hair stackers on the market today, but it is very easy to make one yourself. You can cut the screw end off of a tube of lip protectant (such as Lip-Saver) to make an excellent stacker. Clean it out thoroughly and rub the inside with an anti-static compound such as Bounce. You can also purchase a stacker through a tackle or fly tying shop. A particularly good one is put out by *Streamside Anglers* in Missoula, Montana and is also available through several fishing shops. Another fine one, patterned after a simple U-shaped scoop, is available through the *Dan Bailey Fly Shop* is Livingston, Montana. Dan's Hair Stacker is an excellent choice for the commercial tyer who needs to stack a lot of hair in a hurry.

Be sure to use a heavy thread when flaring hair on flies such as Muddlers or Irresistible bodies. Size "A" or "B" monocord works very well; rod wrapping thread also works. Heavy thread can wear a nick in your bobbin and cause it to cut the thread. Therefore, be sure to examine your bobbin regularly.

Durability is the key to a well-tied hair fly. A drop of good penetrating cement at the base of hair wings or a hair tail will make your fly last much longer. Don't use too much cement because you can turn your good floater into a sinking fly.

Working with hair is not as difficult as it first seems. Don't put too much hair on the hook. Start out with a small quantity and add a little more until you find the amount that is just right. Don't expect to sit down for your first time at the vise and turn out perfect hair flies. Realize that working with hair takes practice and a lot of perseverance.

Deer Hair

I believe one of the most important virtues of deer hair is its ability to display such a variety of textures. Along the back of a deer hide the hair can be very stiff and dark in color. Whereas along the flanks it is lighter and becomes a lot thicker. To understand hair and its use, you must become acquainted with the different types of deer hair available to the tyer.

The Eastern White Tail deer, which is usually where we obtain our bucktails, has body hair characterized by a fine silky texture. It is usually long and is especially hard to work when tying hair bodies. Along the edges of the hide, however, the hair can be used for tying tails and wings on flies such as the Wulffs.

33

The Eastern deer hair can vary in color from a reddish brown or dark brown to almost black. Usually the base of the hair is a light gray. However, I have seen a few hides where the hair has a distinct brownish tinge. For color and texture, especially when tying a fly with deer hair wings, the Eastern deer hair excells.

The white hair found near the rump on the Eastern White Tail deer can be used for tying hair wings. On an older and larger deer the white hair can be dyed and used on bass bugs. The older the deer, the more hollow the hair allowing a thicker body to be obtained.

The Western Mule deer can vary in color also. The body hair is usually a grayish brown during the latter part of the summer, and generally will change to various shades of gray by the time hunting season rolls around. However, the hides of some deer harvested during the archery season (which is usually during the latter half of August) have some interesting brown tones of brown mixing with gray.

One of the most common questions I get asked is "how do you select good deer hair?" This is a difficult task, especially when you are buying hair packaged in a plastic bag, hanging on a display rack. I will try to give some ideas on what to look for.

A young deer killed in the early part of the season, will have a thick coat of fairly even hair. Sometimes the hair will not be long enough for Muddlers or larger flies, but will make fine tying for small dry flies.

Usually the older the deer, the thicker and more hollow the hair will be. Generally try to select hides that have been taken from younger deer and those harvested in the early part of the season. As the season progresses and it gets closer to winter, the deer develop a heavier and thicker coat of more brittle hair. A thick fur-like undercoat also develops as the deer become conditioned for the cold winter months.

If you get hold of a whole hide, examine it carefully. Running along the back will be dark-tipped longer hair. This hair will be stiff and in most cases it will be unusable. Coming down the sides from the back ridge, the hair tends toward a charcoal gray color. In some cases this hair will be very good for tying humpys and other types of hair bodied flies. Further down the flanks of the deer the hair will become softer, thicker and be more adaptable for tying spun, hair-bodied flies, such as the Irresistible. One of my favorite places for obtaining hair for tying Humpies is around the neck. Here you get a good variety of color and also the hair is shorter in length. I might also mention that you can obtain hair from the legs of the deer that is very stiff and can be used for tails on dry flies or antennae and tails on nymphs.

As mentioned before, the tanning of a hide does make a difference in the texture of hair. In Mule deer however, the tanning process can work to the tyers benefit because this tends to soften the hair and make it much more usable. The hides of older animals are often better when tanned.

One of the suggestions I give many beginning fly tyers wanting to learn more about hair is to pay a visit to your local taxidermist. Usually he has several scraps left over from his work. This will give you a chance to examine all different types of hair, ones that are even, uneven, rough, course, soft or silky. If you are fortunate enough to live in an area where there are lots of deer being harvested, check into a place that buys hides. You can usually pay a few dollars and pick up some hides for tying. Buying a whole hide will give you a complete cross-secion of different types of hair, and you will have a chance to look through the hide to find the section best suited for your needs. You can usually find the hide-buying places around processing plants which specialize in handling game meat.

There are several other types of deer hair available: the Coastal Deer, Black-tailed deer, Mexican deer and other smaller sub-species. All will offer hair that can be useful for the fly tyer.

One of the most common problems beginning tyers have is the tendency to cut off more deer hair than they need. When they attach this to the hook the hair twists and turns all over the place. It is better to start off with a small group of hair and add more if needed, until you get the knack of picking the right amount for a particular fly.

Elk Hair

Elk hair is one of the fly tyers best friends. Elk hair has found its way into many of the dry flies we use today. The famous Wulff series of drys, developed by Lee Wulff and made popular by Dan Bailey of Livingston, Montana, makes extensive use of elk hair. Lee uses dark elk for a stiff tail on his Royal Wulff and medium brown elk for the tail and wings on his Gray Wulff.

The Blond Wulff is a perfect example of the use of light elk hair. On this fly both the tail and wings are made from the light flank hair of the elk. Besides being used on the Wulff patterns, both light and dark elk hair can be used to replace hackle fiber tails on many dry flies.

In the early forties, Dan Bailey began to replace hackle fiber tails with elk hair on flies such as, the Light and Dark Cahills, Adams and other popular dry flies. This practice is becoming more popular as the stiffness of hackles continues to decline.

The amazing thing about the elk is the variety of shades of color that are present on the same hide. The colors range from tan, through several browns, to chocolate brown on the legs.

Along the backbone of the elk the hair is long and wirey. This is perfect for ribbing small dry flies and making durable quill bodies on size sixteen to minute size twenty-six dry flies.

On the flanks, the hair is hollow, but not quite hollow and soft enough to be used for Irresistible bodies. The fact that it is somewhat stiff makes it very adaptable for use as wings, Humpy bodies, and tails. When used in a Humpy, the light colored flank hair matches many cream mayfly hatches.

Along the legs, the hair is darker colored and stiff. This is excellent for tails on nymphs and dry flies, and for feelers on some nymph patterns.

The density of the hair depends on the age and sex of the elk. A cow elk provides better hair for tying flies than a large bull. However, a young bull will have more medium and dark brown hair than is found on a young cow.

One of the best ways of obtaining elk hair is on a trip West. Visit one of the taxidermists in a popular hunting area, and you will find they usually will have a large variety of scraps left over from mounting elk heads. These can generally be bought for a nominal sum. Also, during the hunting season, raw elk hides can be purchased inexpensively from hunters. The hide is very thick and I advise you to tan it, because it is hard to dry. In parts of the East, elk hair can be very expensive, but in the Rocky Mountain area, where elk are abundant, the prices are lower and the quality is notably better. One good elk hide will last most fly tyers a lifetime.

Moose Hair

Moose hair is one of my favorite materials to work with. If you have already read my first book, you will notice that I have incorporated moose hair in many of my favorite patterns. In hair flies, such as the Humpy, moose hair makes the most durable tail obtainable. This is because it is much stiffer than elk hair in most cases. The only drawback that moose hair has, when used for tails, is its dark color. The shade changes very little; it is either dark brown or jet black.

However, the location of the hair on the hide is of primary importance in obtaining good tail material. Along the top of the moose hide, better known as the mane, the hair is hollow and very long. Here it will be white all the way up to the tip of the hair, where it then turns into black. However, some of the hair will be black all the way through to the base and will still be hollow.

The mane can be used for quill bodies on flies such as the Ginger Quill and other quill patterns. It makes an excellent substitute for stripped peacock quills, taking a lot less time and trouble. Select one large mane hair that is dark, and one that is mostly light or white. Tie them in front of the tail and wrap them forward forming a light/dark quill effect. I highly recommend lacquering the moose mane body afterwards, as the hair is hollow and very fragile.

As you move away from the mane, the hair becomes shorter, darker and more dense. My favorite place to obtain good hair for tails is along the flanks.

Around the legs, the hair becomes short and very stiff, again providing excellent tail material. On some hides, very beautiful hair is available around the bottom of the leg, where the hair will be silver tipped making a unique and attractive tail for a small Humpy.

I believe this hair should be part of every fly tyers collection, especially for use in western patterns.

Caribou Hair

Although somewhat short in many cases, caribou body hair is the easiest to use for making spun hair body flies. It works well for Irresistible bodies because it packs very tightly and flares much easier than deer hair. Unfortunately, it has one drawback; it is light in color. However, it takes dye readily and some very useful shades can be dyed.

The ends of the hair are somewhat brittle, thus making it inferior for Muddlers due to the fact that it forms a poor collar. It is, however, highly serviceable for bass bugs, especially in dyed colors.

The best way to buy caribou hair is to specify when ordering it what length you need. This depends on what type of fly you are tying. If you tie many clipped hair flies, buying a caribou hide may be a good investment. Most fly tying supply houses carry caribou hair, but taxidermists seem to be the most reliable source.

Mountain Sheep

The hair along the back of the mountain sheep is soft, coarse and excellent for clipped bodies on flies. The Dall sheep has an attractive black and white hair combination that makes a nice salt and pepper clipped body. However, the availability of mountain and Dall sheep hair is very limited. The only places I have found it is from a few taxidermists. Usually the pieces are very small but the quality is excellent.

Calf Tail

This is one of the most popular wing materials available. With polar bear becoming scarce and extremely expensive, the use of calf tail in streamer wings is gaining popularity. Calf tails are easily obtained and rather inexpensive. However, one of its drawbacks is that calf tail hair is sometimes very curled and uneven. It is important to look at a number of calf tails to find hair that is fairly even and straight. The best hair is obtained mid-way through the calf tail to the base of the tail. This hair works very well for wings on flies such as the Royal Wulff, Royal Humpy and other Wulff type patterns.

The higher up the tail the more curled the hair tends to become. If a person is selecting a calf tail for streamer wings, he should look for a shorter tail with longer hair on it. The tails will vary in length and hair characteristics, so when ordering from mail order houses, please specify what length and type of hair you are looking for. The supplier will usually select the right type of tail for your purpose. Calf tails take dye very well and can be dyed a variety of colors. Most supply houses offer them pre-dyed in standard colors.

When using calf tail for dry fly wings, you will find the straighter the hair, the easier it will tie down. Be very careful and use many wraps of thread when tying down calf tail, as it can easily slip out from under the thread. Beginning tyers often use too much calf tail so watch your quantity. You can add to the durability of your calf tail wings if you touch a drop of cement to the base of the wings.

Antelope

Antelope hair, probably the most hollow of all animal hairs, can be used in a variety of clipped fly heads and bodies. Its unique reddish color makes it adaptable to many sculpin patterns, providing a brown clipped head.

The rump of the antelope has clean white hair that is perfect for dyeing a variety of colors. Because of its coarseness, dyed antelope rump hair is highly practical for a variety of bass bugs.

Many fly tying supply houses carry antelope and it is relatively inexpensive. Most western taxidermists have an adequate supply and are usually more than anxious to sell their scraps of antelope hide, as the skin is very thin and does not tan well.

Bear Hair

There are a few types of bear hair available today. Polar bear hair has just about reached the non-available status now and what little is left is very expensive. There seems to be adequate supplies of brown, black and cinnamon hairs available. This hair makes excellent streamer wings and can be used on Muddler Minnows as an underwing. The younger the bear the better streamer hair you will find on it. Sometimes the hair will have broken tips, especially along the back. Therefore, it is best to obtain some medium flank hair. Most people who shoot bear want to make the hide into a rug. When the rugs are trimmed there will always be scraps of hair, but much of this is poor quality and useless to the fly tyer. This accounts for why good bear hair is very hard to find. If you can find some long smooth hair, give it a try.

Porcupine

This prickly critter can be of some use to the fly tyer. Some of his guard hairs will make excellent legs and antennae for nymphs. Also, on small dry flies, one or two guard hairs will make a very stiff tail. Several new patterns use a porcupine quill to form the entire body.

Although it has many uses, it is not readily available in stores. In the Rocky Mountain area, there are many road killed porcupine. You can pull out some of the hair from one of these and leave the rest for the scavengers. Porcupines are not the most pleasant animals to skin. Due to the recent demand, some fly shops are now carrying limited quantities of porcupine quills and hair.

Badger, Coyote and Wolf

The guard hair from these animals makes excellent streamer wings and the underfur can be used in dubbed bodies. Due to the present demand for fur, the price of these hairs have become increasingly higher. All three types of hair can be used for underwings on Muddler Minnows. The underfur of the badger is cream colored and useful for dubbing nymph and dry fly bodies. Badger underfur takes silicone fly dressings very well and makes high floating dry flies. Almost all fly tying shops carry a selection of these hairs. Please note, however, that most hair now marked as wolf is usually taken from a large coyote, as along the back of the coyote the guard hairs are hard to distinguish from the guard hair of his cousin, the wolf. Coyote hair is much less expensive than genuine wolf hair.

WESTERN MAYFLIES

by   Mike Lawson

The following chapter heading is the work of Mike Lawson, the talented professional fly tyer and proprietor of Henry's Fork Anglers in Last Chance, Idaho. When not fishing on the Henry's Fork, Mike is busy inventing flies for selective trout.

Western waters were first thought of as large, swift, brawling rivers typified by the Madison, Yellowstone, Snake, and Big Hole. The patterns developed for such streams were not exactly mayfly imitations, but large, heavily hackled, high floating attractor patterns such as the Goofus, Wulffs, and Trudes, which had as their primary objective good visibility and floatability. These patterns are still top choices in the fast sections of the waters, not only in the West, but through-out the country.

As more anglers discovered waters such as the Firehole, Henry's Fork, and upper Madison, and other western spring creeks, new fly tying problems arose. Since most western mayfly species differ from the eastern species, classic fly tying patterns developed for eastern waters were not adequate for the West. In places such as the Henry's Fork in eastern Idaho, the trout are as selective as anywhere in the world. To be successful, the angler must determine what the trout are feeding on and what imitation will match it.

Fly tyers have created imitations to match the mayfly hatches since the beginning of dry fly fishing in America. Classic patterns like the Horton, Light Cahill, and Hendrickson were all created to match a specific fly hatch. It is significant to realize, however, that these classic dry fly patterns were dressed to match eastern mayfly species.

Recently, new patterns have been developed which match western mayfly hatches. Among these are the sparsely dressed imitations, such as the paraduns and thorax flies with a minimum amount of hackle, as well as patterns with no hackle at all, such as the no hackles. Many new patterns are continuing to be developed to assist the angler in matching mayfly hatches on selective trout waters of the West.

To understand mayfly fishing in the West, one must first understand mayflies. Mayflies have a wide range of environmental requirements. Some species cling to the rubble on the bottom of the swiftest section of the stream. Some like to burrow in the mud and gravel, while others roam freely on submerged aquatic plant life. Some prefer a calm environment with little or no current. Others are free swimmers which can dart through the waters with amazing speed. Most of the better fly fishing streams have a variety of habitat and provide adequate environments for most types of mayflies.

Mayflies are the only aquatic insects with upright wings. Their life cycle consists of four stages — the egg, nymph, dun, and spinner. The nymphs are aquatic forms that live under the surface. Since nymphs never emerge from the water until they are ready to hatch, they are equipped with gills. Duns are winged insects that emerge from the nymph, usually at or on the surface. They float along the water's surface for some distance, drying their wings, then fly off to a sheltered area to molt. Spinners are the second wing form of the mayfly, developing from the final molt. They return to the water to mate, lay eggs, and die. Spinners usually look exactly like the duns, but they have a brighter body and clear wings. For most types of mayflies, it usually takes only 24 hours from the time the dun emerges from the nymphal case until it dies after mating as a spinner. Some species complete their life cycle in only a few months, while some species may take up to two years. In general, however, most species complete their life cycle in one year.

Mayflies vary greatly in size according to the species, ranging from tiny **Tricorythodes** (which can be less than an eighth of an inch long) to the large **Hexagenia** (which can be more than one and a half inches in length). Most species have two pairs of upright wings, with the anterior pair much larger than the hind pair, and they are usually about the same length as the body. Some species lack the smaller, hind wings entirely. All mayflies have two or three tails, depending on the species.

Since I live on the banks of one of the West's mayfly fisheries, the Henry's Fork of the Snake River, I have a first-hand opportunity to try out many mayfly imitations. If you're traveling in the Henry's Fork country of eastern Idaho, stop by Last Chance, Idaho, and visit the *Henry's Fork Anglers Shop* and we can discuss our friend, the mayfly.

DARK GREEN DRAKE

For me, it happened several years ago, before the crowds, before the publicity, before a lot was known about what a true treasure was really there. I had driven by the stream many times and wondered what lie in its waters. The guides and fishermen in West Yellowstone knew the secret and knew the story. Many times, when I wanted to escape the hustle and bustle of the tourist-choked Jackson Hole area, I would drive over Teton Pass and slip down through the long flowing green wheat fields of the Driggs and Ashton farm country. I would hit the main road to West Yellowstone as it intersects right outside of Ashton. The road was not as wide as it is now, and it wasn't as well traveled, but just as surely as now, it brought a person to Henry's Fork country.

One of those early trips to the area was with my grandfather who steered his wood-paneled Ford station wagon along the narrow highway, and he occasionally commented about how he used to fish the Snake River before Palisades Reservoir and how good it used to be. Other than that, he allowed that he didn't know much about Idaho fishing and since he was my constant fishing companion, neither did I.

The tires of the "Woody" rattled the planks of the metal bridge of the upper section of the river and my grandfather glanced to his left and pointed upstream. "Well, that's the old Harriman place. You know the guy that built the Union Pacific? I guess in these parts, they call it the Railroad Ranch. I'll bet there is some pretty good fishing on that place, but the water's too slow for me. It's the same thing like Lewis River up in the Park, and they can have it. I like my rivers fast and surging filled with rushing deep holes." And he drove on through Last Chance, Island Park, Henry's Lake flats and on toward West Yellowstone. I always admired my grandfather because he knew what he liked about fishing, and that was that.

"Grandfather, you got to admit though, that's some pretty good lookin' water we just passed" I said. "Even though it might be slow, I'll bet there's some really large fish in there. Can't we come over sometime and fish it? I hear from a couple of my friends in Idaho that there are some fast stretches farther down. Besides, I think there a few guys that even take float trips." I knew I'd said the right words because my grandfather was a sucker for float trips. He loved to fish out of a moving boat.

Grandpa was the kind of fisherman who liked to fish only a few holes a day. "Fish 'em real good," my grandfather always said, "because you got to at least present the fly to every fish in the pool." This takes a lot of time, sometimes he spent all day long in one hole. I couldn't argue with my grandfather's logic because he caught fish, but as a boy I liked to put on my track shoes, charge up the river and cast to every hole. It was my belief that the more times you exposed your fly to different areas the better chance you had of catching large fish. This used to drive my grandfather batty, but he knew that if he corralled me on a boat, I would stay put and have to fish with him, instead of leaving him to his solitary hole while I charged up the stream. However, even though we took many trips to West Yellowstone, the opportunity never came to float the Henry's Fork with my grandfather.

Several years later, when I became a young guide, I had my first opportunity to fish the North Fork of the Snake (commonly known as the Henry's Fork). It was during the month of June when over in our native Jackson Hole Country the rivers were murky and overflowing from the heavy spring run-off. The only fishing that was available to us was the large deep water lakes and a few select spring creeks and we were thirsty for some new water. A couple of good friends of mine came up with the idea of floating over in Idaho for several days. We loaded up an old military surplus raft and headed over Teton Pass toward Ashton. Since we really didn't know much about the area, we stopped in at several gas stations trying to get some information as to where we should put in our boat. Everyone we talked to pointed us in a different direction. It was almost a scene out of the movie "Deliverance." We followed an Old Timer in his broken-down truck down a dusty dirt road that led to the river. He said, "You can put your boat in here, and you can take out a fur ways down the river. I don't know how far, but I'll make sure the car's there for ya." Being young and inexperienced in such matters, the challenge and thrill of adventure displaced our common sense.

As we launched the boat, I noted how clear the water was compared to the muddy Snake. It was a real treat to fish some clear moving water, instead of the lakes that we had to guide on day after day.

One of the first things we noticed about the Henry's Fork was its width and fairly constant water flow. Right out in the middle, one could leap out of the boat and still not swamp his waders. This is something you could never do on the south fork of the Snake. From the start, we could see why the Henry's Fork had intrigued us. Covered with vegetation, it had to be filled with aquatic insects, but what kind? We really didn't know what to use, and because we were so accustomed to the big hair flies, we naturally started out with them. After an hour of so of fishing, we had no luck.

The scenery was magnificent, with beautiful meadows and snow-capped peaks in the distance. We tried several spots but had not seen a fisherman or a rising fish. We knew there had to be fish in there because we had talked to all the locals who'd explained that there were large fish in there all right, but they were very difficult to catch because their lures kept getting in the moss. We wondered how many people had fly fished the area. Most of the locals were bait and lure fishermen and we thought we might have the edge if there would only be some hatches or something for us to work with.

Finally, one of the group saw a rise, not a big rise, but a rise that at least raised our attention and our hopes for a little action. I had not seen a fish in years the size of this mysterious trout. While we watched him cruise along, he rose again, pointed his nose, and sucked in something I couldn't see. It had to be minute. I jumped out of the boat and held a long line attached to the boat so that both my friends could observe the show the trout was presenting us. A few minutes later he was up again. I was up almost over my waders, holding on to the rope and my friends continued to watch what was happening.

"What kind of trout do you think he is, Jack?" yelled Joe.

"I don't know, I imagine it is probably a rainbow. That's what the Old Timer said was in here. Boy, I've never seen a rainbow that big, what do you think we ought to use?" I replied.

Our selection of flies did not include anything as small as what the fish was taking. One thing that we had learned from fishing up on the Lewis River was that we must be using light tippets. We had 6-x leader that would definitely be light enough, but in those days, 6-x tippet meant less than a pound test, and you had to be careful using something that fragile. Nylon had not proven itself to everyone's satisfaction, and most people were still using gut leader material.

I yelled back to Joe, "Try taking a number 18 Adams and trim all the hackle off, maybe that will be small enough." Joe was a half-converted fly fisherman who would not hesitate to throw a spinning lure whenever a large trout would thumb his nose at flies. I had been working in order to convince him to become an uncompromising disciple of the fly rod, but Joe loved to catch fish and didn't care what he used to do it. But today, he took my advice and he used a rusty pair of clippers to gnaw off the hackle of a little Adams.

He held it up and said, "How does this look to you?" I could barely see it.

"It just might work, Joe, give it a whirl, I'll hold the boat here while you cast" I said.

About this time, an irritating breeze began to stir the air from the southwest. It wasn't enough to make you work hard to push the fly forward, but just enough to make it difficult to keep everything under strict control. Nick was in the front of the boat, ducking down to protect his crewcut from the twirling line that Joe was flinging through the air. Joe had not quite yet mastered the finer arts of fly casting and sometimes the fly would hit the water behind him. Nick knew the safest place to be was on the bottom of the boat. His first cast was about four feet short. I cautioned Joe not to let the fly drag near the fish. I had let go of the rope and the boat had drifted downstream several yards. At this, Joe had lost his footing and fell back, hitting the boat with a big "thud". As he got back up, glaring and obviously mad, our friend the trout slurped another one of the mysterious insects off the surface. Slowly, we pulled the boat back upstream and got it back onto position. Obviously, the trout was so intent on feeding that it wouldn't make much difference what we did, short of dropping a ten-ton anchor right on top of his head. He screamed, "You're lucky you're not walking home, Dennis. Remember, I have the keys to the car." He was right, Joe was the only one old enough to drive and I figured we had better treat him right.

Joe's next cast was right on the money. The fly floated right in front of the trout. The dark green shadow rose up. "Set the hook!" I screamed. Joe stood and froze, motionless, his arms frozen to his side. "Jerk! Jerk! Set the hook!" Nick nearly came out of the boat like a Jack-in-The-Box screaming "Jerk! Jerk!"

His arm shot up into the air, the line tightened, but it was too late. The fly pulled from the trout's mouth and shot back into the air. As a matter of reflex, Joe brought the rod forward as if to cast again back towards the fish. Suddenly, I felt the line brush across my face, and then a twang of pain on the end of my nose. "Ow!" I exclaimed. It felt like a doctor's needle had poked me right in the snoot. I crossed my eyes and tried to focus on the end of my nose, and there I could see a #18 Adam's.

I had let go of the rope and the boat was drifting downstream once again. Joe and Nick were so excited about the fish they had lost that they were doing a lot of screaming and yelling themselves. Joe kept trying to cast, not knowing his fly was gone. I kept leaping ahead in the water trying to grab the fly line as he backcast in my direction. Finally, I made a lucky grab, gave the line a jerk, and pulled Joe backward, knocking him to the floor of the boat. He shot up looking back to see what happened, and there I stood with my hands on my hips, glaring at him with the fly stuck right on the end of my nose. They both burst into jackal-like laughing, pointing at me and continuing to laugh, "We've caught the biggest sucker in the whole river!" I was furious. It took some time before they calmed down enough to come ashore and help me get that stupid Adams detached from my nose.

While on the bank, we decided to regroup our thoughts and have a Coke. Meanwhile, some strange things began to happen out on the river. It was as if someone had blown reveille. Fish began rising everywhere! Rise after rise, the river boiled as the fish slashed away at some large greenish mayflies which had suddenly appeared. Nick reached and caught one and showed it to me. Much to my surprise, it was a large green drake.

We reached in our box and tried to find something that would even possibly imitate it, but no luck. Dumbfounded, we tried several flies with no success. Finally, we settled on using a green bodied Humpy, which we had purchased from the old Boots Allen Tackle Shop back in Jackson. It was big and bushy, but after several modifications made with a rusty old pair of clippers, we were able to cut the flies down to size.

From that point on our success increased. The fish were running large and full of fight and we lost most of the fish when our light tippets snapped as the fish dived for the mossy green vegetation. None of us had ever seen an insect hatch the likes of this one and little did we know were experiencing what has now become a legend — the famous green drake hatch of the Henry's Fork.

While we were woefully unprepared for it on that occasion, in recent years we've been equipped with better patterns and have had better success. One of the best of them is Al Troth's Dark Green Drake.

Al's innovative style has created a green drake imitation that can be most useful for the Henry's Fork and for other streams that hold these big greenish brown mayflies. The colors and size can be modified to match the brown drakes and many others. The parachute style wing allows the fly to float naturally and presents a good silhouette to the wary trout.

In the last few years, I have had chances to look over many green drake imitations, and I'm convinced that Al's is one of the best around. If you plan a trip out West to the Henry's Fork during the second half of June, you should have a dozen of these in your vest.

Oh, yes, I still drive up that road to Henry's Fork country, but it has changed a lot since then. There are now stores and tackle shops to serve the hundreds of anglers who come to fish this classic meadow stream. The waters of the Railroad Ranch have been set aside for some special regulations, including a "fly fishing only" rule. Here is a place where one can fish for large selective trout during a wide variety of hatches. The unique experience gained on the Henry's Fork is one which cannot be learned from books.

Each time I pass through the Henry' Fork country, I think about what man can do to protect what is wild and special so that future generations can have a taste of what we now enjoy.

Bravo, Henry's Fork! Bravo, Idaho! Bravo, Green Drake!

MATERIALS:	Dark Green Drake
THREAD:	Prewaxed 6/0 olive
HOOK:	Mustad 94840
SIZES:	10
TAIL:	Black or dun colored elk hair from rump
RIBBING:	Single strand of canary yellow embroidery yarn
BODY:	Avocado or olive polypro yarn cut into ¼" pieces and olive dyed hare's ear mixed 50-50
WING:	Black polypro yarn
HACKLE:	Grizzly dyed insect green (a yellowish green)

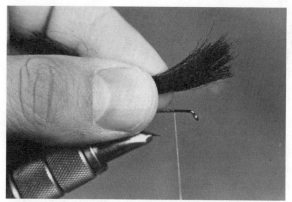

1. Cover the hook shank with tying thread. Cut a piece of black polypro yarn about 2-3 inches long.

2. Tie the bundle of yarn on top of the hook shank, wrap the thread back towards the back of the bundle. Be sure that the back of the bundle of yarn is not past directly above the point of the hook. Cut the excess of the yarn on a taper.

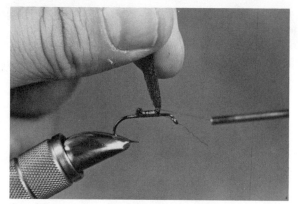

3. Make circular wraps around the wing.

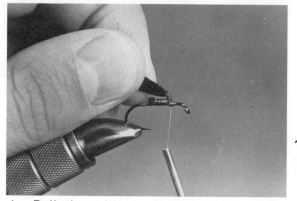

4. Pull the wing back and make several wraps just in front of it to help stand it up.

5. This is the completed wing before final trim.

6. Tie in the tail fibers where the ends of the poly yarn are, and wrap backwards towards the hook bend. The fibers should not be any longer than the shank of the hook.

7. Tie in the ribbing material as shown above.

8. Dub some fur on to the thread and make one wrap of dubbing behind the tail, thereby lifting the tail slightly.

9. Dub the body forward to the wing.

10. Rib the body with a yellow strand of embroidery yarn.

11. Measure two dyed grizzly hackles for length.

12. With the dull side towards you, tie in the grizzly hackles directly behind the wing.

13. Dub over the top of the hackle butts and advance the thread to the eye of the hook.

14. Shows the dubbed base.

15. Lacquer the base of the wing.

16. Begin wrapping hackles clockwise.

17. Make at least 8 turns of hackle.

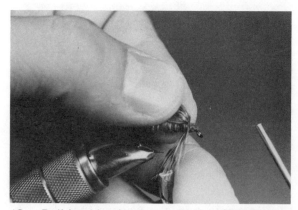

18. Pull hackles back as you tie off and trim.

19.　This is the fly before trimming the wing.

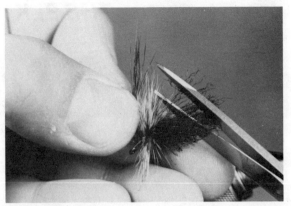

20.　Clip the wing into a triangular shape of the proper size.

21.　Add a drop of lacquer to the base of the wing. This will keep the hackle from coming unwound.

22.　The Finished Fly.

THE ELK HAIR HUMPY

In 1967, at the urging of several of my fishing colleagues, I set upon an effort to improve the Humpy or Goofus Bug. One of the major complaints about the Humpy was its poor durability qualities. It just did not seem to hold up after several fish. At that point I started to experiment with tough elk hair instead of hollow deer hair for the tail. The tail was always the first to be destroyed and without the tail the fly had the tendency to float either on its side or on its head. Our first step was adding stiff brown elk hair, which we obtained from discarded taxidermists' hides. Most of these hides were from the legs, where the hair was dark brown and stiff. We immediately noticed after substituting elk, the tail was much more durable, and the fly would last definitely longer. At this point we felt a need for other colors of Humpies, because the fish-taking champion was relatively limited to the deer natural color, that came in shades of gray, or sometimes a light brown, depending on the type of deer used. Believing in a need for a darker color, we experimented using dark elk for the whole body and wing, but the problem with the dark elk was that it was so stiff that it was hard to fold over and tie properly. Even though a very stiff fly, it sank slowly in spite of loads of Mucilin. Its floatability was not quite up to par. While one day at the vise, I decided to experiment with some of the lighter elk hair, which was more hollow and appeared to be more buoyant, than dark elk hair. Using the dark elk hair for a tail, then the light tan flank for the body, we found a fly that solved the problem of durability and its limitations on color. The light elk Humpy resembled some of the light mayfly hatches, that occur in heavy water conditions. Could it replace the old standby, the Light Cahill? The Light Cahill is an excellent mayfly imitation, but has the problem of being difficult to float in heavy water. Of course, there was always the Blond Wulff, but it seemed to lack the fish-taking qualities that the Humpy seemed to possess. There is almost something mystical about the Humpy and nobody seems to know exactly what this fly imitates. It can represent a number of light colored natural insects, but since it is still a Humpy, it has to be a winner.

In the summer of 1967, several of my friends who were fishing guides, and I started experimenting with the Elk Hair Humpy. We tied it with a light brown elk tail, with a light cream body, and wrapped with either badger or cream saddle hackles. We experimented with different bodies; yellow, red, black, green and cream. That particular year there was an unusually heavy amount of light mayfly hatches and the results were spectacular.

After three seasons of trying the fly, we christened it the Elk Humpy as it richly deserved a place along side of the regular Humpy. Its uses were somewhat limited because of its light color and we found that it was an extremely durable fly that actually outlasted the regular Humpy. The Elk Hair Humpy certainly deserves a spot in your fly box.

MATERIALS:	Elk Hair Humpy
THREAD:	Red, yellow or green monocord
HOOK:	Mustad 94840, 7957B, 7948A, 3906 for heavy waters
SIZES:	8-18
TAIL:	Dark elk hair
BODY:	Light elk
WING:	Light elk
HACKLE:	Badger, grizzly or blue dun

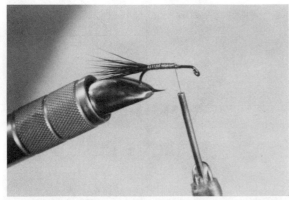

1. Cut out a small bunch of moose hair or elk hock. Stack until tips are even, tie in halfway down the shank and cover with thread.

2. Cut out a small bunch of light elk hair, remove the small fibers and underfur, stack until tips are even, measure for length. The hair should be twice the shank length.

3. Tie in the elk hair bunch on top of the moose hair tail halfway down the shank, make several tight wraps and begin covering over the bunch with thread. This forms an underbody.

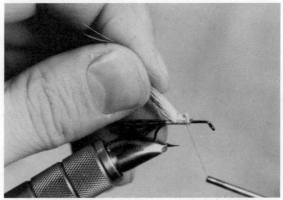

4. Continue wrapping over the elk hair bunch toward the rear of the hook, hold the bunch up in left hand to be sure it does not get mixed in with the moose hair tail. Be sure to wrap all the way back to where the base of the tail is.

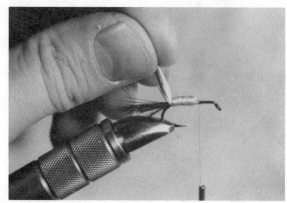

5. Notice the underbody. You should have a nice smooth underbody before you continue.

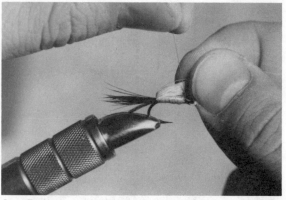

6. Pull the elk hair over forming a hump, be sure to keep the fibers on top of the hook, not allowing them to be tied down underneath.

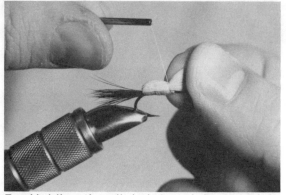

7. Holding the elk hair bunch in your right hand, make several wraps of thread with your left. Pull tight on the third wrap and continue wrapping forward a little bit to form a base upon which to wrap hackles.

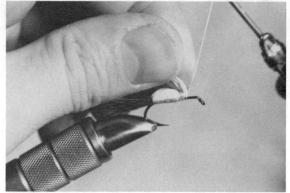

8. Bring the thread in front of the elk hair wing, pull the wing back, and make several wraps of thread just in front of it; this will stand the wing up.

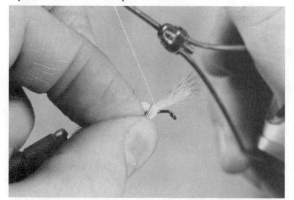

9. Split the wing in two, come between the wings and make several wraps of thread; then come from behind the wings forward between them again several times. This is called "X-ing".

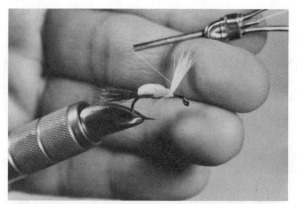

10. Encircle each wing with thread at the base, grouping the fibers together.

11. Encircle the other wing.

12. Pick out two or three badger hackles of the proper size; these can be saddle hackles if you are tying a large fly.

13. Tie the badger saddle hackles in behind the wing with the shiny sides facing the rear.

14. Begin wrapping hackles forward. You should make a total of twelve wraps of hackle.

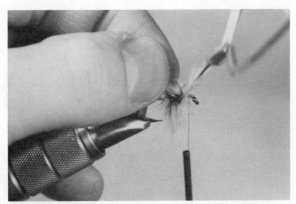

15. Continue wrapping hackles forward. Pull back the wing as you wrap the hackles in front of it. Tie off and whip finish a head.

16. The Finished Fly

BASTARD ADAMS

This particular fly was coined the Bastard Adams by my good friend Reverend Dan Abrams (who, by the way, first gave me the idea for tying this fly). No doubt, many variations of this pattern have been tied by enterprising fly tyers who like the colors of the Adams, but would prefer something with a little bit better floatability.

One of the most frustrating things about fishing an Adams is that it is sometimes difficult to see—especially in the smaller sizes. For a more visible fly of the Adams family you might try a Parachute Adams tied with a white calf tail wing. Another suggestion is to use white calf tail instead of elk hair for the wings in the following instructions.

Tied in the smaller sizes, these can be very effective patterns, yet can be easily seen. Float fishermen who are looking for large flies which suggest a dark natural, yet are highly visible to the angler and have good floating qualities, might give this one a try.

We concur with the words of Dan Abrams who said, "We hope you won't have to ever call this fly a bastard."

MATERIALS:	Bastard Adams
THREAD:	Black
HOOK:	Mustad 94840, 7957B
SIZES:	10-18
TAIL:	Dark elk
BODY:	Dubbed muskrat
WING:	Dark elk
HACKLE:	Brown and grizzly mixed

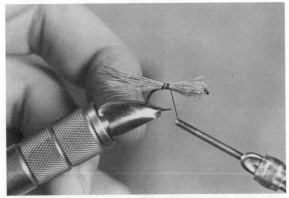

1. Cut out a small bunch of elk hair, stack until all tips are even. Tie the elk hair in just above the point of hook with several tight wraps.

2. Clip the elk hair bunch halfway down the shank and cover with thread.

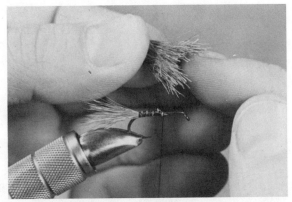

3. Cut out another bunch of elk hair, remove the underfur and small fibers.

4. Stack the elk hair so the tips are all even.

5. Measure the elk hair bunch for length. The wing should not be longer than the shank of the hook. Hold the elk hair bunch on the top of the hook with the thumb and forefinger one-third behind the eye, make several tight wraps, securing it to the hook.

6. Trim the hair butts so that they meet the front of the tail.

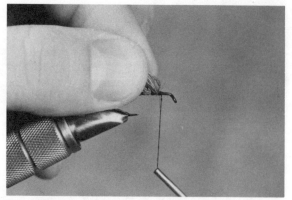

7. With the thread in front of the elk hair bunch, pull back the hair and make several wraps just in front of it. This will stand up the hair.

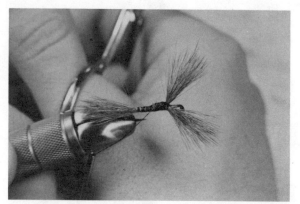

8. Separate the wing, making two equal wings. Come between the wings with the thread toward the back of them, then from behind the wings come between them toward the front. This is called "X-ing".

9. Encircle one of the wings with several wraps of thread, just at the base of the wing.

10. Encircle the other wing in the same way as the first one.

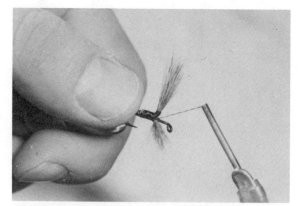

11. This shows the completed wings, notice how encircling the wings groups the fibers together.

12. Bring the thread back to the base of the tail. Apply enough dubbing to the thread to form the body.

13. Dub a nice tapered body to halfway down the shank.

14. Pick out a grizzly and a brown hackle in the correct size.

15. Tie the hackles in with the shiny sides facing the back.

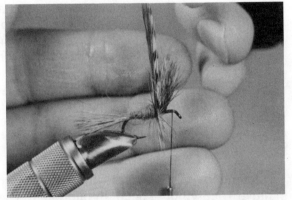

16. Wrap the hackles, making twice as many wraps in front of the wing as behind. Tie off hackles and whip finish.

17. The Finished Fly

FLOATING NYMPHS

By Bonnie and René Harrop

Bonnie and René Harrop are two of the most exciting fly tyers I've ever met. When not in St. Anthony, Idaho they can be found testing some of their inventive patterns on the Henry's Fork. The following is a reprint of an article they wrote for Fly Tyer Magazine.

The question of fly selection during a hatch of mayflies is often more than simply picking the appropriate dry fly particularly when the hatch is very heavy. This is especially true on the Henry's Fork of the Snake upon which I have had the good fortune of spending a great deal of my fishing time.

Tremendous hatches of mayflies ranging from the large and clumsy Brown Drake to the diminitive **Tricorythodes** occur throughout the season on this great river. Heavy angling pressure has caused the trout that inhabit this stream to become highly sophisticated and selective and if an angler is going to fool one of the big rainbows his offering as a rule must closely represent whatever insect or insect stage that the trout are feeding on.

Many of fly tying's greatest innovations have been born on the Henry's Fork.

My experience has shown that during a heavy hatch the trout prefer to feed on the mayfly as it emerges from the nymph case on or just beneath the surface. It is at this point that the mayfly is most vulnerable and the trout feed on the emerging dun in preference to the floating dun.

It was with this in mind that I set out to design a fly which would effectively imitate this elusive stage of the mayfly ... no longer a nymph yet not quite a dun either.

The first step was to go to the aquarium where I could observe the hatching process. It was here that I discovered that often the wings of the freshly emerged fly remain rolled up tightly against the top of the thorax for a surprising length of time. Except for the color, the basic configuration of the fly was very similar to the nymph. The answer was simple ... all that I had to do was to tie a basic nymph pattern only substitute the heavy hook for a fine wire dry fly hook, use buoyant materials for the various parts of the fly and use the same basic colors of the appropriate dun pattern.

After satisfying myself that my theory was valid I began tying the flies for my customers, calling them floating nymphs. The term floating nymph is actually a misnomer for even though the fly looks and is tied like a nymph, what we are actually imitating is the freshly hatched dun with the wings not yet erect. For example, if the dun were to have olive legs and tail, a yellow body and medium gray wings the same colors would also apply to the emerging dun.

The technique used to fish the floating nymph is the same that one would use to fish any dry fly ... that is to dress the fly with a good floatant and deliver it gently above the feeding trout. A long drag free float is mandatory. Even though the fly has proven itself and can often be the difference between success and failure there are several drawbacks. A trout feeding on this stage of the fly often moves about in search of the helpless fly and it is sometimes difficult to get the imitation over him. The low silhouette of the fly makes it difficult to see making it difficult to fish it effectively at a greater distance than twenty feet.

At any rate the floating nymph is worth keeping in mind the next time your favorite dry fly is not producing the kind of results you would like it to.

FISHING THE
GREEN DRAKE EMERGER

Of all the places I've ever fished the Henry's Fork of the Snake has to be my favorite. My idea of a perfect day is to pack a lunch and spend the entire day fishing the Harriman Ranch with my husband.

One of my fondest memories is of a beautiful summer day in early July. We were up early in order to be on the river in time for the first hatch of the morning. When we arrived at the river I was sure that we would have super fishing for there wasn't another fisherman in sight which is highly unusual on this famous stretch of water. I hurried into my waders, vest, etc., anxious to make that first cast.

The river was alive with rising trout as far as I could see but I knew the best fish would be working the far bank. Taking a firm grip on my wading staff I eased my way into the stream and began working my way across. The water was covered with pale morning duns so I paused at midstream and selected a size 18 Gray-Yellow No-Hackle and attached it to my 5x tippet. Scanning the undercut bank I quickly spotted a good trout working near a partially submerged log. Keeping low, I worked my way into casting position ... twenty feet out and slightly above the feeding trout. My first cast was short and I let the fly swing down and away from the fish before making my pick up for the next cast. The next four or five casts were either too short or the fly would drag before it reached the feeding fish. Finally I aimed a cast slightly farther upstream than I'd been casting and the fly landed gently, not more than an inch from the grass. I knew immediately that the cast was good and when the trout rose confidently and inhaled the little fly I experienced the excitement of the first fish of the day. Immediately upon feeling the barb the rainbow made a long run and cartwheeled sixty feet below me. One more short run and a couple of jumps later I landed the plump sixteen incher.

For the next two hours René and I had great sport as the trout fed ravenously on the little may-flies.

Noon found us munching salami and cheese under an old willow tree about a mile downstream from our starting point. For the past twenty minutes I had been watching the feeding activity of what seemed to be a very large trout and I was anxious to try for him.

After working my way into position I paused to study the water. There were still plenty of pale morning duns on the surface but there was also something else. I didn't need a close examination to see that the big slate winged olive duns were none other than the Western Green Drake, the fly that made the Henry's Fork famous. With total confidence I picked a size ten green drake dun from my fly box and tied it to my leader. After four or five tries the fly finally landed in the feeding lane and I tensed as the fly approached the big trout. I couldn't believe it when the fly floated over him untouched ... the cast and drift were perfect. Three times I covered that fish and three times I got the same result ... refusal. It seemed as though the big trout was thumbing his nose at me as he continued feeding, totally ignoring my offering. He must be feeding on something other than green drake duns I thought as I frantically searched my fly box. Suddenly something caught my eye and there tucked into the corner compartment was what I hoped would be the answer. With trembling hands I managed to tie the fly to the tippet and began working the line out toward my waiting friend. Damn — it's short I swore under my breath as the fly touched the water. I raised the rod tip slightly to pull the fly under and began to make a slow retrieve away from the trout. Suddenly there was a swirl and my rod tip was jolted violently toward the water. Somehow the fragile tippet held and I felt the heavy throbbing of the big fish as he tried to figure out what was going on. It didn't take him long to decide that whatever it was he didn't like it and slowly he started off across the broad flats. My reel was running in smooth, audible clicks and I was beginning to relax when he suddenly accelerated causing both me and the reel to scream. I watched in awe as two feet of trout catapulted into the air, his bulk shattering the stillness as he crashed into the mirror like surface. "I'll never land him," I thought as I fought to retrieve line. "He'll play with me for a while but in the end he'll be the winner." By now René had moved down stream from where he had been fishing and was busily snapping pictures and shouting orders. "Keep the rod tip up — Give him line" — Just what I needed. After what seemed like hours the fish began to show signs of weakening and I thought just maybe I had a chance. Grudgingly he began to give ground and as I glanced upstream I realized that until now it had been me who was givng ground — we were more than a hundred yards down stream from where I had hooked him. I wanted to scream when his head finally came up and as I worked him into shallow water I couldn't believe it — I was going to land him.

After a few quick photos I eased him back into the water where I worked him gently in the current. "What did he take?" my husband asked. "My green drake emerger," I answered proudly. "The one with the marabou wing." "Beautiful," he said. By that time the big trout had regained his strength and as he eased out toward midstream I gazed out over the river to where the sun was illuminating the Tetons and had to agree, it truly was beautiful.

MATERIALS:	Green Drake Emerger (Dry)
THREAD:	6/0 pre-waxed yellow
HOOK:	Mustad 94833
SIZES:	10

TAIL:	Grizzly hackle fibers dyed chartreuse
BODY:	Olive Spectrum
RIBBING:	Bright yellow floss
CASE:	Dark blackish brown Spectrum
THORAX:	Same as body
LEGS:	Grizzly hackle fibers dyed chartreuse

MATERIALS:	Green Drake Emerger (Wet)
THREAD:	6/0 pre-waxed yellow
HOOK:	Mustad 3906B
SIZES:	#10
BODY:	Olive seal fur
RIBBING:	Fine oval gold tinsel
WING:	Dark blackish brown marabou
TAILS AND LEGS:	Amber colored fibers from Hungarian Partridge tail feather

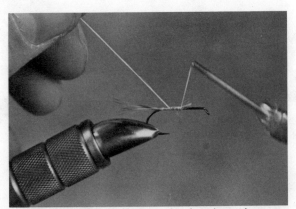

1.   Attach the thread to the hook and cover the rear half of the hook with thread. Tie in 8 to 10 stiff grizzly fibers at a point directly over the barb. Tie in a four inch piece of yellow floss at the base of the tail.

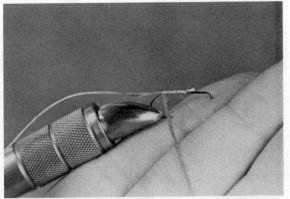

2.   Apply enough Spectrum dubbing to form the abdomen.

3. Dub a nice tapered abdomen forward. Be sure to make one turn of dubbing behind the floss. Notice above where the abdomen stops.

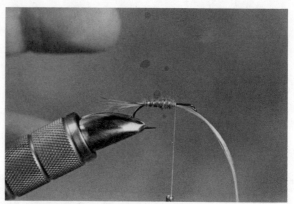

4. Spiral the floss through the abdomen forming the rib.

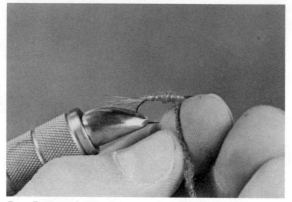

5. Dub a fairly large amount of dark brown Spectrum onto the tying thread.

6. Slide the dubbing down the thread forming a ball.

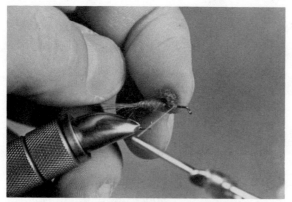

7. Secure the ball to the hook shank.

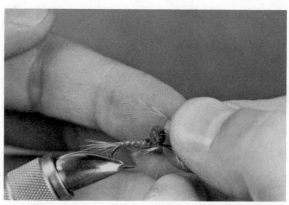

8. Tie in four or five grizzly fibers on each side of the fly ahead of the fur ball to form the legs.

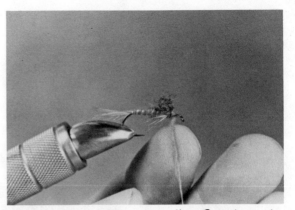

9. Note the above picture for the legs and the ball. This ball represents the splitting wing case.

10. Apply a little more olive Spectrum to the thread. Finish off the thorax and whip finish a head.

11. The Finished Fly

AP NYMPH SERIES

The AP Nymph Series was developed by Mr. Andre Puyans, a talented professional fly tyer from Walnut Creek, California. Andre's creative patterns have been a boon to fly tyers and fly fishermen in the United States and other parts of the world. This big burley man with an out-going friendly nature looks to be more at home in an Oakland Raider football uniform than in front of a delicate fly-tying device. However, don't let Andre's appearance fool you. His fingers are nimble and his skill is hard to match.

Andre's frustration with many poorly developed nymph imitations and artisticly detailed nymphs which can take so long to tie, led him to develop the AP Nymph Series. In my opinion this has been the first logical approach to nymph tying in many years. Andre considered three aspects of importance to the trout: size, shape and color in that order. Many hours were spent analyzing the importance of the mayfly nymphs in the trout's diet. To quote Andre, "obviously a nymph that spends most of his life under a rock, then crawls out of the stream to hatch has little importance to the trout's diet, because he is not available as a food unless dislodged by high water or the like. We then must concentrate our efforts of fly tying imitation on the more mobile species, those nymphs that swim and crawl around quite actively."

To tie the proper shape of a mayfly nymph, one must be familiar with its general body proportions: the abdomen is generally about 50% of the total body length, the thorax at about 40% and the head making up the remaining 10%. By conforming to these natural proportions you provide accurate and realistic imitations. In the past many nymphs have not followed these proportions, but the AP Nymph Series has.

When imitating any insect it is important to consider the insects texture. Material used to imitate this texture must give the appearance of being alive. To accomplish this, Andre has used the aquatic furs such as muskrat and beaver to give a life-like appearance in the water that is far superior to synthetics and land-locked animals.

Another important aspect is the tail. Natural nymphs have two or three tails which are tapered or hair-like filaments. However, as Andre points out, the trout does not seem to care about the actual number of tails but it is very important to tie the flies sparsely for a more realistic imitation. Too many nymphs today are tied with a heavy tail, thus distracting from the natural appearance. Many are also tied with too fat a body destroying the natural silhouette. We sometimes have an inclination to overdo so that our fly is more buggy or attractive to the wary trout.

One of the most important things Andre has developed in the AP Series is the legs. He is careful to note that most modern nymph imitations use tiny traces of hackle normally appearing on the underside of the fly. Andre's legs are tied to the sides, providing a more life-like appearance.

Many nymphs seem to have a problem with the head. They are generally small, shiny (from lacquer) and a totally different color from the rest of the fly. Andre points out that a natural nymph has a larger head which is the same color as the body. He accomplishes this by dubbing the head with the same dubbing as he used for the body.

Following the lines of his shape, size and color relationship, Andre's goal was to limit the number of patterns possible while using a complete color system that would represent most natural insects. I believe that the important contributions of this fly are that it is a simple pattern with relatively easy materials to obtain that can be tied in a relatively short period of time and is as effective as a more complex pattern. Andre's creativity proves that sometimes, what appears to be simpler can be better.

Maybe someday you will be passing through the beautiful green meadows that lead up to the fabled Henry's Fork in Eastern Idaho, where you may spot a figure casting a long delicate line. As you move closer you will see a burley man with a pipe tucked securely under his lip, concentrating, watching each cast, looking for that magic rise. More than likely it will be Andre Puyans, fishing one of his favorite waters. When he has finished you might slip up and tell Andre "thank you" for his AP Nymph Series, then quietly slip away leaving him to the solitude of the river.

MATERIALS:	A.P. Muskrat No. 2
THREAD:	Gray 6/0 pre-waxed
HOOK:	3906B or 9671
SIZES:	8-16
TAIL:	Dark moose hair
BODY:	Dark muskrat
RIBBING:	Gold wire
THORAX:	Dark muskrat
LEGS:	Dark moose hair
CASE:	Dark moose hair
HEAD:	Gray 6/0 prewaxed or dubbed muskrat

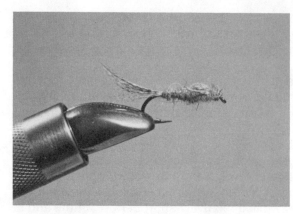

MATERIALS:	A.P. Olive
THREAD:	Olive 6/0 prewaxed
HOOK:	Mustad 3906B
SIZES:	8-16
TAIL:	Finely marked dyed olive mallard flank
BODY:	Beaver dyed medium olive
RIBBING:	Gold wire
THORAX:	Beaver dyed medium olive
CASE:	Finely marked dyed olive mallard flank
LEGS:	Finely marked dyed olive mallard flank
HEAD:	Olive 6/0 prewaxed varnished or dubbed with olive beaver

MATERIALS:	A.P. Peacock and Pheasant
THREAD:	Black 6/0 prewaxed
HOOK:	Mustad 3906B or 9671
SIZES:	8-16
TAIL:	Pheasant center tail section
BODY:	Bronze peacock herl
RIBBING:	Copper wire .006"
THORAX:	Bronze peacock herl
LEGS:	Pheasant center tail section
CASE:	Pheasant center tail section
HEAD:	Black tying thread, varnished

MATERIALS:	A.P. Beaver
THREAD:	Gray 6/0 prewaxed
HOOK:	Mustad 3906B
SIZES:	8-16
TAIL:	Dark moose hair
BODY:	Dark beaver dubbed
RIBBING:	Copper wire .006''
THORAX:	Dark beaver dubbed
LEGS:	Dark moose body hair
CASE:	Dark moose body hair
HEAD:	Dark beaver dubbed

MATERIALS:	A.P. Black Beaver Nymph
THREAD:	Black 6/0 prewaxed
HOOK:	Mustad 3906B
SIZES:	8-16
TAIL:	Dark moose hair
BODY:	Dyed black beaver
RIBBING:	Copper wire 006''
THORAX:	Dyed black beaver
LEGS:	Dark moose body hair
CASE:	Dark moose body hair
HEAD:	Black tying thread or dubbed black beaver

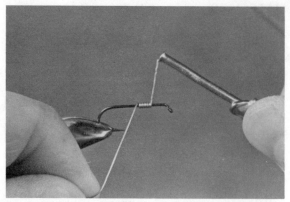

1. Weight the thorax with medium lead wire as shown above.

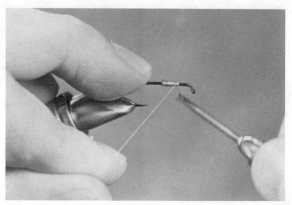

2. Attach thread to the front of the hook.

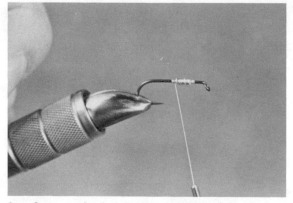

3. Secure the lead with the thread as shown above. Wrap forward and behind.

4. Tie in enough material for the tail, wing case and legs. Tie this in just to the rear of the weight. Please note the amount of material used is selected for the proper sized wing case.

5. Thin the tail by cutting out half the tail material.

6. Advance the thread to the rear and make a couple of wraps beneath the tail to lift and spread it.

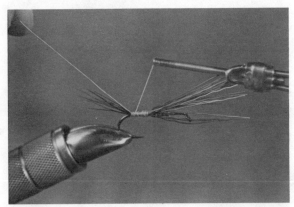

7. Tie in the ribbing wire on the side closest to you.

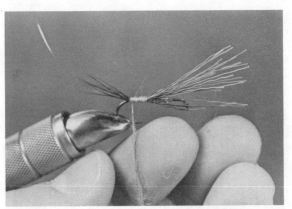

8. Dub on some muskrat for a body.

9. Dub a tapered body.

10. Wind the ribbing forward spacing evenly. Wind several times in front of the wing case and trim.

11. Shows the completed body.

12. Apply more dubbing to the thread for the thorax.

13. Dub the thorax slightly larger than the body.

14. Form the wing case by pulling the hair over the thorax and tie down with 6 to 10 turns of tying thread.

15. With the tying thread just in front of the thorax, separate out 3 hair fibers on one side and bind back with thread.

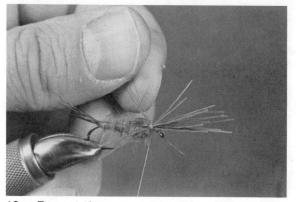

16. Repeat the same procedure on the other side.

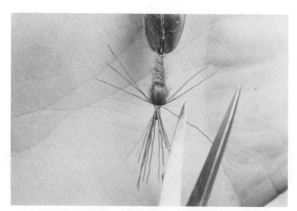

17. Shows the legs in position from the top.

18. Clip off the excess moose hair.

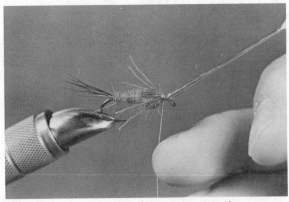

19. Touch a drop of lacquer to the wrap.

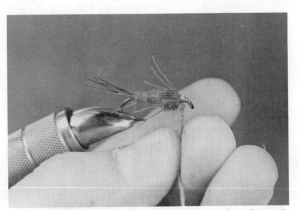

20. Apply some more dubbing to the thread and dub a head just in front of the thorax.

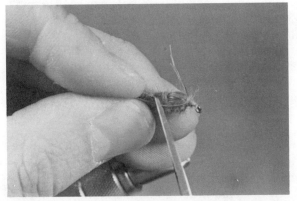

21. Clip the legs off just to the rear of the thorax.

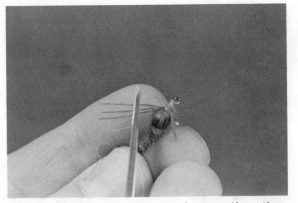

22. Repeat the same procedure on the other side.

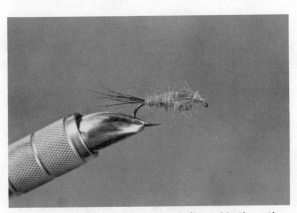

23. Shows the completed fly. Notice the proportions and the length of the legs.

THE PHEASANT TAIL NYMPH

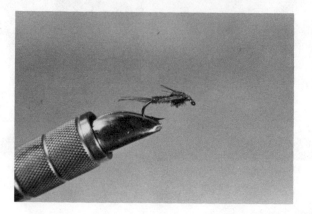

Every once in a while a pattern appears out of nowhere that is so simple and intriguing that it becomes a classic, and nobody quite knows why. This is the case of the Pheasant Tail Nymph. This English pattern is touted in Frank Sawyer's book **Nymphs and the Trout** as being an effective chalk stream pattern which can be used to imitate the smallest may flies.

A closely guarded secret among many spring creek fishermen in the Rocky Mountain area, the Pheasant Tail Nymph has proved to be an effective fly which should be in every angler's vest. Not only does it have a natural appearance in the water, it is also a rather easy pattern for the fisherman to tie.

The Pheasant Tail Nymph was introduced to me by my friend and fly tyer, Al Troth, who claimed that he had no time for laborious flies which required the intricate procedure of tying knots on tiny legs and painting intricate patterns on the wing pads of his nymph patterns. Al explained to me that he could not see how a trout could detect any of these little time-consuming additions to a fly. As a fellow professional fly tyer, I knew what he was talking about.

Besides tying flys on a commercial basis, Al and I also like to go fishing. And when we tie flies up for our personal use, we want to tie them as fast as possible and get on the stream. If we have to take a great deal of time to construct a fly, it is harder for us to fill the box. I'd rather spend that extra time out casting to a rising trout.

Based upon my extensive experience as a fishing guide, I have become convinced that the fisherman's skillful presentation of a good suggestive pattern is more important than worrying about the minute details of intricate legs, pulsating gills and mottled wing pads on my imitations. Hence, my attraction to the simple Pheasant Tail Nymph.

What makes this fly such a deadly killer? Its natural shape resembles many of its natural counterparts found in most of the western waters. It is sparse, easy to cast, readily sinks, and retains its slim silhouette. I urge that you discover for yourself just how effective the pheasant tail nymph can be. It doesn't take much time to tie up a bunch of these little critters, and if you happen to know a small, glassy spring with finicky rainbows that rise only on special occasions, it just might do the trick. Well, don't just stand there — get tying!

MATERIALS:	Pheasant Tail Nymph
THREAD:	6/0 Pre-waxed tan
HOOK:	3906
SIZES:	10-14
TAIL:	Pheasant tail fibers
RIBBING:	.005'' dia copper wire
BODY:	Pheasant tail fibers
WING CASE:	Pheasant tail fibers
LEGS:	Pheasant tail fibers
THORAX:	Peacock herl over layers of copper wire

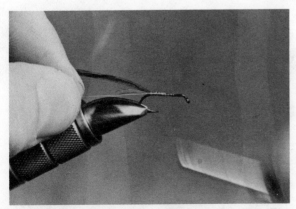

1.   Cover hook shank with tying thread. Tie in strands of pheasant tail for the tail. Tie in a piece of copper wire 5-6'' long. Tie in a second bunch of pheasant tail for the body.

2.   Wrap the pheasant tail forward, tie off. Rib it with copper wire and tie off. Do not cut the wire. The body should come approximately two-thirds of the way up the shank of the hook.

3. Tie on a section of pheasant tail for the case. Make it long enough to form the case and bend back for the legs.

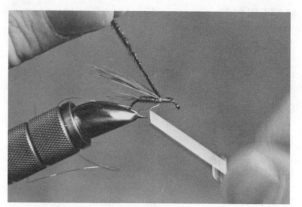

4. Tie two strands of peacock herl.

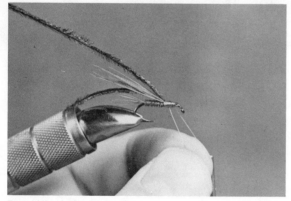

5. Wind three or four layers of copper wire to form a heavy thorax.

6. Pull peacock herl fibers forward and then tie off with thread. Wrap thread backwards to the middle of the hook.

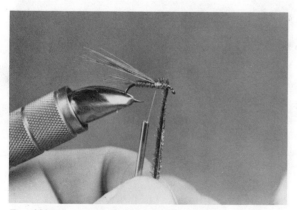

7. Wrap peacock herl backwards to the wing case material; tie off with thread.

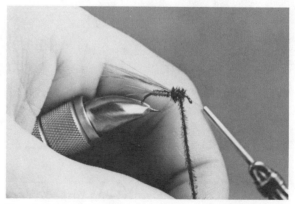

8. Advance thread forward. Wrap peacock herl forward to the eye; tie off and trim.

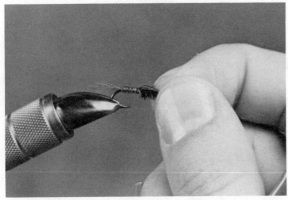

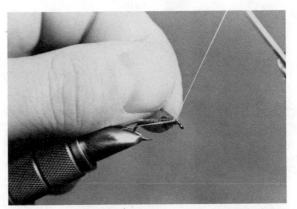

9. Pull pheasant tail fibers forward and tie off.

10. Pull pheasant tail fibers backwards into two equal bunches, one on each side of the body. Wrap thread backward a bit to secure the legs. Whip finish and trim.

11. Trim the legs so that they are ⅔ the body length. This is the finished fly.

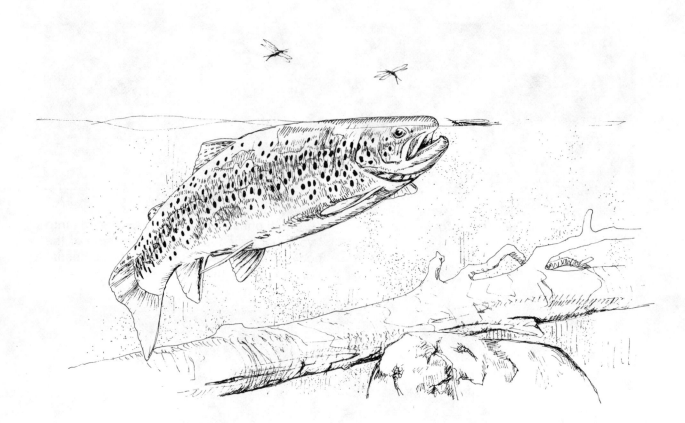

THE STONEFLY OF THE WEST

The elusive stonefly has lured anglers from all parts of the world, who dream of catching big trout. The frenzie feeding pattern of trout that accompanies the hatch of the large stoneflies on many of our western rivers usually provides some of the most exciting and memorable fishing available in the West today.

However, in spite of the opportunities provided by the large stonefly hatch, many anglers are disappointed by their success. We hope that with the showing of new patterns and methods of fishing them, it might help improve your luck.

Bud Lilly, "Mr. Stonefly" from West Yellowstone, Montana, is a famous fishing tackle provider and one to the most knowledgeable fly fishing authorities and guides in the West today. He has agreed to provide us with an insight into the mysteries of the "Stones". We would like to offer you some of Bud's feeling and pointers on the stonefly hatches on western rivers. Your chances of success will be greatly increased if you have some knowledge of the insects themselves, the nature of the hatch, how the trout feed, and the characteristics of the stream.

The most common of the large stoneflies, the **Pteronarcys californica,** develops from eggs to mature adults in 3 years. After hatching from the egg, the nymph migrates from the steam to the banks, and the adult emerges from the nymphal shuck and clings to branches, logs and rocks along the river's edge. After the mature adults mate, the females take to air, deposit the fertilized eggs into the stream, and the 3 year cycle begins again.

The nymphs in the various stages of development will always be found in the stream, but the concentration of nymphs as they prepare to crawl from the stream generates the gluttonous feeding sprees of the trout. This mass emergence of adults is called the hatch. The appearance of the hatch and its upstream movement are determined by several factors. The water temperature, the color of the river, and the air temperature seem to be the conditions that dictate exactly when the stoneflies will hatch. One who is not familiar with these factors should depend on the suggestions of a local expert or the experience of anglers who have visited these western rivers in the past.

Usually the hatch begins about the same time each year. It can be earlier with unseasonably warm weather or low stream flows. A late spring with high water and cold weather can retard the hatch a few days or, in some cases, for weeks. Again, having a good reliable source will help you in planning your trip.

The greatest numbers of the hatched adults ordinarily remain along the stream section for 4 to 6 days. However, conditions will affect the rate of progression upstream. The stoneflies require oxygenated water so that fast moving water over gravel and boulder strewn river bottoms are where the nymphs develop in greater numbers.

Happily, stoneflies keep civilized banker's hours during the hatch. Contrary to the habits of many other hatching insects, the major flight of stonefly adults is mid-day. This allows the fisherman those precious early morning hours of sleep and some needed time in the evening to visit the local watering holes that seem to mark the western fishing resort towns.

After the sun has warmed the air and the adults have dried their wings and mated, the flight begins. There will be some feeding activity on either side of this mid-day period, and it is well worth fishing. Evenings can be an exceptionally rewarding time to fish, especially with late evening hatches of insects such as mayflies and caddis. To the fish, variety also can be the spice of life.

As the nymphs begin to crawl from mid-stream to the banks, many are washed loose and tumble along the bottom of the stream. The trout feed on these drifting nymphs with great vigor. This "happening" is always well upstream from the main body of the adult hatch. Some enterprising anglers employ heavily weighted, dark-colored nymph imitations, which we will describe later in this chapter. Dead-drifting these big imitations along the bottom can set off some intriguing action.

Be sure to use a short line for more precise control, and don't be afraid to use plenty of weight on your fly or leader.

Trout will feed on nymphs until they are gorged. During the stonefly hatches, I have caught many trout which had big insects dripping out of their mouths when caught. When the adults first begin their egg laying flights the trout may be full and ignore them. Sound advice is to fish the area for several days. Success will depend on your consistence and perseverence.

One of the most exciting and memorable times in a fly fisherman's life is the time when the stoneflies first start twirling and the air is filled with these miniature helicopters. Everywhere you look, the "stones" are in the air. They are on your rod, in your boots and between your glasses but when that first trout rises and the adrenalin starts to flow, the feeling is hard for anyone to describe. This is what memories are made of. At the outset of the hatch, you will find that the smaller trout are on the move, and even the Rocky Mountain Whitefish are getting into the action. Be patient! Keep working! Soon the big trout will take their turn.

In some of our western rivers, which are fringed with many small side channels, the feeding may begin there. Sooner or later the really big trout will take up the prime feeding locations by logs, large boulders or in heavily flowing currents over submerged rocks. Surprisingly, in spite of the many natural stoneflies that are covering the river, you may find the trophy size fish can be very selective, even though their smaller friends are very careless. There is always the problem of natural competition, and your imitation can get lost in the crowd of naturals floating by.

Careful observation and pinpoint casting may be the difference between a trophy trout and just an average size fish. Most often the larger fish will seldom move more than a couple of inches for the large stoneflies in the heat of the hatch. In areas where the larger trout have been fished for quite a bit, you may find that smaller, lighter leaders may be the most practical for conditions and a smaller, more sparsely dressed fly sometimes will work better than a heavily dressed imitation. Notice that most of the naturals will ride very low in the water.

Sometimes a larger, lazier trout will prefer a drifting, drowned adult. This can be matched by a sparsely clipped adult imitation, unweighted nymph or in certain cases, a streamer. Size, contour and color may be more important in those cases. Be sure to watch for hatches of smaller stoneflies that sometime follow the main event. These also can provide great fishing, with hook sizes going down as small as 10's and 12's.

A suggestion passed on to me by Jack Hemingway, is to carry a small, light pair of binoculars. One can scan the water and watch the large trout rising. In many cases the big trophy fish make very little disturbance on the surface, and with just the rise of a nose may take in a large stone. With the help of some binoculars, you can distinguish at great distances the difference between a smaller, more active trout and big, lazy monster you are looking for. A little place in the vest for a small pocket pair of binoculars may be one of the best investments you ever make.

Even during the height of the hatch, it is important that you are careful with your casts and wading. It is easy to disturb the fish in spite of the tremendous activity that is going on. Caution should always be taken in fishing for large trout in spite of what their feeding pattern may be. A fly picked up too soon might pop the water and could easily put down the rising trout that might have been the trophy of your trip.

The western rivers that produce the salmon, trout, willow or some of the other local nicknames given to the stonefly often baffle the first time angler. Learning where the feeding trout can be found in the stream is also a problem. The help of a person familiar with the area is invaluable. If you can't find someone to assist you, use common sense. Trout feeding on nymphs will seek out riffles that lead to the holding areas of the river. The shallow riffles are easily overlooked by many anglers. Deeper runs can be productive when the trout are not actively feeding on nymphs. Hatched adults fall or are blown to the water along the banks. Trout move into feeding stations to intercept floating insects, taking them off the surface in slashing rises.

Rivers which flow through rocky-bottomed canyons are sometimes referred to as "pocket water" stretches having sizable rocks which create a pocket of water behind the boulder. It is a favorite spot for feeding fish. Many of the warier trout will remain in the middle of the river behind rocks for even further security. Fishing this water can be a problem. The round, slick rocks make wading difficult, and the current may be very deceiving. What looks like slow-moving water might indeed be a current heavy enough to knock even the strongest wader off his feet. It is recommended that one be equipped with a staff and a good pair of felt soled waders. Aluminum cleated sandals which fit over your wader is another accessory you should consider. These could save your life.

Top-feeding trout are not easily detected in rough, broken riffles in many of the fast, rushing mountain streams. A certain amount of practice will be required to learn how to read the river and locate likely spots where the trophy trout are busy gathering in the little floating critters. In some cases it may only be a flash of reflected light or the dorsal fin or the flip of a tail you'll see. Many times you will be casting blindly and catch the sight of a feeding fish out of the corner of your eye. One of the most important things in fishing is to develop an eye which is keyed to such detail.

I like to walk along a section of river observing every hole and every pocket before I even cast a line. Many people try to fish too much water. It is better to take a smaller stretch of river and fish it well than spend hours hopping from rock to rock trying to fish the whole river in one day. Conditions change throughout the day. A hole may see completely dormant, and an hour later may be a mass of rising trout. It all depends on conditions and time of day.

When fishing our western rivers, especially with the large stonefly imitation of sizes 2 through 8, you will find it difficult to keep from getting line drag from the contrary currents. First of all, don't cast too long a line, and learn to keep a little slack so that the fly will drift naturally. Teach yourself to work the cross-stream drifts in order to reach trout rising under overhanging brush or near undercut banks.

Often you will find that casting an imitation downstream can be a very effective way of getting a proper drift to your fly. Experiment! Use the first cardinal rule of fly casting; don't cast more line than you can effectively handle. It doesn't serve any purpose to cast a long line and then have a fish rise to the fly and have too much line out. You can not pick it up in time, and you end up not only spooking the fish, but trying your patience as well. Sometimes a very careful long wade will be more effective than casting 90 feet to a rising fish that you will never hook.

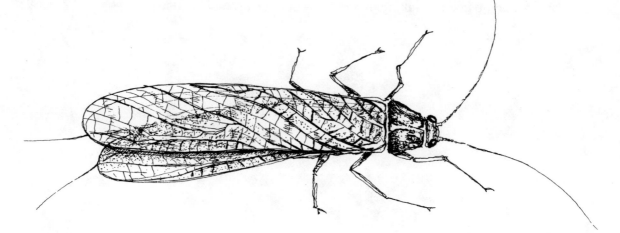

If you are planning a trip to fish the great salmon fly hatches, I would like to give you some suggestions to consider, and some approximate dates for when these stonefly hatches may occur. There are many tackle shops and guide services which can give you further information in the areas you plan to fish. The Henry's Fork of the Snake River in Idaho from mid-May to early June is a well known spot. The river is usually clear, but can be high. Don't forget the great green drake hatch which occurs from mid-June to the end of June. The fisherman can plan a very exciting fishing trip to this area. Due to the high quality of the fishing, the angler must be prepared for large crowds which can be somewhat disconcerting. All one needs is a small portion of water to have the fishing of a lifetime. There are shops that offer guiding service and local information in Last Chance, Idaho.

The Big Hole River in Montana is another well known spot to be the first week of June to the third week of June. The river can be high and roily during the early part of the hatch, but persistant anglers can still take large trout. Access on certain parts of this river may be difficult due to the natural terrain. Floating sometimes can be the best way of fishing it. There are guides available in Wise River, Dillon and West Yellowstone.

Melrose, Montana, is an interesting small village to use a headquarters for your attack on the Big Hole. Last year I observed a large 6 pound grandfather of a trout taken on a Royal Wulff, 4 days after the main stonefly hatch had passed. This river can be good during and after the hatch.

During early June to early July, try the Clark's Fork of the Columbia, Rock River and the Blackfoot River in western Montana. The dates vary according to the weather fluctuations on the western slope of the Continental Divide. High water sometimes can be a big problem. In considering a visit to this area you should contact local guides and tackle shops in Missoula, Montana.

The Yellowstone River in Montana and Yellowstone Park is another popular place in early July to early August. When high, discolored water during the first stages of the hatch in the lower part of the Madison proves discouraging, try the clear sections of the Yellowstone in our first national park. Special regulations have helped to improve this fishing in recent years. Many of the cutthroats will average over 2 pounds.

One should write the National Park Service at Yellowstone National Park for copies of the current fishing regulations, since they do change from year to year. Some stretches of this water are fly fishing only.

The Madison River in Montana is probably the best known of all stonefly rivers and is usually good from mid-June to mid-July, but is high and roily until late June in some areas. There is excellent nymph fishing when the water drops and clears. The upper reaches of the Madison in Yellowstone Park provide both good nymph and dry fly fishing.

Float boat fishing is permitted on most of the rivers, except in Yellowstone National Park. There are some special regulations on the Madison River now, and others are being considered. Writing to the Montana Fish and Game Department will give you the information on floating regulations.

Wading to fish the hatch can still be considered the best method to reach trout in most sections of the river. Floating, however, will provide you with transportation to areas that are not serviced by roads and can provide you with the chance to camp overnight and see different parts of the country. It also can provide an effective way of following the hatch if one has the time and facilities to do such.

Recommended equipment will include both floating and sinking lines spooled on a good single action reel with plenty of backing. The graphite rods of today provide the power to throw the large stonefly imitations without a great deal of effort. Line sizes 6, 7 and 8 are suggested. These rivers seem to be magnets for strong winds, so be sure to practice throwing large flies into the wind before venturing out on some of these streams. Here, again, the new graphite rods make the chore of casting into these blowing gales a little less strenuous.

We hope these suggestions and information will be useful to you when planning your trip to the western stonefly rivers. We hope that the patterns that we are going to show you on the following pages will help you create special moments of your life. We have taken great care in selecting these patterns that will both effective to fish and a joy to tie. Good Luck!

THE JUGHEAD

No matter where you travel in this great and varied fishing world, you always come upon a town where, within that town lives a certain person whose legend far precedes him. The West Yellowstone area of Montana is gifted with many of these legends. Who knows if any or all of the stories are true, but they add variety to the sport we know as fly fishing. One of these individuals is Pat Barnes.

Pat has spent 34 years floating the Yellowstone Park and Madison River area. Along with his wife Sig, they have helped the visiting angler through their small, but complete, tackle shop for many years. When I first walked into their shop as a young man, I saw Sig sitting at a strange looking sewing machine set up that allowed her to whip through flies at lightning speed. The vise twirled around as she sat for hours, day after day, tying Sofa Pillows.

The Barnes' introduced me to the world of commercial fly tying, since I sold some of my first flies to this fishing couple. They were critical, demanding and helped me improve my skill. As we all changed and grew a little older, we went our separate ways. I still, however, kept in contact with the Barnes'.

The Sofa Pillows were the fly tyers' first attempt to imitate the huge stoneflies commonly known as salmon flies which populate many western streams. It was a popular fly with fishermen because it was so highly visible, floated through the swiftest currents, and matched the size of the natural insects. Also, its silhouette was a good representation of the natural insects shape. This was a good fly for the fly tyers, too, as it gave them a chance to use their surplus of large brown hackle that seems to accumulate.

The Sofa Pillow soon became the Improved Sofa Pillow. It was at that time that a friend of the Barnes' introduced them to the Jughead. This new and exciting fly is fast replacing both the Super and Regular Sofa Pillow.

The Jughead was first tied by Betty Hoyt, a friend and talented novice fly tyer. Fly tyers have always had trouble with the Sofa Pillow because of the necessity of wrapping four or five hackles to support the fly. Betty replaced these hackles with a clipped deer hair head and the Jughead caught on. Pat's enthusiastic fishing guides started tying the Hoyt version for their own use. Many found it easier to cast and it out-floated most other stonefly imitations. In the ensuing times several things were added, such as palmered hackle on the body and elk hair under the squirrel tail wing. This improved the visibility and floatability of the fly, allowing it to be used from both a boat and from the shore with ease.

After all these years as a West Yellowstone native, Pat has finally set out to make new stories about himself. Like a number of American trout fishermen, he now spends his winters down south in New Zealand and Australia. However, when summer approaches West Yellowstone country he migrates back up to enjoy the excitement of the mystical stonefly hatches of the Madison River country.

MATERIALS:	The Jughead
THREAD:	Black monocord for body and black A monocord for head
HOOK:	79580 or 9672
SIZES:	4-10
TAIL:	Elk hair
RIBBING:	Brown neck or saddle hackle tied palmer over body
BODY:	Orange 2 ply yarn or orange polypro yarn
WING:	Red fox squirrel tail
UNDERWING:	Elk hair (optional)
HEAD:	Clipped deer or antelope body hair

1. Tie in a clump of stacked, stiff light brown elk hair. Be sure to tie hair in very securely.

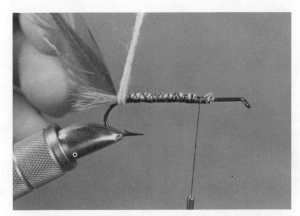

2. Tie in two strands of orange polypro yarn. Also tie in a large brown saddle hackle with the glossy side facing the tail.

3. Wrap the orange yarn forward approximately two thirds down the shank, tie off and trim.

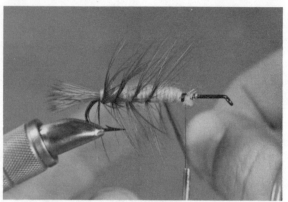

4. Palmer the brown saddle hackle forward in even spacings, tie off and trim.

5. Trim all the hackle off the top portion of the body, and also trim the hackle even with the hook point around the rest of the body.

6. Select a dark brown clump of heavy body hair from along the back of an elk. The hair should be long and wirey. Measure for proper proportions.

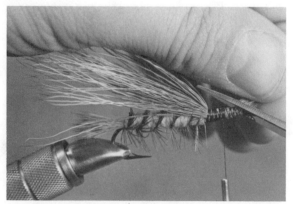

7. Tie in the elk hair securely, as it easily twists. Trim the hair butts and wrap over them with thread.

8. Lay over top of the elk hair a small wing of fox squirrel tail. Tie in securely.

9. Trim the butts at an angle and cover them with a few wraps of thread. Add a drop of penetrating cement.

10. Tie on heavy "A" monocord. Add a drop of lacquer.

11. Lay a large clump of trimmed, light gray deer body hair or antelope hair on top of the hook. Make 3 or 4 tight wraps, securing the hair and allowing it to spin around the hook.

12. Lay another clump of hair in and repeat step #11.

13. Pull back the hair and make a couple of wraps just in front of it.

14. If necessary, add a third clump of hair to fill out the head. You may only need two clumps for a smaller fly.

15.   The hair should form a ball as above.

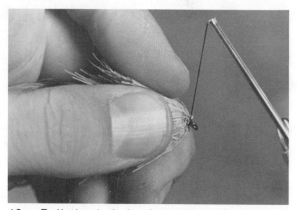

16.   Pull the hair back; make a few wraps just in front of it. Whip finish a head.

17.   Trim the hair flat on the bottom.

18.   Trim around the side toward the top forming a cylindrical head. Notice that the scissors do not trim all the way back.

19.   Finish trimming the head in the above manner. This keeps you from cutting the squirrel tail wing.

20.   This is the finished fly ready for the stream. The head should resemble the shape in the above picture.

JACKLIN SALMON FLY

Bob Jacklin lives in the heart of the stonefly country, West Yellowstone, Montana. What better place to experiment with new fly patterns, than the Madison River country, home of one of the largest and most important salmon fly hatches that occur in the United States. Within a few short miles, Bob has over seven major rivers that have excellent salmon fly hatches. Naturally, with this kind of exposure, Bob has experimented with a variety of materials, and he has created a very bouyant and life-like salmon fly imitation.

Bob believes his fly has several advantages over the standard common ties, such as the Sofa Pillow. He designed it to have two important qualities for the patterns to be used in heavy western waters — good floatation and durability. In order for the angler to compete with the blanket hatch of natural stoneflies floating down the river, he must constantly cast and re-cast his fly, hoping to put it right over the top of a rising fish. This calls for a durable imitation, because the time taken to tie on a new fly could mean the difference between a large fish and no fish at all.

It also must be a good floater in order to stay up in the rough western rivers. The moose hair body, which is liberally coated with Pliobond, assures good floatation and durability.

Bob wisely incorporated the elk hair wing set at such an angle that it becomes an easily spotted indicator as it drifts through the choppy water. Durability, visibility, floatability and just downright fishibility make the Jacklin Salmon Fly an imitation that one should consider when preparing for salmon fly hatches.

The Jacklin Salmon Fly can be tied in a variety of colors by using either dyed elk or moose hair. This makes it possible to imitate a number of different salmon flies, such as the small golden stones that occur in many areas. Also, if changed a bit, it can be fished as an effective grasshopper imitation.

While Bob freely admits that all salmon fly patterns will work sometime or another, his pattern has some advantages which should be considered when choosing a fly for your western or eastern adventures. We tend to agree with Bob and offer his selection for your next trip to stonefly country.

MATERIALS:	Jacklin Salmon Fly
THREAD:	Prewaxed orange monocord
HOOK:	Mustad 94840 or 9671
SIZES:	4-8
RIBBING:	Pre-waxed orange monocord
BODY:	Moose dyed orange, tie some strands in an upright position in the wing
WING:	Light elk hair tied at 45°
HEAD:	Grey deer body hair

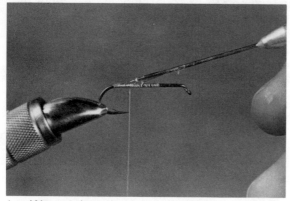

1. Wrap tying thread to provide a smooth base. Lacquer the thread with a bodkin thoroughly.

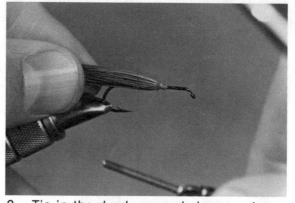

2. Tie in the dyed moose hair securely approximately one-third back from the eye. With thumb and forefinger, pull back tightly on the hair.

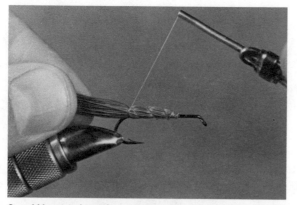

3. Wrap tying thread back towards the bend of the hook, evenly spacing the wraps. At the bend of the hook, make several wraps of thread to secure the hair to the bend of the hook.

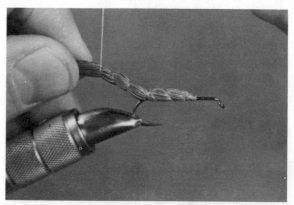

4. After securing the hair proceed to wrap evenly backward past the hook bend toward the end of the hair. The thread should be wrapped at a slight angle with firm pressure as shown above.

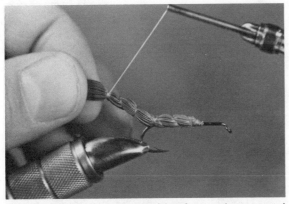

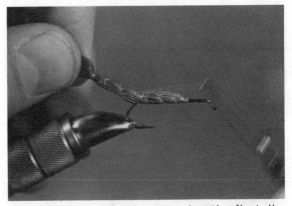

5. End your segmented body as shown and make several wraps of thread at the end of the segmented body to end and secure the segmentation. Be sure to leave enough moose hair to be folded back forward in the upcoming steps.

6. Wrap forward, criss-crossing the first ribbing of thread, forming an "X" pattern. Continue "X-ing" your thread until you have returned to the start of the body. Be sure to pull each wrap securely into the body.

7. With thumb and finger push remaining hair forward, evenly on both sides.

8. Hair should be facing forward as shown above.

9. With thumb and forefinger pull hair forward so that it covers the first body.

10. Repeat the same thread method as in the first few steps and advance the thread over the first body towards the far end of the tail.

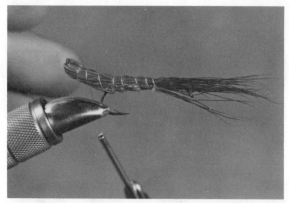

11. After reaching the base of the tail wrap a couple of extra wraps and advance thread back towards the start of the body again forming the "X" pattern.

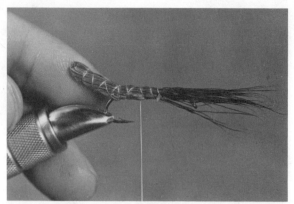

12. This is an example of the "X" pattern body.

13. After "x-ing" the body, pull up the remaining tuft of moose hair. Make four or five wraps of thread around this circularly, parachute style.

14. After completing the circular wraps, pull the hair back and make a few wraps of thread just in front of it.

15. Cut out some light elk hair, neatly stack it and measure for length.

16. Hold the elk hair on top of the tuft of moose hair. Tie down securely and cover the butts with thread.

17. Cut out a small clump of light elk hair or deer hair. Trim the hair butts even and hold them against the wing with your right hand. With your left hand, make a couple of wraps of thread over the hair base flaring the butts. Trim the hair butts and cover them with thread.

18. With hair tied forward, begin to pull back the strands evenly around the eye of the hook in a flared fashion as shown above.

19. Pull back on the flared hair forming a bullet head as shown above.

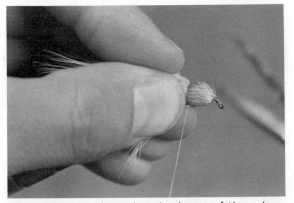

20. With the thread at the base of the wing, make several tight wraps securing the bullet head.

21. Continue wrapping until bullet head is secured. Fly should appear as above. Pull thread forward and wrap thread over the remaining exposed portion of the hook eye. Whip finish and lacquer.

22. With bodkin lacquer the extended tail of the salmon fly.

23. Lacquer the bullet head with a penetrating cement.

24. The completed fly.

TROTH SALMON FLY

This pattern is Al Troth's answer to the large stonefly hatches that occur on many of our western rivers. The durability, visability, and floatability that are incorporated into this effective pattern make it useful for float fishing as well as bank fishing.

As with many patterns, it may be advisable to make a few changes which will allow this pattern to more effectively match the stonefly hatches in your area. For a body material, light elk hair can be used in various dyed colors. When changing the body color be sure to make the rest of the fly consistant in coloration.

Next time you're out West chasing after some of the elusive stonefly hatches, bring along a few Troth Salmon Flies. This may be the ticket to catching some of the large trout that surface feed on these juicy morsels.

MATERIALS:	Troth Salmon Fly
THREAD:	Brown Nymo and Orange Nymo
HOOK:	79580
SIZES:	4-8
TAIL:	Brown or black elk or deer
RIBBING:	Orange Nymo
UNDERBODY:	Pumpkin orange polypro yarn
BODY:	Orange dyed bucktail or cream elk rump dyed orange
WING:	Brown or black hair from elk or deer
TOPPING:	Fluorescent orange calf or buck tail
HEAD AND LEGS:	Dark brown elk or deer flank hair

1. Using the lighter colored tying thread wind on a layer of thread over the hook shank and tie in the tail.

2. Build up body padding with polypro yarn (see figure 2 for proportions).

3. Tie in a large bunch of body hair by the tips ⅓ of the shank length back from the eye.

4. Double the tying thread by forming a loop, make at least 12 inches long. Whip finish the bobbin end.

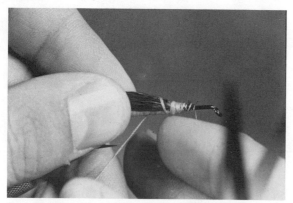

5. Begin to spiral the thread backward.

6. Continue to spiral the thread backward, be sure to keep firm pressure on the thread.

7.   Make a half-hitch at the end of the body securing it to the hook.

8.   Pull the hair toward the eye of the hook.

9.   Spiral the thread forward forming a segmented body. Be sure to use firm pressure.

10.   The completed body should appear as above. Be sure to tie off firmly.

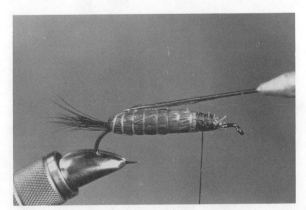

11.   Tie off hair, whip finish and coat with pliobond cement to make more durable. Tie in the dark tying thread.

12.   Tie in wing hair using tight spiral wraps at the front and becoming looser toward the rear. Note the length of the hair in the above picture.

13. Add fluorescent hair for topping in the same manner as the wing, then use a thin spar varnish at the base of the wing.

14. Tie in hair for the head and legs, holding it in your right hand. Clip the butts short and cover them with thread as you wrap the tying thread toward the base of the wing.

15. Pull hair back to form a round head. Make hair long enough so that the points reach to the point of the hook.

16. Wind a few turns to hold hair firmly in place. Whip finish.

17. Clip excess hair from top of wing.

18. Varnish the head. This is the completed fly.

PICKET PIN

From its emergence on the West Coast as a steelhead pattern, the Picket Pin's fame has spread across the United States. This unique fly has stood the test of time proving effective in small streams as well as large rivers.

Several variations of the Picket Pin have emerged from Montana. Here, it is tied on a longer shank hook for use on some of the massive stonefly hatches. Although it has recently been replaced by some of the newer patterns, I hope this effective fly will make a resurgence back into the mainstream of Montana fishing.

Eastern anglers have found this pattern useful for Atlantic salmon and for trout in many Pennsylvanian streams. I hope you'll give this classic pattern a try.

MATERIALS:	Picket Pin
THREAD:	Black
HOOK:	Mustad 9671
SIZES:	4-10
TAIL:	Golden pheasant tippet fibers
RIBBING:	Brown saddle or cock hackle
BODY:	Several peacock herls
WING:	Light elk body hair
TOPPING:	Gray or red fox squirrel tail
HEAD:	Peacock herl

97

1. First tie in several strands of golden pheasant tippet. Then attach three to four strands of thick peacock herl, tying them in at the bend of the hook, as shown in the above picture.

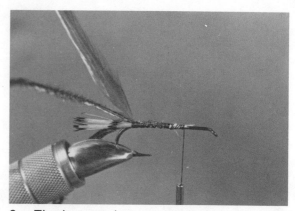

2. Tie in one brown saddle hackle with glossy side facing the back of the hook; be sure to tie in the vein of the hackle securely to the body.

3. Carefully wrap the peacock herl forward over the thread towards the eye of the hook. Gold wire can be ribbed to secure the peacock herl if desired.

4. Tie off peacock herl approximately ¾ of the way down the hook, as shown above.

5. Palmer hackle forward.

6. After palmering hackle forward to the end of the body, wrap several turns at the front of the hook to add a thicker hackle than that palmered over the body.

7. Lay on top of the hook a neatly stacked group of elk hair, either light or dark in color, with the proportions as shown above.

8. Switching hands, tie hair securely right next to the end of the hackle. Be sure to tie down the hair securely and tightly. A small clump will remain as shown above. Trim and move the thread forward to cover most of the hair.

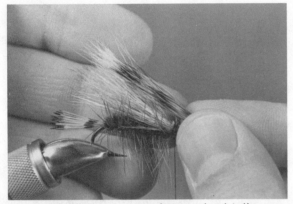

9. Select either gray or fox squirrel tail; even hairs and lay on top of elk hair. This should be accomplished with a very small amount of hair to top the fly out.

10. Trim and tie down securely, dropping a small amount of lacquer to secure the hair.

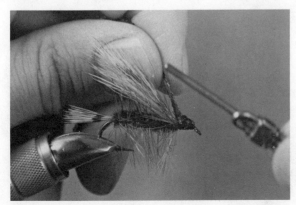

11. Tie in two to three strands of peacock herl.

12. Wrap the peacock herl forward forming a head. This is the finished fly.

THE BITCH CREEK

There are questions which seem to pop up wherever I travel. Questions such as: "What are your favorite flies?", "If you are limited to one fly what fly would it be?"

Once, while visiting a fly fishing club in Washington, a person asked me, "If you were limited to one nymph, what nymph would you choose?" I thought about it and several flies ran through my mind: the Hare's Ear nymph, a variety of caddis nymphs, a stonefly nymph, the Montana Nymph, and the Bitch Creek nymph. I gave some thought to the flies I had used in lakes, creeks and streams and had produced well, under a variety of conditions. One pattern kept flashing through my mind — the Bitch Creek Nymph. I thought about the times on the Beaverhead River and the Big Hole River when the Bitch Creek had saved the day.

"Yes, it would be the Bitch Creek!" I exclaimed.

There is probably not a more versatile nymph available today. Tied in different sizes and different materials it could represent a variety of aquatic insects, and the wiggly rubber antennae and tail are definitely a fish enticer. That question caused me to reflect more deeply on the merits of the pattern. "It is an especially good brook trout fly," I thought to myself. I remember a time when fishing a high mountain lake, nestled back among the Wind River Mountains which was filled with nice-sized brook trout. The fly that I had the most luck with was the black and yellow Bitch Creek.

Thinking about that experience caused me to remember another occasion when I was fishing for golden trout in a lake high in Wyoming's Wind River Mountains; a #14 Bitch Creek nymph turned the trick when nothing else seemed to work. I also recall the time on the Green River when just before dark I let a #2 all black Bitch Creek drift under a big log and just as I began to twitch it back into mid-current, a six-pound brown nearly took the rod out of my hand.

There was also the time of the massive salmon fly hatch on Montana's Big Hole River when I was introduced to a new technique using this pattern. I tied a large fluttering stonefly dry pattern on the tip of my leader, but also attached a Bitch Creek as a dropper. The two fly system was a real struggle to cast, but on almost every drift I would either get action on the surface to the stonefly dry, or the sunken Bitch Creek would attract some attention below.

I have to rate the Bitch Creek as one of the most versatile flys available. It can be used in lakes, streams, and spring creeks. I've tied it in a variety of different colors — yellow and green bodies with an orange or yellow thorax — and they all work. If you are heading toward some Rocky Mountain trout waters, be sure to have some tied up. It should be the flagship of your nymph fleet.

MATERIALS:	Bitch Creek
THREAD:	Yellow monocord
HOOK:	Mustad 9672
SIZES:	4-12
TAIL:	Rubber legs
UNDERBODY:	Lead wire optional
BODY:	Yellow chenille with strip of black chenille over back
RIBBING:	Yellow monocord
THORAX:	Black chenille
LEGS:	Soft brown hackle (hen hackle preferred) and gray ostrich

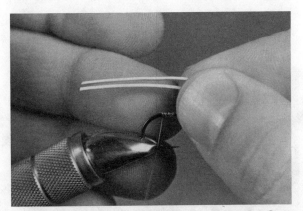

1. Cover the hook shank with thread. Cut off about a two inch piece of rubber hackle.

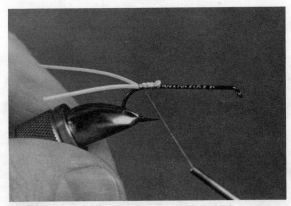

2. Take the rubber hackle and fold it over so that it forms two pieces as shown above. Tie in the rubber hackle on top of the hook directly above the hook point.

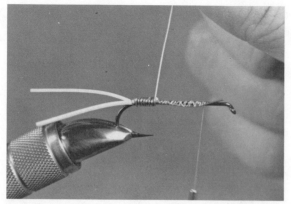

3. From the beginning of the bend start to wrap thin lead wire, wrap this forward to about the middle of the shank of the hook.

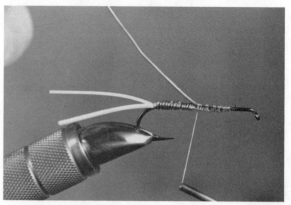

4. Tie in heavy lead wire, starting just behind the eye of the hook and tie back to where the thin lead wire stops.

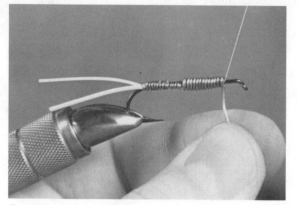

5. Wrap the heavy lead wire forward and tie off. Be sure to leave some room for the head and antennae.

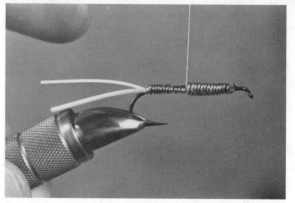

6. Bring tying thread back towards the rear of the hook all the way to the bend.

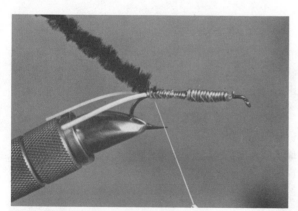

7. Tie in black chenille directly above where the tail was tied in.

8. Tie in yellow chenille and ribbing directly above where the tail was tied in. The yellow chenille should be on top of the black chenille.

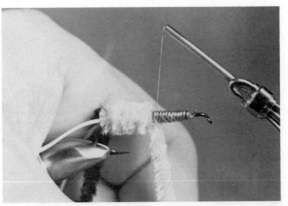

9. Wrap the yellow chenille forward to the middle of the shank of the hook.

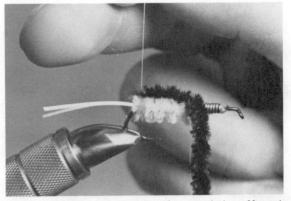

10. Shows wrapping the chenille forward and how far it should be wrapped.

11. Pull the black chenille over the top of the yellow chenille forming a back, tie off but do not clip. This black chenille will also form the thorax.

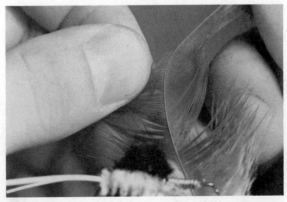

12. Advance the ribbing forward tie off and trim.

13. Shows the fly after the abdomen has been formed.

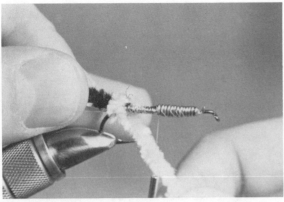

14. Select a saddle hackle of the proper length pull the fibers off one side of the hackle.

15. Tie the hackle in front of where the chenille body stops.

16. Tie in an ostrich herl.

17. Wrap the black chenille forward, tie off and trim.

18. Wrap the gray ostrich herl forward, tie off and trim.

19. Wrap the saddle hackle forward.

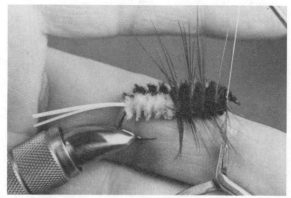

20. Tie off and trim.

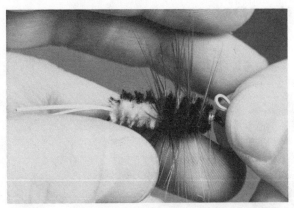

21. Cut a two inch piece of rubber hackle, double it over as with the tail.

22. Place the rubber hackle on top of the hook and tie on. Cover thoroughly with thread, this will form the antennae and also the head.

23. Pull back the antennae and whip finish.

24. Clip the black chenille back as shown above.

25. Shows the completed fly.

GROVE NYMPH

This particular nymph pattern was first shown to me by Rich Anderson of "Streamside Anglers" of Missoula, Montana. It was developed by one of their fishing guides working for them during the summer, Grove Hull.

Rich fondly spoke, "This man is definitely an exceptional person. With Grove Hull you can go down the river, and can have all the tea you want from wild roots. He will identify every bird. Grove hunts with a falcon and has served roast rattlesnake to his clients. Right down the line, he is as close to being able to live with the land as any guide in the Rocky Mountains. Not only that, but he gives fly casting lessons to some of the best known casters in the country Rich recounted that he was by far the "best guide we've ever had the pleasure to work with." My curiosity was set in motion, I had to meet this gentleman, for being around Grove Hull was in itself a truly unique experience.

I asked Grove why he fished. His first answer was for the "recreative parcel of it. The re-creation of a body's mind, spirit and soul. It's something that's enjoyable and there is a challenge to it, which is a part of the whole thing. It's sort of like a golf game, when fish aren't hitting even when you are casting, casting is a part of it. There are the esthetics of the casting, doing a cast rather well, even if the trout don't rise and did this cast make a par on this riffle, or whatever? A little bit of that is satisfying. These are the main reasons. I am not a scientific fisherman and I only know Latin names for a half dozen insects. I like to fish some well-tied flies and fine rivers. The Henry's Fork and spring creeks are the places I really enjoy because of the challenge of those places. Whether a fly is tied with three hackle turns or four doesn't make any difference to me. Whether I know the Latin name of the insect doesn't either. If it's a green and olive job, that's close enough for me. It seems to me the fish have kind of an edge on. It's like we are doing all this stuff and pretending that what we are doing, all the things in our civilized life, are important, but when you come to the fish, he is just trying to stay alive. It doesn't matter whether he is 3 inches, 18 inches or 24 inches, they are all fighting as if it was their last venture on earth, and so I like to fish. I enjoy the birds along the river as we are floating down. I like to listen to the water and see the light reflecting off the water. There are just so many facets to what you are doing by being there. It just seems to be more real than most things we do."

Grove is a young man with a passion for fly fishing. He took up fly tying at the same time he learned to fish. As he says, "Most of you guys have been fishing all of your lives. I happened to get into it because some of my friends at the university did. I have had a hell of a lot of catching up to do and it beat the hell out of me. I couldn't catch a fish, couldn't buy a fish, but I learned and kept with it."

Grove loves to guide and loves both teaching the client, and, in his words, "Learning things from them I never even knew I had learned. One of the reasons I like to guide is the great experiences. I had a ten year old kid on the Smith River who hadn't fly fished before and I wanted him to catch a big fish, so I worked. This was a four or five day float, and I helped him with his casting and worked! And worked! Finally on the last day we pulled up behind this rock. I had never caught a big fish there. The boy cast and pulled out a five pound brown. His father looked at him and said, "It's your fish." He looked at the fish and then at me and gently put the fish back. He wanted it to live, and that's why I guide."

From this simple approach, Grove Hull developed his nymph. More out of frustration than design, he felt for the nymph he was trying to imitate, the patterns were not representative enough. Using materials easily obtained, and with simple methods he created a very realistic and life-like imitation of the stones that hatch in the Missoula area. For this we thank Grove and for getting interested in fly fishing.

MATERIALS:	Grove Nymph
THREAD:	Brown monocord
HOOK:	Mustad 79580 (you must bend this one) or 37160
SIZES:	2-10
TAIL:	Brown round monofilament
UNDERBODY:	Lead wire
BODY:	Olive brown wool yarn
RIBBING:	Dyed brown flat monofilament
WING CASE:	Olive brown wool yarn
THORAX:	Light tan wool yarn
LEGS:	Partridge divided and cemented into three legs on each side
ANTENNAE:	Dyed brown round monofilament

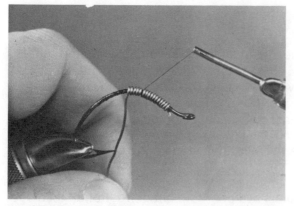

1. Wrap medium weight lead around the hook shank covering the forward part of the shank. Make a number of wraps of thread through the lead to help secure it to the shank.

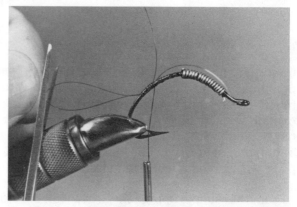

2. Take some brown dyed monofilament and form a loop. Tie the loop in and trim the end, notice proportions and where the tail should be.

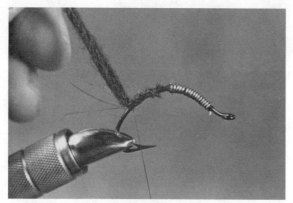

3. Tie in some dark spun angora yarn on top of the hook where the tail starts.

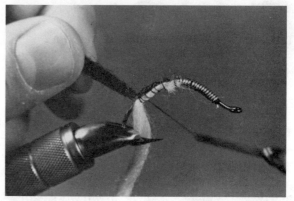

4. Beneath the hook tie in some light angora yarn. It should be tied in so that it ends at the same place that the dark yarn does.

5. Tie in a strand of brown dyed flat monofilament.

6. Make one wrap behind the light yarn, then wrap forward to approximately halfway down the hook.

7. Tie off the dark yarn forming a loop, then pull the tan yarn forward.

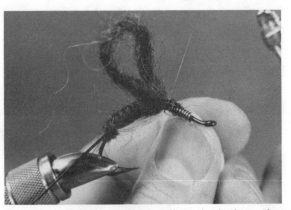

8. Tie off the tan yarn directly below the point where the dark yarn is looped, this will form an underbody. Do not trim the yarn.

9. Rib the flat mono forward in even spacings. Tie off and trim. Select a pheasant breast feather and trim off all the fuzz at the end of the vein.

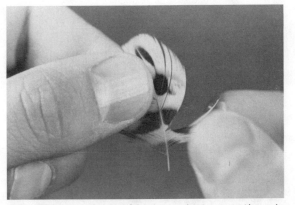

10. Place a drop of lacquer between thumb and forefinger. Separate the feathers into 6 legs, 3 on each side.

11. This is what the completed feather looks like.

12. Tie in the breast feathers securely by the butt. The light side should be facing up.

13. Wrap the tan yarn forward covering the remaining portion of the hook, be sure to leave enough room to tie off and form a head.

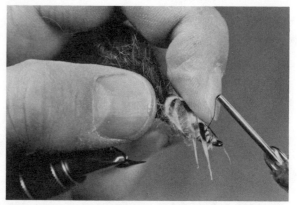

14. With forefinger of the left hand, push forward on the breast feather and tie it down.

15. Pull the dark angora yarn forward and tie down forming a wing case.

16. Take a piece of brown dyed thin monofilament and double it to form two antennae, be sure the curves are out as above.

17. Tie the monofilament directly on top of the head so that it forms "V" like antennae. Trim the antennae and whip finish a head.

18. The Finished Fly.

THE POOR HELGY

The hellgramite, which is found on almost all of our western rivers, is especially popular in Colorado. The talented fly tyer, Jim Poor, who resides in the suburban Denver area, showed me this effective hellgramite pattern. It has the fine qualities of being an effective, representative helgy imitation, yet, it is one of the simplest nymph patterns to tie. While many of the new complex nymph patterns are painstakingly tedious to tie, this one is a breeze to put together. It can be an effective pattern for the tyer who doesn't have the patience to sit down and take 20 minutes to tie an effective looking nymph, then lose it on a backcast two minutes later.

One effective fishing method is to roll this nymph along the bottom with a lead line, but, please note that it is disgustingly easy to lose a fly in the rocks of a streambed. You won't feel so bad losing this fly. The Poor Helgy can be tied in different colors by varying the materials slightly to imitate various colorations of the natural in your particular stream.

Mr. Poor has always been a practical fly tyer and his patterns represent that fact. When visiting Denver, be sure to see Jim at his "Angler's All" shop, and discuss Colorado fishing with the master.

MATERIALS:	Poor Helgy
THREAD:	Black monocord
HOOK:	Mustad 9672
SIZES:	4-10
TAIL:	Dark moose body hair
UNDERBODY:	Lead wire
BODY:	Dark moose body hair
RIBBING:	Black monocord
CASE:	Black magic marker (waterproof)

THORAX: Tan chenille

LEGS: Brown saddle hackle

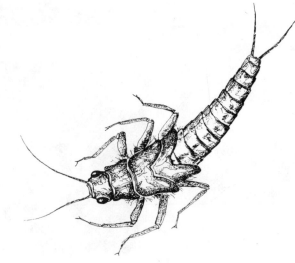

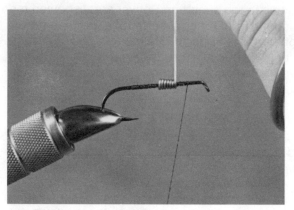

1. Beginning halfway down the shank, wrap a piece of heavy lead wire to ¼ back from the eye.

2. Select out a bunch of dark moose hair. Remove the underfur and small hairs.

3. With the thread directly above the barb, tie in the moose hair with several tight wraps.

4. Shows the moose hair tied in with several tight wraps.

5. Separate the bunch of moose hair in half at the rear.

6. Make several wraps around each bunch of moose hair forming a forked tail.

7. Shows the forked tail.

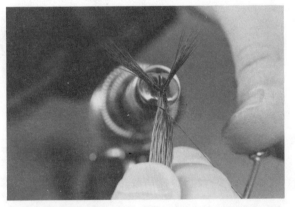

8. Advance the tying thread forward in several even spacings.

9. Tie off the moose hair bunch as shown above. Notice the even spacings.

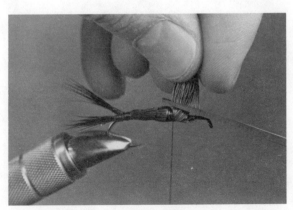

10. Trim the moose hair butts.

11. Cover the trimmed ends with thread forming a smooth base upon which to make a thorax. Note that the body ends approximately halfway down the shank of the hook.

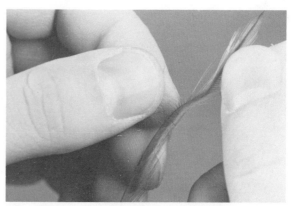

12. Select out a saddle hackle, remove the fibers from one side of the hackle.

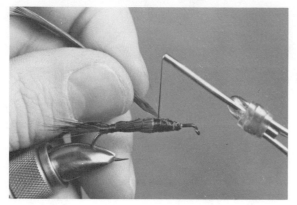

13. Tie in the hackle where the body ends.

14. Tie in a three inch piece of chenille. Lacquer the thread. This will form a tacky base on which to wrap the chenille.

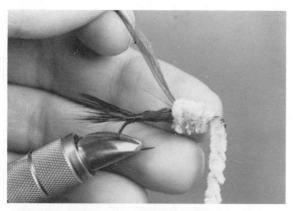

15. Wrap the chenille forward, tie off and trim.

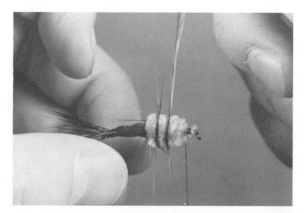

16. Wrap the saddle hackle forward, tie off and trim.

114

17. Trim the saddle hackle along the top of the thorax.

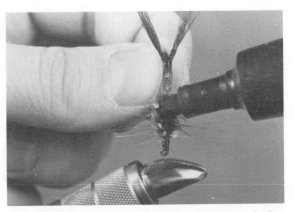

18. With a dark waterproof marker, mark the top of the chenille as shown in the above picture.

19. Thoroughly lacquer the moose hair body.

20. The Finished Fly.

CHESTNEY'S STONE NYMPH

This interesting nymph pattern was shown to me be by Jim Chestney. He gives credit for the original idea and the development of this fly to Jack Michievicz of Phoenixville, Pennsylvania. Jack put him wise to a wonderful cotton chenille, which gives superb breathing action. Jim first showed this unusual chenille, and I was very impressed with its feel. The cotton chenille is softer, more lifelike, a completely different appearance in the water than the chenille that we have been accustomed to using for the past many years. This material is available through Jack at his tackle shop in Phoenixville.

Even though mono was originally used for this pattern, we now use latex exclusively. Latex gives some fantastic colorations when painted with waterproof felt point markers. A good selection of these felt markers should be in every fly tyers collection of materials. They can be obtained from many fly fishing supply houses or from most art studios. The reason I selected this particular stonefly pattern is that it represents another series of species found in many areas of the West. Most of the emphasis on stoneflys in our area is given to the larger **Pteronarcys** and **Acroneuria** species. There are many other areas which have smaller species of stoneflies which this pattern will effectively imitate. I suggest you check out the availablity of the stoneflies in your area and see if this pattern might work for you. One suggestion is to change the color to match the stones for your area. I feel this fly is effective enough to deserve a special place in your fly box.

MATERIALS:	Chestney's Stone Nymph
THREAD:	Tan
HOOK:	Mustad 9671, 9672
SIZES:	6-10
TAIL:	Two fibers from a goose quili dyed light brown
UNDERBODY:	20 lb. test mono tied in at each side to give a flat body
BODY:	Deep yellow fur dubbing with pale latex strip wrapped over top, darken top with dark brown felt pen

RIBBING:	Dark brown buttonhole twist thread
CASE:	Mottled turkey section
THORAX:	Light brown cotton chenille
LEGS:	Small finely barred feather from the wing of a quail, grouse, woodcock, etc.
HEAD:	Mottled turkey quill section and cotton chenille (same as in thorax)

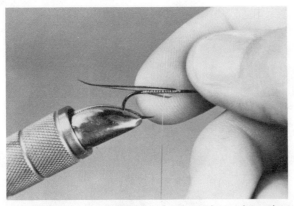

1. Wrap a small base of tying thread to the middle of the hook. Cut out a light brown dyed goose quill fiber. Measure for length. Hold between thumb and forefinger of left hand along the side of the hook and tie in securely.

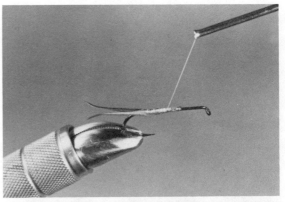

2. Repeat this with the other goose quill fiber, cover the fibers with thread to where the bend begins. Notice how the curves of the fibers are both facing out.

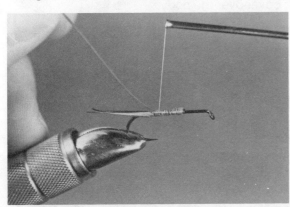

3. Beginning one third behind the eye tie in two pieces of 20 pound monofilament along the sides of the hook. Thoroughly cover these with thread. Cut these off just above the barb.

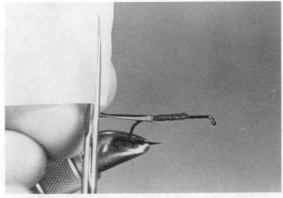

4. Cut a three inch strip of thin latex approximately ¼" wide.

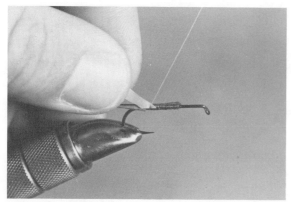

5. Taper the end of the latex and tie in just above the barb.

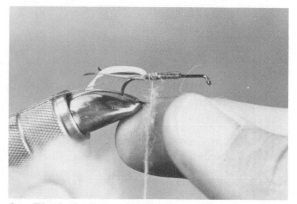

6. Tie in a three inch piece of dark brown buttonhole twist thread. Dub on some deep yellow dubbing.

7. Place a drop of vinyl cement on the under-body. While still tacky, pull the buttonhole twist thread to the side with right hand and make one turn of dubbing behind it, then begin to dub a body forward.

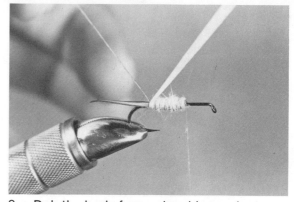

8. Dub the body forward making a nice even taper to approximately one third behind the eye. Grasp the latex in the right hand and thread in the left hand, pull the latex and begin to cover over the body.

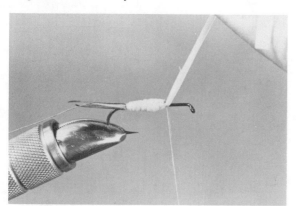

9. Stretching the latex, wrap it forward over-lapping with each wrap. Tie off and trim.

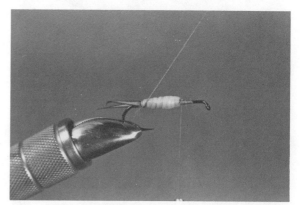

10. Rib the body spacing evenly and pull tight with each wrap. This will help secure the latex to the hook.

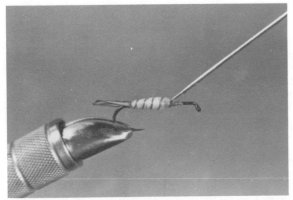

11. Tie off and trim the ribbing. Place a drop of lacquer on the cut ends. This will keep the stretched latex from pulling out.

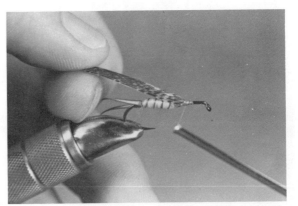

12. Cut out a mottled turkey section approximately ¼" across. Tie in just in front of the body. Put a drop of lacquer on the wraps.

13. Pull out a hen chicken saddle feather. Prepare as in the above picture.

14. Tie in the hen feather by the tip.

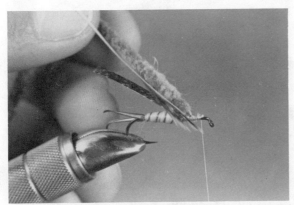

15. Cut out about a 4" piece of light brown cotton chenille. Tie this in just in front of the hen feather.

16. Wrap the cotton chenille forward forming a fat fuzzy thorax. Tie off and trim.

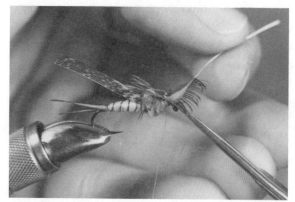

17. Pull the hen feather over the eye, tie off and trim.

18. Pull the mottled turkey feather over the eye forming a wing case, tie off but do not trim.

19. Lay a two or three inch piece of cotton chenille over top of the turkey feather. Tie in using an "X" method.

20. Make a simple over-hand knot with cotton chenille and pull tight.

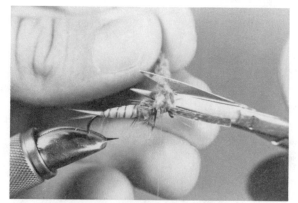

21. Trim off short.

22. Pull the turkey feather back over the cotton chenille and tie off. Pinch this feather in and cut into a notched wing. Pull the thread beneath the eye, whip finish and trim.

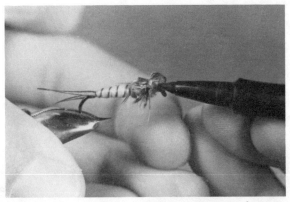

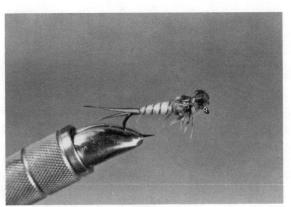

23. With a dark brown waterproof pen, darken both eyes and coat them with a drop of lacquer. If you wish, you can also darken the top of the abdomen.

24. The Finished Fly

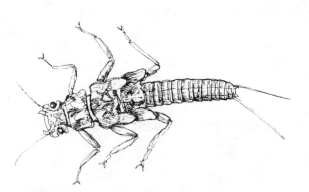

BROOK'S STONE

Charlie Brooks is a unique individual. He is an interesting and a truly western writer and fisherman. His book, **Larger Trout for Western Fishermen**, is a fine classic in western angling literature. Charlie is a practical fisherman, and his flies reflect a simple, straight approach to fishing. His imitations are easy to tie, and most important, work very well. Brooks believes in large flies, as he has said many times before "that few trout take many size 28 nymphs. Maybe small trout do eat such insects, but if you are fishing for fingerlings, you are reading the wrong books." Charlie fishes for large fish, and knows his business. His advice to the visiting angler, "pick the flies that represent the basics of the trout's diet". He contends that you are best fishing larger flies which consist of the greatest percentage of the fish's diet. This is the way to take large fish. Charlie's Stone will represent the **Pteronarcys** and **Acroneuria,** which is prevalent in a lot of our western rivers. It is a big fly for big fish, and it should be tied heavily weighted.

I recommend Charlie's nymph for fishermen who want a nymph that will work well in deep heavy water, and will sink to the bottom. This fly will represent the larger stonefly nymphs and is easy to tie, effective, and very durable. It is practical like the man who invented it. We recommend everyone who fishes the West to have a couple of Charlie's books. Another book: **Nymph Fishing for Larger Trout** is a definate must for the western fisherman. I don't think you will be disappointed in Charlie's nymph.

MATERIALS: Brook's Stone

THREAD: Black monocord

HOOK: Mustad 9672

SIZES: 4-10

UNDERBODY: Heavy lead wire

BODY: Black fuzzy yarn, heavy

RIBBING: Brown dyed flat nylon monofilament

GILLS: White or light gray ostrich herl

LEGS: One grizzly and one brown dyed grizzly

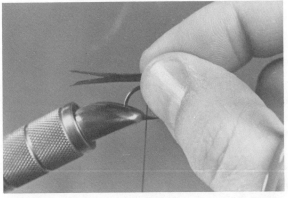

1. Select two goose quill fibers, match these up so they are equal in length and so that the concave sides are facing away from each other as shown in the above picture.

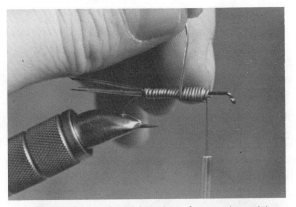

2. Tie in the goose quill tail in the middle of the shank of the hook. Note that the fibers lie along and not on top of the hook.

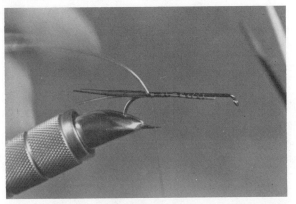

3. Tie in some medium or heavy lead wire, size depends upon the size of the hook and how fast you want it to sink.

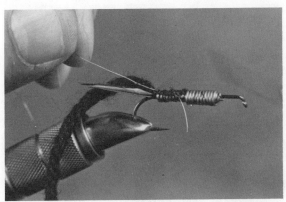

4. The bobbin should be in a forward position. Wrap the lead forward then back over itself to halfway down the shank. This will make a heavier thorax. Wrap the thread back over the lead wire to secure it.

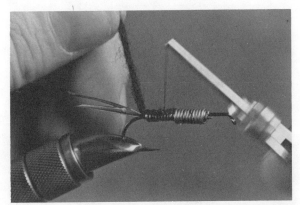

5. Tie in the yarn at approximately the middle of the shank of the hook and wrap the thread backwards over the yarn.

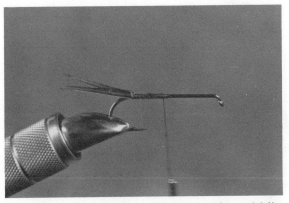

6. Tie in a piece of gold wire the same place the yarn was tied in. Advance the thread backwards over the gold wire to the tail, bring the thread forward again.

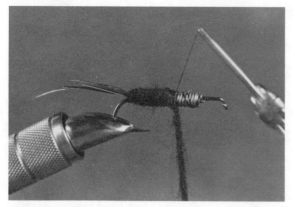

7. Wrap the yarn forward and tie off in the middle of the hook; do not clip.

8. Rib the abdomen with even spacings of gold wire, tie off and clip.

9. Select one grizzly and one brown hackle.

10. Pull the hackle fibers off of one side of each of the hackles.

11. Tie in both hackles in front of the abdomen, tie in two pieces of ostrich plume.

12. Place a drop of lacquer where the ostrich plumes and hackles are tied in. This will cement the yarn to the hook and keep the materials from slipping.

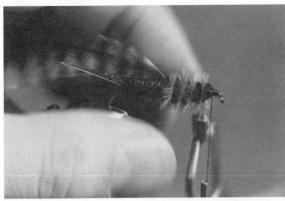

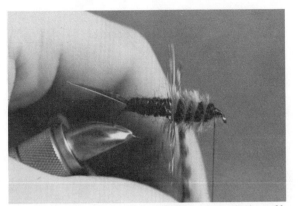

13. Wrap the yarn forward forming a fat thorax, tie off and trim. Wrap both of the ostrich plumes forward, tie off and trim.

14. Wrap both hackles forward and tie off and trim. Whip finish and lacquer the head.

15. Shows the completed fly.

THE CADDIS

What has caused this new resurgence of interest in our old friend the caddis? One of the many reasons is a keen interest in entomology by today's angler, and the approach to more realistic imitations of the natural insects that inhabit our streams.

The constant push by new fly tyers and anglers for a more natural and representative pattern has caused us to take a more scientific look at our fishing methods and flies. This keen interest in a closer study of aquatic insects has brought some interesting facts to light. Probably one of the most common insects in trout water is the caddis, and in many cases, it is one of the least understood.

Since most caddis flies share a similar silhouette, most of our imitations can be tied in the same manner. By using different materials, and varying the color and size of our patterns we can effectively imitate most caddis naturals we run across.

In the following chapter we have tried to pick out some of the new and effective caddis patterns. For further study, I can recommend a couple of books which will enhance your investigation of this amazing little insect. One particularly good book, **The Challenge of the Trout**, by Gary LaFontaine offers several chapters on western caddis fishing, its theories, imitations and general information on fishing the various hatches that occur on our Western rivers.

Another excellent book which will give you further insight into the hows and whys of the caddis, and how it relates to the fisherman is the book, **THE CADDIS AND THE ANGLER**, by Solomon & Leiser. There have been many articles written in magazines, and almost any copy of the **FLY FISHERMAN MAGAZINE** you pick up will have an article on the caddis.

The increasing interest in this particular fly and the development of new materials has brought about an enlightened age of even further realistic caddis imitations. There has been a recent surge of interest in emergent pupae. Out of this have come new realistic patterns and methods of fishing them.

Caddis and all their imitations have always been around, but recent interest has formed a new field for the fisherman and fly tyer. I have included, in the following chapter, several patterns which have proven to be very productive and interesting to tie.

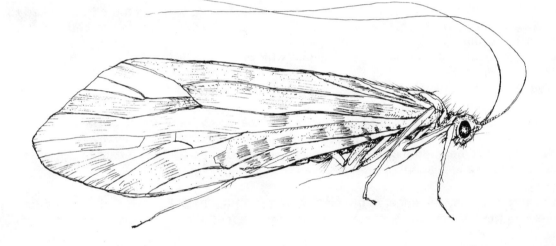

THE ELK HAIR CADDIS

This particular morsel was developed by Al Troth, to match the various western caddis hatches occurring in his beloved Montana streams and many other parts of the West.

My first experience with the Troth Caddis came while fishing with Al on the Beaverhead River near his home town of Dillon, Montana. He introduced me to the caddis to be used as a floating dropper fly, while fishing a large Girdle Bug nymph pattern. The high riding Elk Hair Caddis would also serve as a strike indicator on a dead drift of the nymph.

As we drifted around each bend of the river, I laid my clumsy Girdle Bug into the deep pockets where the large browns lay. The drift of the boat would cause the Girdle Bug to swing deep under the cut banks, while the bouyant Elk Hair Caddis floated above it on the surface. After a few minutes of splashing the large Girdle Bug into the fish-laden pockets, I had my first large brown on. He raced to the middle of the river and then with one powerful run came back upstream, passed the boat and headed for a grass-covered bank.

In an effort to keep the angered brown from reaching the bank I pulled hard, ripping the ugly Girdle Bug from his mouth. He then dashed, unimpeded, into the safety of the green mossy bank.

The line had drifted back towards the boat as we continued floating down the winding river. I started stripping in the slack, and was looking for the next busy looking pocket and suddenly I heard a loud "slurp" and glanced up just in time to see my Elk Hair Caddis disappear. I raised my rod to tighten the line and made sure I had the hook securely in the jaw of the fish. A few minutes later we boated a nice pound-and-a-half rainbow that had plucked off the little caddis. This he did after the large brown had freed itself from the Girdle Bug and fled the scene.

This "two-fly" concept led me to think back to some of the two fly fishermen I had known in my boyhood days around Lander, Wyoming. Some of the oldtimers who came into my father's shop bought flies that were snelled with leaders, so they could easily attach them to the line. They always preached the two-fly concept but I had found such a rig more awkward to cast. However, on that day with Al Troth, I found that the use of two flies can offer a totally new dimension in trout fishing. A nymph or streamer on the end of the line can be used to drift underneath banks while a floating dropper can attract fish feeding on the surface.

A year later, on the Big Hole River, a fishing companion of mine, former Under Secretary of the Interior, Nat Reed, plucked off a six-pound-plus, brightly colored brown on a #10 Royal Wulff, used as a drop in a similar two-fly system. Meanwhile, forgetting the lesson of the previous year, I continued to fish with a single fly with somewhat less spectacular results. Nat's prize fish had first swirled at a Montana Nymph and then rose to the Royal Wulff, as if to refuse the nymph and take the dry instead. A very interesting situation.

I leave it to you to determine whether this method could be used in your area. From a boat it has its advantages, but it also has its disadvantages. I've seen more than one fish lost because one of the flies had caught in the net and caused trouble in landing the fish, resulting in a trophy released prematurely.

Several experiences later I had a chance to recognize another value of the Elk Hair Caddis. I was floating Montana's Beaverhead with Bill James, a friend and fishing guide from Dillon, Montana. This tall, burley, good-natured fellow has a special place in his heart for this river.

It was an early fall day and there was a particularly large adult hatch of crane flies in all sections of the river, blanketing the water and skating with the breeze which the trout were niftily picking off the ruffled surface. These were large trout, and their dorsal fins cut the water like sharks as they cruised in search of the dancing crane flies.

I tied on a #8, brown bodied, Light Elk Hair Caddis, and within minutes I started tying into fish. Before the float was over, I had boated many nice-size browns, taken from the banks and several rainbows taken from the middle of the stream.

The technique I was used to was to skate a Mucilin-dressed Elk Hair Caddis across the water and utilize the breeze to help propel the fly. This action brought trout careening across the water in an effort to nail the large caddis. It was amazing. They were taking the Elk Hair Caddis for a crane fly! I didn't know if it was the size of the fly, the coloration, or the action that was bringing them. All I know was the fish were coming.

One of the strangest events of my fishing career occured on this same trip. On this paticular stretch of river, the current ran under a large tree and then fanned out into a placid deep hole just below it. Our boat drifted to the edge of the hole and I was false casting just before dropping the caddis near the edge of the tree. Suddenly, out of nowhere, one of the most beautiful rainbows I had ever seen in my life, jumped three feet out of the water in an attempt to nail the airborne fly. That fish would have tipped the scales past the 10 pound mark!

Bill James and I just sat in the boat, shaking our heads. When something like that happens silence speaks more eloquently than words.

We pulled to the bank and cast to that spot time and time again. Nothing happened, but those are the kind of experiences which bring a fisherman back to such a river. Every time I return to the Beaverhead, I will think about the flying rainbow decorated with the deep red slash along its side. I will recall the gaping mouth which almost — but not quite — clamped on the false cast fly. It's just one sight I'll never forget.

I recommend Al Troth's Elk Hair Caddis as one of the most versatile fly patterns to be had. Whether floating on the water or waving in the air, trout can't seem to resist it.

MATERIALS:	Troth Elk Hair Caddis
THREAD:	Danville tan 6/0 pre-waxed
HOOK:	Mustad 94836, 94840
SIZES:	8-16
BODY:	Hare's ear dubbing
RIBBING:	.005'' dia gold wire
WING:	Cream colored elk flank hair
HACKLE:	Dark brown or furnace

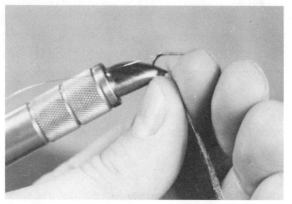

1.   Tie in a 4'' piece of gold wire at the bend of the hook.   Apply some dubbing to the thread.

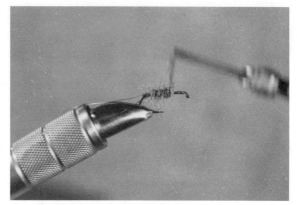

2.   Begin dubbing a body forward.

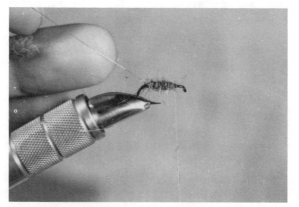

3.   Finish dubbing the body.   Notice the above proportions.

4.   Tie in hackle at the eye of the hook allowing 1/5 of the shank to tie in the wing.

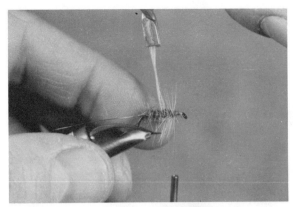

5. Palmer the hackle backwards.

6. Tie the hackle down with three turns of wire at the bend. Trim the hackle.

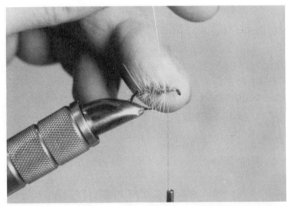

7. Wind the wire up through the hackle and tie off at the eye. Do not cut the wire, work it back and forth until it breaks forming a curl that keeps it from slipping.

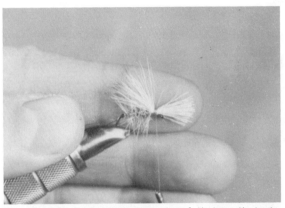

8. Cut out a small bunch of light elk hair. Remove the small hairs and underfur; stack until even. Holding the wing between thumb and forefinger, tie in the wing with several loose wraps. Then make several tight wraps to hold the wing in place.

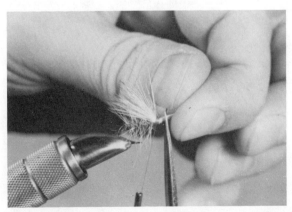

9. Clip the fibers off even with the eye. Whip finish and lacquer.

10. The Finished Fly.

THE GODDARD CADDIS

With the caddis being so important in the trout's food chain, I believe it is imperative for a person to have a wide variety of caddis patterns in order to match any different type of situation. One problem with most caddis patterns is poor floatability. Many of the older caddis patterns were tied sparsely, and until the recent emergence of the elk hair caddis patterns, they floated very poorly in heavy water. Not all our western rivers are placid streams. We have tumbling, mountain brooks, and larger, swift rivers, such as the Madison and Snake. On these it is important to have a pattern that floats high and dry.

One day while thumbing through a magazine called **ANGLER**, (a fine colorful, publication out of California) I happened upon a column called "Fit to be Tied," written by Andre Puyans. The article was interesting and captured my imagination. The column described a fly developed by John Goddard, a well-known English fly tyer, and a fishing companion of his, Cliff Henry. With the help of Andre and his knowledge of spun deer hair they developed an interesting and functional fly, that I think fills many of the gaps left in the various caddis imitations.

Its style is simple and fashioned after the famous Irresistible fly, which has been around for some years. The shape really seems to be the key. Its clipped deer hair body is shaped to suggest a caddis wing. This, along with its superior floatation immediately made the Goddard Caddis a pattern to be reckoned with. The fly has broad appeal and can be used anywhere from the United States to Alaska, South America, New Zealand and Canada.

Of the many new caddis flies offered on the market today, this one offers one of the most exciting dimensions that has come along in many a year. Its tent style, clipped hair body can be formed with caribou hair, deer hair and even antelope hair on larger sizes. Different colors can be achieved by using dyed types of antelope and deer hair, along with many natural shades. By also switching hackle colors the tyer can devise an almost endless variety of imitations. Its floatability and visibility along with the ease of tying will make the Goddard Caddis a standard pattern in the years to come. This British-American effort will bring hours of pleasure to anglers throughout the world.

MATERIALS: Goddard Caddis

THREAD: Black "A" monocord and tan 6/0 pre-waxed

HOOK: Mustad 94840, 7957B, 7948A

SIZES:	8-14
BODY:	Natural deer hair marked with waterproof pen
WING:	Natural deer hair
ANTENNAE:	Brown hackle stems
HACKLE:	Brown or red game

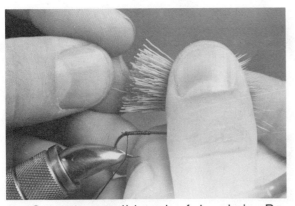

1. Cut out a small bunch of deer hair. Remove underfur and small hairs. You should have black "A" mono tied to the hook now.

2. Lay deer hair over the top of the shank of the hook and hold with thumb and forefinger.

3. Make one loose wrap around the deer hair, then on the second wrap, begin to pull. Pull tightly on the third wrap.

4. Wind thread through the hair forward.

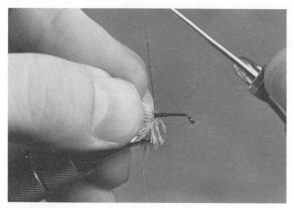

5. Make several wraps just in front of the hair pulling back as you make the wraps.

6. Select a second bunch of hair, clip the tapered points.

7. The second hair clump is spun in front of the first batch as in step 3. The hair should cover about two-thirds of the hook shank leaving at least one-third for a hackle.

8. Compress the hair clump with thumb and forefinger.

9. Make a couple of half-hitches in front of the second hair clump.

10. Take the fly out of the vise.

11. Trim the bottom flat.

12. Trim the top at an angle. It should be larger toward the rear.

13. Clip the body into a cone shape.

14. Shows the cone shape of the body.

15. Cut the wing at an angle to form a tent shaped caddis wing.

16. This is the finished body and wing shape.

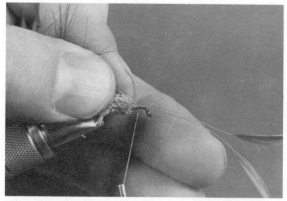

17. Attach the tan 6/0 pre-waxed thread in front of the body and tie in antennae, these should be on top of the hook with the hackle curves facing away from each other.

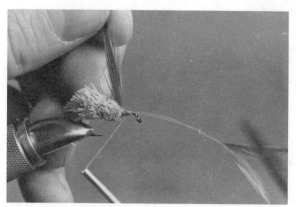

18. Attach hackles just in front of body.

19. Wind hackles one at a time. Be sure hackle size is not over one and a half hook gaps.

20. Tie off hackles, whip finish.

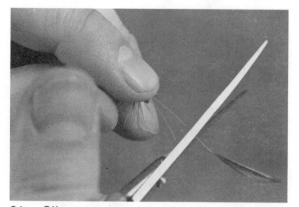

21. Clip antennae. Lengths should be 2-2½ times the hook gap.

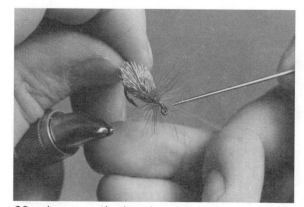

22. Lacquer the head and antennae.

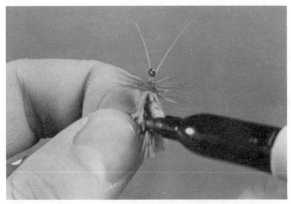

23. Color the underbody with a "Panatone" permanent marker.

24. Shows the completed fly from top.

25. Shows completed fly from the side.

POOR'S CADDIS

In this day and age it is hard for the tackle shops to keep pace with the many changes and innovations of the fishing business. New flies, equipment, and other angling accessories make the specialty fly fishing shop an important part of the angler's enjoyment of the sport. Two innovative gentlemen who have kept their customers on top of this entangled fly fishing business and Jim Poor and his partner Bill Shappel, of "Angler's All" in Denver, Colorado. Through their tackle shop in Littleton, Colorado, they offer expert advice about the nearby Colorado fishing waters, and have outfitted their esteemed clients for trips all over the world.

Jim, who escapes to the fine trout streams of New Zealand each winter, is possibly the finest fishermen and tyer of small flies I know today. And when I say small, I mean very small. Jim cut his teeth on the South Platte River south of Denver, which is considered by many to be one of the finest quality fishing waters to be found today. This is a place where anglers can test their skill with very small dry flies, which at times may be as small as size #24 or even smaller. After being involved with the Platte River, for over forty years, Jim's practical fishing experience with tiny fly patterns is unequaled. Jim has tutored me in many different facets of the fishing business, including everything from the art of selling a fly rod to the best place to buy fly leaders. I have paid close attention to his advice, because when he talks, the wise angler will listen.

What Jim is to the art of angling, Bill Shappel is to the business side of the sport. Jim told me that he brought Bill into the department because he loves the outdoors and fishing, but more important, he had the business skill and training that Jim needed for his growing clientele at "Angler's All". The combination of these talents reflect the quality of their shop, which is widely known as a haven for the visiting angler and a place where knowledge can be freely exchanged.

Oh yes, Jim might be a little crotchety every once in a while, but wouldn't you be if you had some of the finest fishing in the world only 30 miles away and you had to be stuck in a shop?

Jim and Bill are in constant contact with their tyers. They are told of changing fishing conditions and get new ideas from their clients. Together, with a group of young energetic fly tyers and fishermen, they form a staff of knowledgeable, courteous people that allow a free exchange of fishing ideas. No secrets kept here; when a new fly pattern is developed it is freely exchanged among friends.

The Poor Caddis has been a pattern born of such open exchange, and it has been found to be very productive in Colorado waters. Bill designed the pattern himself, taking the ideas of many of his angling friends. They developed a fly that differs from other caddis patterns in several ways. It can be modified to fit most any caddis hatch, especially the small caddis patterns that hatch in rivers such as the South Platte.

Bill felt this fly should only be named after the friend and business partner who had come to mean so much to him. Come and enjoy an experience with the Poor Caddis.

MATERIALS: Poor's Caddis

THREAD: White or cream 6/0 pre-waxed

HOOK: Mustad 7948A, 94840, 7957B

SIZES: 10-16

RIBBING: Badger hackle tied palmer style

BODY: Cream dubbing

WING: Turkey tail feather section

HACKLE: Badger hackle

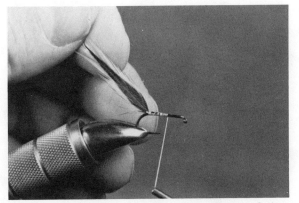

1. Tie in the hackle above the point of the hook. Wrap back over the hackle butt to the bend.

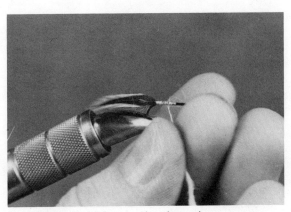

2. Apply dubbing to the thread.

3.   Dub a tapered body two-thirds of the way up the shank toward the eye. Be sure to lift the hackle and make a wrap of dubbing behind it.

4.   Palmer the hackle forward to the end of the body, tie off and trim.

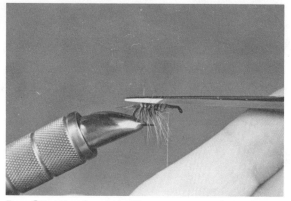

5.   Clip the hackle fibers on top of the body very short.

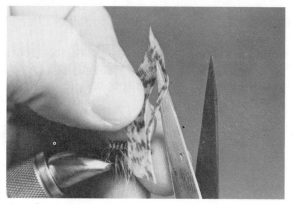

6.   Cut out a piece of turkey quill approximately ¼" wide.

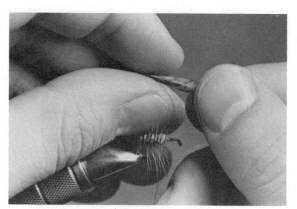

7.   Fold the wing in half.

8.   Trim the wing at an angle as above.

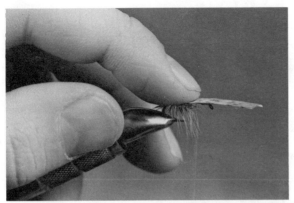

9.   Hold the wing on top of the hook and tie in with several wraps.

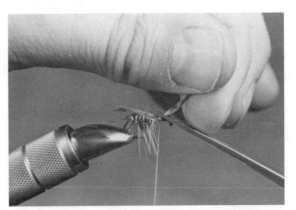

10.   Trim the excess butts at an angle and cover them with thread.

11.   Pull the fibers off the butt of a badger hackle and tie in at the base of the wing.

12.   Wrap the hackle forward, tie off and trim. Whip finish a head.

13.   Notice the shape of the wing.

14.   The Finished Fly

COLORADO KING

This group of flies is one of the wonderful inventions of the innovative fly tyer George Bodmer from Colorado Springs. Originally tied as an attractor pattern, anglers have found it to be productive over a broad range of fishing conditions. The Trude-style wing has a silhouette suggestive of either caddis flies or stoneflies. However, if the wing is tied at a greater angle, it can be a useful mayfly pattern.

Using elk hair instead of deer hair will make a much more durable fly. The body color can be changed to imitate various caddis or stone flies in your area. I suggest you give George's pattern a try when some of those fluttering caddis have you wondering what to use.

MATERIALS:	Colorado King, Brown
THREAD:	Brown 6/0 pre-waxed
HOOK:	Mustad 94840
SIZES:	8-18
TAIL:	Dark moose body hair tied in a "V" style
BODY:	Brown hare's mask fur
WING:	Dark deer body hair tied trude style, could also use dark elk
HACKLE:	Brown tied palmer over body

MATERIALS:	Colorado King, Light
THREAD:	Yellow 6/0 pre-waxed
HOOK:	Mustad 94840

SIZES:	8-18
TAIL:	Moose body hair tied in a "V" style
BODY:	Dubbed yellow rabbit fur
WING:	Light deer body hair or elk hair tied trude style
HACKLE:	Grizzly tied palmer over body

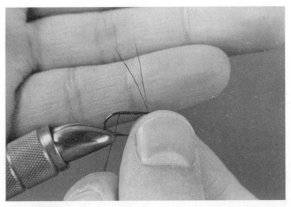

1. Select two stiff strands of dark moose hair. This should be obtained from body hair and not moose mane.

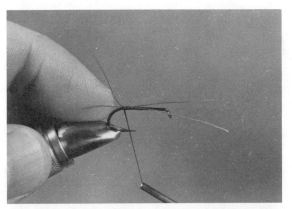

2. Tie in both strands on top of hook, using a finger to separate the tail into a V-shape.

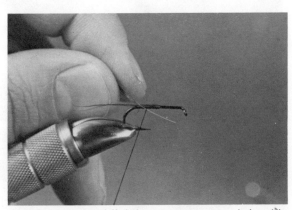

3. Select a reddish-brown game cock hackle and tie in securely at the tail.

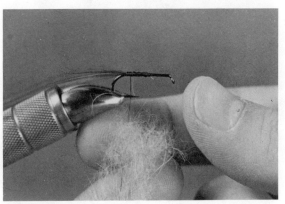

4. Dub in soft underfur.

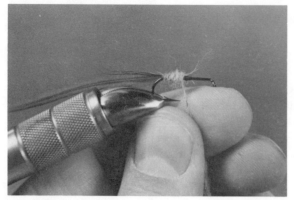 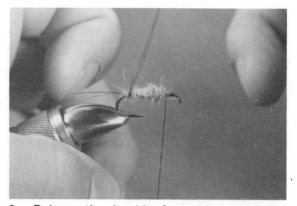

5. With thumb and forefinger twist the fur gently around the thread, making several wraps in between twists. Lift the hackle and make one wrap behind it.

6. Palmer the hackle forward toward the eye. Notice proportions and try to match as per our picture.

7. Continue wrapping the hackle towards the end of the body, keeping the proper gap between wraps.

8. Tie-off and trim your hackle and lay a small base of light thread towards eye of hook.

9. Lay a small bunch of neatly stacked hair directly over top of hook, match proportions as shown in the picture. Notice the thumb and forefinger, as the hair should be loosely held between them.

10. Switch hands using the thumb and forefinger of the other hand and bring the bobbin over top of the hair and tie the hair down tightly. The cut end of the hair should flair as shown in the picture.

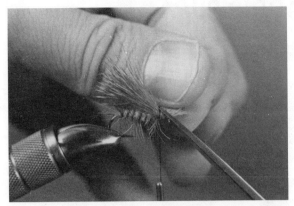 

11. With thumb and forefinger of your left hand, pull the hair away, and at a slight angle, trim with scissors. Be careful not to trim the thread and make sure that the thread has the hair securely tied down before trimming. This will prevent twisting.

12. Wrap tying thread towards the eye of the hook in a neat fashion, tapering the head and covering all of the hair. Then with a bodkin, lacquer the forked moose hair tail and add a drop of lacquer to the base of the hair and the head.

13. The Finished Fly.

SPARKLE CADDIS PUPA

Gary LaFontaine is a clinical psychologist who has been intensely involved in trout research. He is now widely accepted as an expert on caddis and their imitations.

The Sparkle Caddis Pupa is an outgrowth of Gary's masters thesis on the selective feeding response of trout. Here he found that the more distinctive the physical appearance of an insect type, the more selectively the fish keyed on it. In this respect, the shimmering air bubbles carried under the pupal sheath by an emerging caddis fly were one of the strongest visual characteristics.

This research prompted Gary to experiment with various materials to find something that was not only translucent, but also reflected light like an air bubble. The Sparkle Caddis Pupa incorporates both of these properties into an extremely productive fly. The Sparkle Caddis is tied in a variety of colors, depending upon the caddis found in your area. I hope you will find this pattern as useful as many others have.

Gary has told me that he expects his new book **CADDIS FLIES**, to be out by Christmas of 1980. This is the culmination of ten years of research on caddis flies. I think that both this and his other book, **THE CHALLENGE OF THE TROUT** would be excellent additions to your angling library. I highly commend Gary on his work.

MATERIALS:	Sparkle Caddis Pupa (Emergent Grannom)
THREAD:	Brown 6/0 pre-waxed
HOOK:	Mustad 3906B, 7957B, 94840
SIZES:	12-14
BODY:	Olive/brown rabbit fur blend
OVERBODY:	Chocolate brown "Sparkle" yarn
WING:	Brown dyed deer hair
HEAD:	Brown marabou

MATERIALS:	Sparkle Caddis Pupa (Local)
THREAD:	Black 6/0 pre-waxed
HOOK:	Mustad 3906B, 7957B, 94840
SIZES:	10-18
BODY:	Mix of tan "Sparkle" yarn and tan rabbit
OVERBODY:	Tan "Sparkle" yarn
WING:	Light brown deer hair
HEAD:	Brown marabou

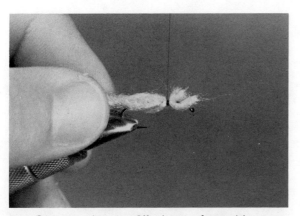

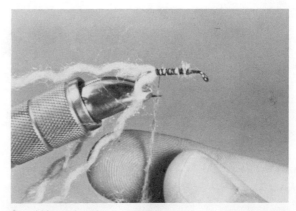

1. Cut out about a 3" piece of sparkle yarn. Separate out several strands; the amount of strands depends on the size of the hook. Tie these in approximately ⅓ back from the eye.

2. Wrap back over the sparkle yarn to the bend of the hook. Apply some of the sparkle fur dubbing.

3. Dub a body forward, notice the above proportions.

4. With a comb or toothbrush fray the sparkle yarn.

5. Continue to brush the sparkle yarn until it is completely frayed as shown above.

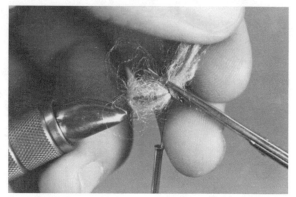

6. Pull the sparkle yarn forward completely surrounding the hook. Tie off and trim. Cover the exposed ends throughly; place a drop of lacquer on the wraps.

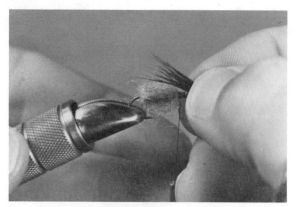

7. Cut out a small bunch of dyed deer hair, measure for length.

8. With the thread just behind the eye tightly tie in the deer hair bunch. Make a few wraps backward loosely to keep the deer hair bunch from flaring.

9. Trim the ends and cover the exposed ends with thread.

10. Cut out several strands of marabou, tie in at the base of the wing.

11. Place a drop of lacquer on the thread base; wrap the marabou forward; tie off and trim.

12. Shows the completed fly. Notice that you can see the body through the sparkle yarn sheath.

STILL WATER INSECTS
AND
ATTRACTOR PATTERNS

As angling pressure continues to increase on many streams, a number of stream fishermen are turning to lakes to expand their fishing skills. This has caused a surge of interest in dragon flies, leeches, and crayfish. In the following chapter, we have offered some imitations which will enhance your lake fishing experience.

The advent of the belly boats to the lake fishing scene has allowed the angler greater mobility at less expense. Spotting a fish and maneuvering into the proper position in one of these float-ables adds a certain challenge to lake fishing that has not been satisfied with normal wading and boat fishing methods.

Aside from belly boats, there is a certain challenge in fly fishing the still waters due to the variety of methods which can be used to take trout. Imitating mayflies and midges has often resulted in some worthy catches. While streamer fishing has been the traditional method of taking lake trout, nymph fishing has recently become popular and resulted in some trophy catches.

One commonly overlooked nymph is the dragon fly. While it is almost impossible to imitate the adult dragon fly buzzing over the water's surface, it is easy to match the shape of the nymph. This fat, juicy nymph represents a good meal to the wary trout.

While the damsel flies are more common in still water, many species exist in slow currents. They are agile swimmers and are found clinging to vegetation in many slow currents. Their slender, minnow-like appearance makes them a challenge to imitate, but their importance in the food chain makes it a worthwhile proposition.

Probably of the greatest importance in this chapter are the attractor patterns. You're on the stream, you look around, and nothing seems to be happening. What do you do? Many anglers reach for their fly boxes and pull out an attractor pattern. These flies are often used as fish locators when the trout don't seem to show any activity. Even if your quarry doesn't take the fly, as long as he comes up and looks at it, you've located him.

We hope that the attractor patterns in the following chapter will help you in those hard to fish occasions.

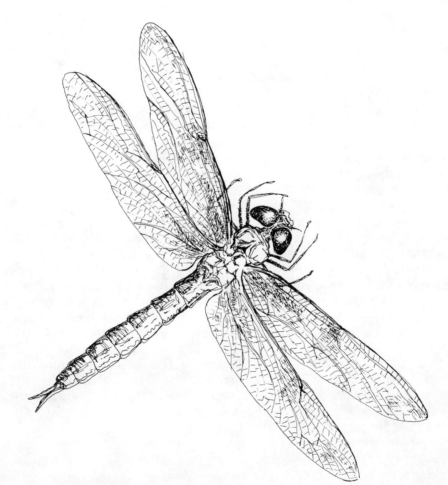

THE GIRDLE BUG

You haven't lived until a number two weighted Girdle Bug thumps you on the back of the head. I first had this experience on the Beaverhead River in southwest Montana. It was my first exposure to the famous Girdle Bug hatch. I always thought the Girdle Bug was more of a joke than a real fly. Everytime I looked at the fly, I found it hard to believe it could actually catch fish. Its white, rubbery legs and that plain, simple, black body made it look more like a crappie fly than a trout fly. I don't think I'll ever forget my first trip to Dillon, Montana.

On the way over, we had dodged thunderstorms in a small 150 Cessna, and it felt good to be on the good earth. We descended into a beautiful, wide, green valley with several ribbon-like rivers, bisecting the carpet-like farm fields. A friend of mine, Bob Fravel, a local wholesale sporting goods salesman and Montana fishing addict, had given me the lowdown on the famous Girdle Bug hatch of southwest Montana. He had enticed me into visiting the Beaverhead Valley to find out for myself if it was truth or myth.

Bob was there to greet me and he introduced me to two of his friends, Jim and Rod Harrison, who operated a sporting goods store in Dillon. They had a group of young fishing guides who were well-acquainted with the river and who were fun to be with. For example, one of the guides, Monty, lived in Dillon all his life and had fished the river since he was a small boy. He knew the river like the back of his hand and, more importantly, he knew most of the brown trout by their first names. In addition to being excellent fishermen, they were the craziest guys I had ever been around. They made fishing so much fun that the actual catching of fish was secondary to the good companionship and comraderie that fishermen often share.

These three crazy guys were about to take me on a discovery adventure with a Girdle Bug as the guide. We went screaming up the highway pulling a trailer with a rubber raft and an aluminum Johnboat, and finally pulled on to an old, rusty bridge just north of Dillon along the famed Beaverhead River. Out came the trusty fly rods and all the needed equipment. After setting up my eight and a half foot graphite, Jim untangled a leader and said, "Na, I think you probably need one of these here leaders that we tie up special." It was absolutely the heaviest leader I have witnessed. It had to be at least 15 pound test, tied in three sections. Protesting, I exclaimed, "Wait a minute, isn't that getting a little bit carried away?" The surprised guide glanced at me and laughed, "If you are going to fish my river, you'll learn to love these leaders." Firmly I spoke, "That's a little bit heavy for me. I'll stick to what I normally use." Shaking his head, he whispered, "You'll see."

I noticed Jim's head was covered with some strange wriggly creations which seemed to engulf the tattered long-billed fishing cap. "What do you use up here?", I questioned. "Oh, we use several flies, but mainly we use the ole Girdle Bug." The bearded guide plucked off his antique hat and threw it to me. There were Girdle Bugs that were black and green, and some with orange bellies, red bellies, green bellies, and the wildest assortment of colors you ever saw, and all were tied with bouncy latex legs. I remembered hearing about the Girdle Bug and how effective it was on certain lakes around the central Montana area, but every time I saw one, I thought it to be more of a joke than a real, viable pattern.

I started with one of my old favorites, the Marabou Muddler. As we drifted down the current making short casts, I cast my Marabou Muddler and very carefully worked it through the many pockets protected by overhanging brush. I would see a dark shadow drift out, follow the fly, refuse it, and dash to the safety of the undercut banks. My fishing companion in the front of the boat had already hooked two fish on the huge, ugly Girdle Bugs. Both fish weighed over two pounds and had fought admirably.

As we journeyed downstream, it became apparent why they used the heavy leaders. The thick brush extended to the water's edge, waiting to grab a poorly cast fly. The crafty browns lay underneath the bank and the imitations had to be put within a couple of inches of the brush to be effective. During mid-afternoon, we worked the overhanging willow banks, where the languid, lazy browns took advantage of the shaded cover in little pockets sheltered by the brush. After parting with a handful of streamer flies, I grudgingly gave in and decided to try the methods of these young fellows. With a bright gleam in their eyes, they handed me a size 2 Girdle Bug, black with an orange belly.

It seemed rather strange to be throwing this big leaded monster at those browns. It almost felt like I was lobbing 8 inch howitzer shells at the poor, defenseless trout, but after the next bend, I found that these fish were neither poor nor defenseless, as one bright colored brown came skyrocketing out of the willow bank. It gave an aerial display that would rival any wild rainbow. This prime example of a Beaverhead bully brown was a glistening fish of about three and a half pounds.

This was my introduction to a pattern for which I've developed a particular fondness. As the next couple of days passed, I learned more about fishing these funny, wiggly critters with Al Troth. Al's theory about the Girdle Bug's success on the Beaverhead is that is represents the many crane flies that hatch early in the morning.

Rolling slowly out of bed at four o'clock in the morning is a severe shock to my body because back home one seldom went fishing before ten o'clock. But here I was, sleepily greeting a wide-eyed Al. You have to get up early to catch the crane fly hatch before the sun peeks over the mountains. A cold chill was in the air, but a quiet, eerie feeling came over me as we drifted through the twilight and gently made our sneak attack on Al's special, placid pools of the Beaver-head. As we were waiting for the warmth giving sun, Al recounted the most effective method to fish the Bug was to cast it slightly upstream and let it drift down underneath the banks, giving a pumping action by moving the rod up and down while stripping ever so slowly. With the pumping action of the rod, the legs would wiggle and give the appearance of a live, squirming, little critter sliding into the trout's lair.

When fishing out of a moving boat, cast slightly upstream to compensate for the movement of the raft and let the actual drifting of the boat help move the fly downstream in a natural dead drift, stripping the line slowly. Many anglers make the mistake of casting downstream and retrieve the fly upstream towards the boat. However, there are moments when a downstream cast in fast, rough water can compensate for the quick drag when pocket casting in such a current. The fly should remain motionless until you drift past the fly and the current swings your line around and drags it back into mainstream.

A sudden splash brought us to reality as the noble browns started their feed. We quickly forgot the chill as we grabbed our rods. An early morning mist covered the dark, grey pools, and as the sun's first rays brightened the haze, a fin broke the water a foot from the rocky shore. The cruising fish swirled again, engulfed a doomed crane fly. Carefully, I laid a cast several feet in front of the moving wake, and gently pumped the rod up and down to coax the Bug to wiggle just a slight bit. The hidden submarine crashed through the air with the Girdle Bug attached to his hooked jaw. The fish made one bone-jarring jump after another from one end of the flat pool to the other. Soon it was over but on that particular morning, I had experienced those magical moments which make you glad you're a fisherman. Never again would I laugh at that strange, wiggly-looking fly called the Girdle Bug, nor would I ever decisively call it "just another bass bug." It's funny how one's opinion can change when a fly takes a few large browns. We fly fishermen are truly contradictions of ourselves!

MATERIALS:	Girdle Bug
THREAD:	Black monocord
HOOK:	Mustad 79580
SIZES:	2-10
TAIL:	Rubber legs
UNDERBODY:	Lead wire
BODY:	Black chenille with a light brown chenille belly, many other color combinations may be used
RIBBING:	Fine silver oval tinsel
LEGS:	Rubber legs

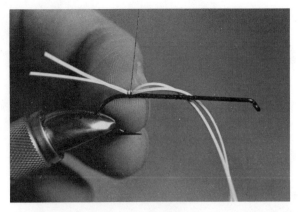

1. Cut two three-inch pieces of rubber leg material and place side by side and tie them onto the hook directly above the barb.

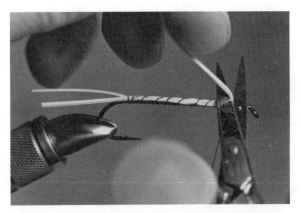

2. Wrap the thread forward covering the rubber leg pieces and forming an underbody.

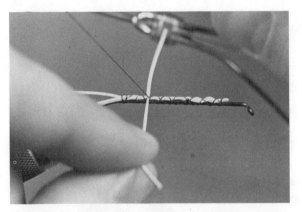

3. Cut a two-inch piece of rubber hackle. Lay this across the hook about one quarter of the shank up from the bend. Tie in securely using an X-ing method, as previously described in the book.

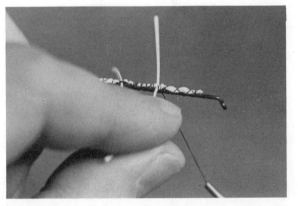

4. Repeat step #3, this time tying it in halfway down the shank.

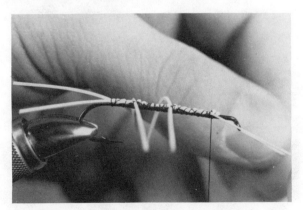

5. Repeat step #3, this time tying it in one-quarter behind the eye.

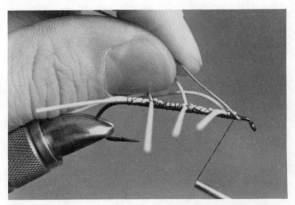

6. Just behind the eye, tie in some medium or heavy lead wire.

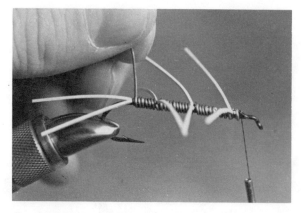

7. Wrap the lead wire backwards to the base of tail, as shown above.

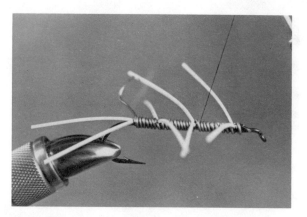

8. Advance the tying thread backwards to the end of the lead.

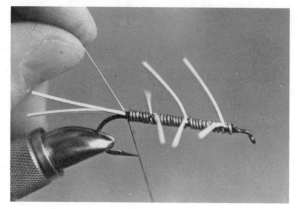

9. Tie in the ribbing material.

10. Tie in the black chenille and the yellow chenille; the black should be on top.

11. Lacquer the lead underbody after advancing the thread forward to the eye.

12. Wrap the chenille forward being sure not to cover the rubber legs; the rubber legs should be in the position as shown above.

13.   Pull the yellow chenille under the body as shown above. Tie off and trim.

14.   Rib the body forward. This will secure the light chenille belly.

15.   Rib all the way to the eye, tie off and trim.

16.   The Finished Fly.

BAILEY'S DAMSEL

Probably the most interesting and useful insect of the order "Odonata", is the damsel fly. This resident more commonly associated with still water, such as lakes and ponds, may also be found in certain types of streams, such as spring creeks and slow moving bodies of water. In the lakes and slow water, they are usually found clinging to underwater vegetation, while in streams they are found clinging to rocks. The damsel fly nymph is a fragile, slender, fish-like insect. Their bee-like eyes are quite noticable and their bodies are quite colorful. They are expert swimmers with three broad gill plates, which considerably aid their movement.

At hatching time, damsel fly nymphs flee from their dwellings to hatch into adults above the water's surface. At this particular time they are most vulnerable and can touch off a feeding frenzy attracting a multitude of still water anglers.

After the damsels become adults they seldom stray far from the water's edge, making them a prime target for cruising trout. This, of course, lends itself to numerous adult imitations which can provide some fantastic fishing. Another vulnerable time in their adult life is when the female damsel fly deposits her eggs below the water's surface. At this time a wet fly pattern can produce some surprising results.

There are a number of damsel fly imitations available. Some of them are quite complicated and use a variety of materials to achieve one of the most distinguishing characteristics of the damsel fly, the eyes. The use of plastic beads, nylon fishing line and other materials to represent the prominent eyes of the nymph is common in many patterns. Also there are several nymph patterns which create movement by using a hinged body.

We offer you here a very simple and a quite successful imitation of a damsel fly. This one is tied by the famous *Dan Bailey Fly Shop* of Livingston, Montana. Bailey's Damsel will be easy for you to tie and experiment with. We also have shown three other patterns of damsel flies, that you can tie up and test.

Using the damsel fly can be a rewarding experience. Of primary importance to the angler, however, is learning to recognize them and to pick suitable imitations for the various damsel fly hatches. This will take experience and patience. If you have a favorite lake, pond or other body of water frequented by damsel flies, try experimenting with some of the patterns we have offered here. You may want to vary the body color to match the damsel flies in your area. Good luck! You may find a whole new world of lake fishing that you never knew was even there.

MATERIALS:	Bailey's Damsel
THREAD:	Black monocord
HOOK:	Mustad 9672, 9671
SIZES:	6-12
TAIL:	Pale olive marabou
UNDERBODY:	Lead wire
BODY:	Several peacock herls
RIBBING:	Gold mylar tinsel and gray ostrich
CASE:	White floss
THORAX:	White floss
LEGS:	Brown hackle

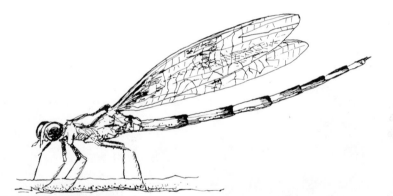

MATERIALS:	Elk Hair Damsel
THREAD:	Black 6/0
HOOK:	Mustad 94831, 94840
SIZES:	10-12
BODY:	Light elk hair dyed blue (Royal Blue works fine)
WING:	Elk mane or other straight non-hollow hair
HACKLE:	Light blue dun

MATERIALS:	Green Fair Damsel Nymph
THREAD:	Green monocord
HOOK:	Mustad 9672
SIZES:	8-12
TAIL:	Three peacock sword fibers
BODY:	Green crewel yarn
RIBBING:	Fine oval gold tinsel
THORAX:	Same as body
HACKLE:	Medium green dyed grizzly hackle

MATERIALS:	Wright's Green Damsel
THREAD:	Yellow 6/0 prewaxed
HOOK:	Mustad 79580, 9672
SIZES:	8-10
TAIL:	Mallard flank dyed green
UNDERBODY:	Lead wire
BODY:	Green marabou
RIBBING:	Fine gold wire
CASE:	Mallard flank dyed green
THORAX:	Mallard flank dyed green
LEGS:	Mallard flank dyed green

1. Cover the hook shank with thread, clip out a small bunch of marabou for a tail.

2. Halfway down the shank tie in the marabou and cover it with thread toward the bend.

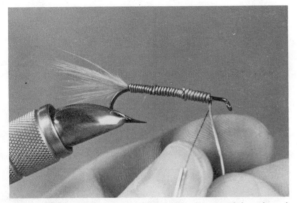

3. Beginning at the tail wrap thin lead weighting two-thirds of the way up the shank of the hook. Wrap heavy lead the rest of the way up the shank of the hook leaving a little room at the eye of the hook for the head.

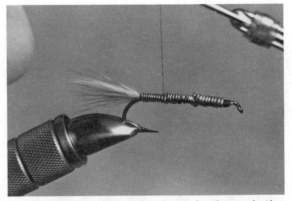

4. Bring the thread backwards through the lead to the tail. It is also a good idea to lacquer the lead at this point.

5. Bring the thread forward to halfway down the shank and tie in two peacock herls, advance the thread to the tail.

6. Bring the thread forward to the middle of the hook and tie in the gold ribbing, advance the thread backwards over the ribbing towards the tail and forward again.

7. Tie in a piece of ostrich herl and advance the thread backward to the tail.

8. Lacquer all the above tied in ends. The thread should be in the middle of the shank. Begin wrapping the peacock herl forward forming the abdomen or body.

9. Continue wrapping the peacock herl forward forming a thick abdomen. Tie off in the middle of the shank.

10. Advance gold ribbing forward in even spacings and tie off.

11. Advance the ostrich herl ribbing forward in even spacings and tie off.

12. Cut two pieces of four-strand floss approximately three inches. Tie these in the middle of the shank of the hook.

13. Separate one of the pieces of four strand floss.

14. Tie in a saddle hackle for ribbing.

15. Wind the lower piece of four strand floss forward forming the thorax.

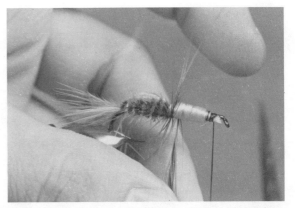

16. Wind the saddle hackle forward ribbing the thorax and forming the legs.

17. Tie off the saddle hackle.

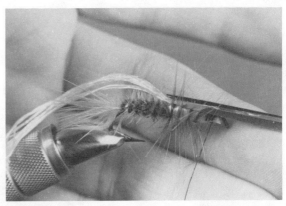

18. Clip the saddle hackle on the top of the thorax.

19. Pull the four-strand floss over the thorax forming the wing case and tie off.

20. Cover the remaining ends with thread forming a nicely tapered head. Whip finish and lacquer.

21. Shows the completed fly.

ASSAM DRAGON NYMPH

This is one of Charles Brooks's killer nymph patterns. A fly so simple that its simplicity is probably its number one virtue. This fly is one of the easiest to tie, but one of the most difficult to find materials for. Charlie's recommendation is that the body material be seal **fur**, not seal hair, which is harsh and translucent like polar bear or other types of silky hair.

Seal fur is taken from the Alaskan Fur Seal, which is managed by a strictly controlled program, administered by the U. S. Fish and Wildlife Service. It is not an endangered species as is believed by many Americans. The Alaskan Seal fur is a dark brown, almost black. The Eastern fur bearing seals are slaughtered while young and their pure soft, white fur is dyed to resemble the Alaskan Fur Seal. We do not advocate the use of the fur from baby seals, but rather from the larger and older Alaskan Fur Seals, (from which only the males are harvested). The best way to obtain this fur is to go to furriers and buy whatever scraps are left over from making coats. According to Charlie, to be most effective the fly should be made of the seal. However, there are other materials which can be substituted to get close to the desired effect. Otter (which is also tough to get), mink, muskrat, beaver and other furs will produce a fairly good effect. Dying or bleaching the fur allows you to achieve the colors necessary to match many dragon fly hatches. The sizes of the fly can be varied to match the great variety of dragon fly nymphs that dot the Washington, Oregon, Montana and Idaho flat lands which have substantial populations of these insects. Some are large — nearly two inches long — and have thick, wide bodies, providing a real mouthful for most trout.

Dragon flies are fairly easy to find. Although they are not strictly lake flies, abundant populations can be found in ponds and lakes across the country. An ideal place to look for hatches of dragon flies are the many slow moving spring creeks that dot the farms and country-side of the western mountain states. One fact to be carefully noted is that the dragon fly is a prime food source while in the nymph stage, but when the fly matures it is no longer an important part of the trout's diet. I have seen many adult fly imitations, but very few of them have become effective patterns.

I recall an incident while fishing Brumby's Weir, a low, slow-moving stream in Tasmania, and a place where dragon flies are a major source of food. There were fish ranging from three to five pounds, leaping through the air like porpoises and snapping at the hovering dragon flies as they darted and dashed over the pond. There was a huge hatch of these adult mini-monsters as they propelled along like little helicopters. The trout were going berserk, and the frustrated fishermen were standing on the bank wondering what to use. There was a group of about eight or nine anglers all trying different flies, different methods with no results. The fish were cruising in between the weeds looking for dragon flies that were hovering above the reeds.

Night-fall soon ended our frustrations and we cruised back into the little town of Kressy and asked our good friend and local fly tyer, Noel Jetson, if he had any suggestions. Noel had lived on the banks of Brumby's all his life and was known as one of Tasmania's premier tyers. He turned around and said, "Auie, we have the proper fly." Then he proceeded to dump about 30 or more flies on the counter. They were the wildest looking things we have ever seen. He exclaimed, "These represent over twenty years of work. All of this time I've been trying to invent an adult dragon fly imitation that really works, and none of them have. The only fly that I think will work would be one that had a small propeller, which would enable our patterns to hover over the water."

He cheerfully reminded us that the fish taken in Tasmania were taken on the dragon fly nymphs. Then, he proceeded to show me six or seven very interesting patterns to match their local dragon flies. He told us the only hope of catching the fish was to use the juicy buggy nymphs before the naturals had a chance to become adults. This flying steak dinner has to be one of the trout's most treasured meals and I believe if you have a hatch of dragon flies in your area, you should be tying some of these nymphs. Charlie's Assam Dragon is one of the best around, and the proper use of it can provide some exciting times in dragon fly territory.

MATERIALS:	Assam Dragon
THREAD:	Black monocord
HOOK:	Mustad 9671
SIZES:	4-8
BODY:	Strip of seals fur on hide 1/8" × 1/4" or mink
HACKLE:	Soft grizzly dyed medium brown

1. Trim a thin piece of hair using a tape knife or lance.

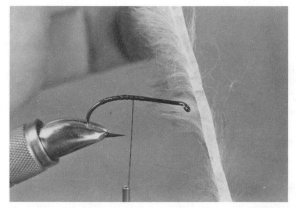

2. Shows a lateral view of the hair. The hide should be flexible and tanned, not a rough dry hide.

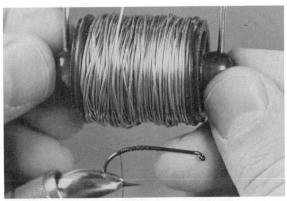

3. The above picture shows a loaded lead bobbin.

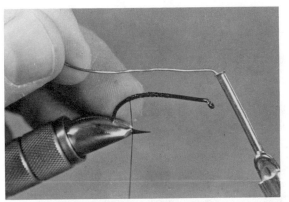

4. Take the lead bobbin and pull out a couple of inches of lead.

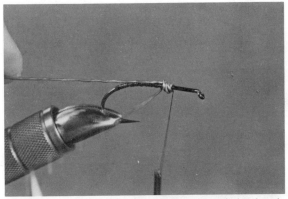

5. Tie in lead and wrap back toward the back of the hook like you would with your wrapping thread.

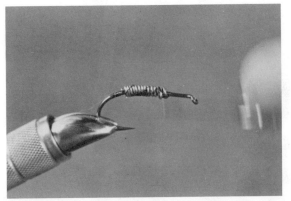

6. Trim the lead, wrap backward with the tying thread over the lead. Securely fasten the lead to the hook with thread.

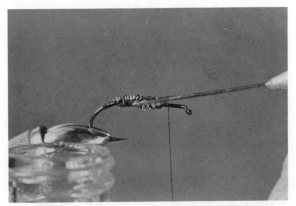

7. Completely lacquer the lead with a fast drying cement.

8. Tie in the fur at the bend of the hook, with the hair on top.

9. The hair is tied in at the bend of the hook as shown in the above picture. With your thumb and finger pluck out the fur.

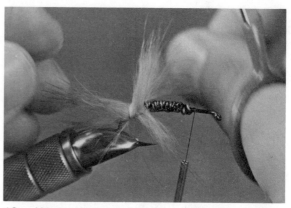

10. Wrapping towards you, wrap the fur forward.

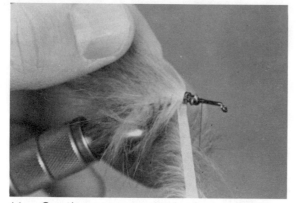

11. Continue to wrap the fur forward pulling back on the fluffy underfur; the hide should cover the hook evenly and should not overlap.

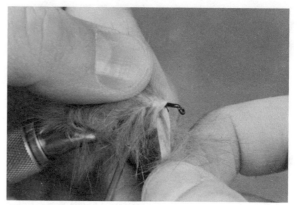

12. Just before the eye, tie off and trim the fur.

13. At the front of the hook tie in a partridge hackle at the base and wrap it forward forming a collar.

14. Tie off with your thread, whip finish and trim. This is the finished fly.

THE WOOLY BUGGER

To the amazement of many anglers, (including myself), the Wooly Bugger seems to have the special merit of producing well in the slack waters of western spring creeks and sloughs.

Bud Lilly suggested that I ask John Bailey about this fly. John just shook his head and said, "I don't know why it works, but it does. It's as simple a fly as one could ask for when it comes to the tying vise, yet, it is effective. When nothing else seems to work on Armstrong Spring Creek, "the Bugger is a killer."

George Anderson, one of John's guides and store employees joined our discussion about the Wooly Bugger. George is a very competent nymph tyer who loves to fish the spring creeks flowing through the fertile valleys that are in the Yellowstone River country. He had the same story to tell. The Bugger really works on spring creek trout!

George made the interesting observation that the way a Wooly Bugger is put together just might be the reason it works so well. It is important that the tyer uses very thin chenille and some good soft hen hackle to tie this pattern. Good hen hackle is just about as hard to find as a good grizzly dry fly neck. George suggested checking with companies that sell soft hen hackle for legs on streamers or for tying the new Matuka fly series. The appearance of good soft, wet fly necks back on the market is due to the interest in Matukas and some of the fuzzy nymphs that are being tied today. It is always good to check with any fly shops, especially around commercial tyers that may be discarding these necks over the better dry fly necks.

George stresses that the important thing about this fly is to have good soft hackle and be sure to wrap the lead only on the front of the hook, (and not throughout the whole fly). This forces the fly to ride with the eye down and the tail up. He believes that this gave the fly a good representation of the crane flies which are prevalent in many of the spring creeks. George stressed again, "Be sure to fish the fly extremely slow, working it along the bottom with slow, short jerks and letting it drift down to the working fish." Another suggestion is to try the Wooly during the middle of the day when hatches have thinned out a little.

From my own experience in fishing spring creeks, I have noticed the crane flies emerge just as the first rays of the morning sun hit the water. I suggest that if you know a place that has crane flies, give this a try early in the morning, especially if the brown trout are in residence. Try it again in the evening — just before dark. I feel that it is very important to make sure that a very slow retrieve is used along with a subtle lifting movement in order to properly imitate the movement of the crane fly nymphs.

Around the West Yellowstone area we find that people use it also in some of the larger lakes which contain crane fly larvae. It goes back to the old adage that plain and simple things often work the best. The Wooly Bugger certainly proves that point.

MATERIALS:	Wooly Bugger
THREAD:	Black monocord
HOOK:	Mustad 79580, 9672
SIZES:	4-12
TAIL:	Black ostrich herls
UNDERBODY:	Lead wire
BODY:	Green chenille
RIBBING:	Blue dun neck or saddle hackle palmered over body

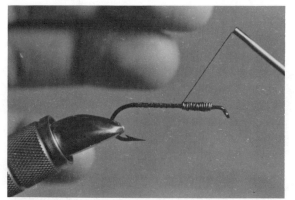

1. Cover the shank of the hook with thread. Wrap lead wire over the first third of the shank of the hook; be sure to leave room for the head.

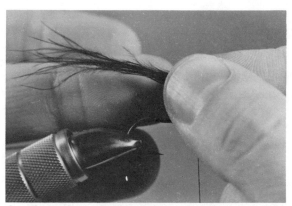

2. Select a small clump of black ostrich.

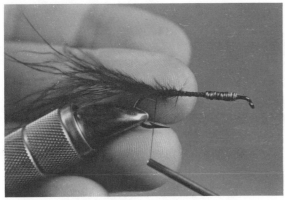

3. Tie in directly above the point of the hook.

4. Tie in chenille directly behind the lead weight, wrapping the thread backwards over the chenille to the beginning of the bend of the hook.

5. Select a hackle of the proper size.

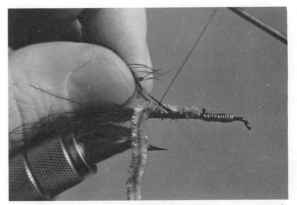

6. Tie in the hackle by the point instead of by the butt directly above the point of the hook.

7. Shows the hackle tied in.

8. Wrap the chenille forward. Be sure to make one wrap behind the hackle.

9.   Tie off the chenille.

10.   Clip the chenille to form a tighter body.

11.   Hold up the hackle with the right hand and pull the fibers off one of the sides with the left hand.

12.   Wrap the hackle forward.

13.   Tie off and trim.

14.   The Finished Fly

OSCAR LEECH

By Bruce E. James

My alarm rang at 6:30 that morning. I was to meet Jack Dennis and Dan Abrams at Jack's house for a short session of photographing flies. We wanted to do a leech pattern for the book, but neither Jack nor I was very impressed with any of the possibilities open. Finally, after a couple of cups of coffee and a slightly overcooked breakfast, I gathered up my bags of materials and hopped in the truck.

Dan was his usual jovial self that morning. Aside from being an excellent photographer, he really should be a movie director. With a "Hold your bobbin up" or "Your scissors are in the way," Dan managed to direct us through another fly. As is common with many things, sometimes a new pattern is a combination of ideas you have already seen with your own twist added. We had been tying several of Al Troth's patterns using art foam as an underbody. Jack liked the look of a strip of fur wrapped around the hook to form the Assam Dragon. I liked the idea of a marabou tied on top of the hook shank and using beads for eyes, both of which I had seen before. All of these we meshed together to form the dreaded monster, Oscar Leech.

Oscar Leech has an incredible lifelike motion when stripped through the water. Even though we haven't tried this pattern I remember Jack's remark, "This would be dynamite on the Green."

When tying Oscar Leech several things should be remembered. The strip of rabbit skin used must be very pliable in order to wrap it around the hook. To accomplish this, use a warm water dye bath and rub mink oil into the skin after it has slightly dried. Also, be sure to leave enough monofiliment outside the beads so that when the ends are burned they will form big enough buttons to keep the eyes on.

We hope you will try this fly in your area and let us know how well it works. Jack is anxious to try it on some big browns, who seem to like this sort of fly.

MATERIALS: Oscar Leech

THREAD: Black monocord

HOOK: Mustad 79580

SIZES: 2-6

UNDERBODY:	Lead wire and art foam
BODY:	Black dyed rabbit fur on the hide
WING:	Black marabou
HEAD:	Two plastic beads fused to coarse monofilament, head covered with black ostrich and eyes painted with black lacquer

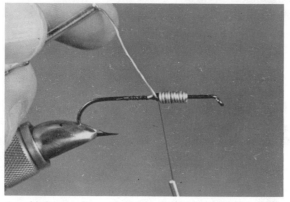

1. Using a floss bobbin make approximately 12 wraps of heavy lead as shown above, tie off and trim.

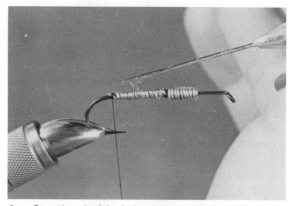

2. Starting behind the heavy lead wrap some lighter amp lead towards the rear of the hook, trim and securely fasten. Then lacquer all the lead with a penetrating cement.

3. Tie in several strands of black marabou to form the tail.

4. Tie in a strip of art foam at the beginning of the tail.

5. Taper art foam forward as shown above. Be sure to leave ¼ of the shank length for the head.

6. At the top of the fly tie in small plume of black marabou, Matuka-style on top of the hook.

7. Repeat process (step #6)

8. Continue to repeat step #6 and #7 spacing plumes of black marabou evenly on top of the hook.

9. The completed wing should appear as above.

10. Return the thread evenly back through the divided Matuka-style wings to the start of the tail.

11. Trim, using a scalpel or tape knife, a thin strip of dyed black rabbit or other similar fur. The strip should be long enough to wrap the full length of the hook.

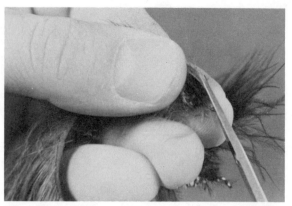

12. Strip the fur off the front end and notch. Note that the hair fibers point back from that end.

13. Tie in the strip of fur at the base of the tail, where the fur has been slightly notched. Be sure to tie it in securely.

14. Wrap the strip of fur as you would any chenille or wool in between the Matuka/Maribou wings, wrapping it forward towards the eye. Notice the skin will lay right on the art foam and the fur will be protruding outward.

15. Tie off the fur at the end of the wing, as shown above.

16. Wrap heavy amp lead at the front of the hook forming a head. Trim lead and tie off.

17. Tie in a small strip of art foam at the base of the wing.

18. Wrap art foam forward covering the lead. Wrap the thread back and forth over the art foam to secure it to the lead.

19. With a water-proof, black felt tip marker, color the art foam a dark black.

20. Tie two pieces of monofilament on top of the art foam head; these will hold the eyes.

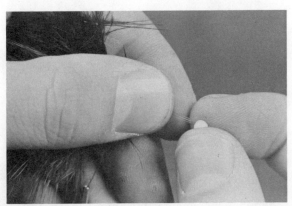

21. Take both pieces of monofilament and insert a glass bead. The bead must have a hole in it.

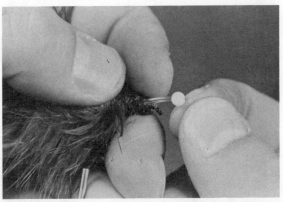

22. Shows the bead on the monofilament, with your forefinger, push it all the way to the base of the monofilament.

23. With a lighted match, carefully singe the monofilament until it melts back to the glass bead.

24. Be careful not to burn the mono too far down or you might burn your finger. Notice the eye above.

25. Repeat the same method on the other side of the fly.

26. Burn the eye on the other side.

27. The completed eyes should appear as above. You will find the eyes to be quite durable and very realistic.

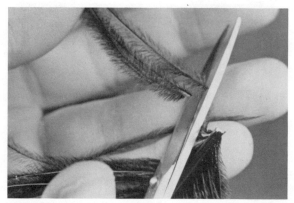

28. Trim out some black ostrich herl from a large furry plume.

29. Secure the ostrich behind the eyes.

30. Wrap the ostrich herl forward, wrap him between the eyes forming a furry head.

31. With a match stick or paint brush, drop black lacquer on the tip of each glass eye.

32. The completed fly ready for a swim.

33. Mr. Oscar Leech after a swim in the water; a very realistic leech imitation.

JIM'S CRAYFISH

Whether you call them crawdads, crawdaddies, or crayfish these crustaceans are prevalent in certain areas in the United States, New Zealand and Australia, and many anglers don't realize they should be considered an important part of a trout's diet.

I was greatly impressed by this pattern first shown to me by Jim Chestney. It was the first really authentic imitation I had ever seen of the mystical little creature which I felt confident about offering to a finicky trout.

While fishing the Whakarewa River in New Zealand, I had my first opportunity to see fresh water crayfish in a trout stream environment. The Whakarewa is a beautiful river which was 15 to 20 feet in width and it winds through a small, intimate valley in New Zealand's north island sheep country. The stream plunges through many small farms and sheep ranges of the Whakarewa valley. It is a classic, meadow stream reminiscent of the eastern farm country chalk streams. Large ferns and other exotic plants dot the stream bank, and in some cases provide cover for the trout. The stream is filled with rainbows ranging from a pound up to six pounds. As in most New Zealand streams the fish are usually found singularly, and sometimes there are great distances between fish, however most trout average better than 3 pounds.

While working through the meadows and casting to each one of the runs on the Whakarewa, I glanced down in the shallows and spotted what looked to be a crayfish. I scooped up the little critter and discovered it was exactly what I had known in Missouri as crawdads. The color was a little darker than what I remembered, but it was definitely a crayfish. I brought the little crustacean to an angling mate, and asked him what he knew about it. He made the comment that it is considered quite a delicacy for hungry trout, but that nobody had yet come up with a good fly to imitate the crawfish. He said that some people fish with them live, but in most areas that was against the law. Having mentioned it was a good saltwater bait, we tried to think of any patterns that might be good imitators.

As we walked back to the car, we climbed through a narrow gorge, where the water was quite deep and the current tumbled through it very swiftly. From our vantage point, ten feet above the water, we could see a hugh rainbow resting near the shelter of some streamside brush. Every once in a while, we'd see the fish rise to the top of the surface and then retreat back into the deep water underneath a bush. We couldn't see what he was feeding on, but we assumed it was nymphs. There seemed to be no way to land the trophy, but I thought we would have a little experiment. We drifted several nymphs down through the hole, but nothing seemed to attract it.

I got to thinking about the crawfish, and how effective the Kiwi had told me it could be. I looked in my box for the biggest, ugliest nymph that I had, and in one corner of the box lay a great big size 2 hard cased Helgramite. It was a crawly, ugly critter, a couple of inches in length, and fat in diameter. It resembled the crayfish (especially the dark colored ones) and I showed the fly to my friend, who immediatley turned his face in disgust, and said "No self-respecting New Zealand fish would take that!" It was impossible to get a very good cast and the only way to get a fly to the fish was by dangling the fly in the water and let it drift quickly through the little pockets. It was almost like cane pole fishing, because you would lift the fly up and dab it back in the water. With no chance of landing the fish, I still wanted the challenge of hooking him. About the second time of doing this the huge dark shadow of the rainbow rose up and devoured the fly. My rod tip sprang into the air, but due to the bad angle, the fly pulled out of the fish's mouth. However, it proved to me that the fish definitely had taken the nymph for a crawfish. The largest nymph in the stream was a size 12, and this fly is infinitely bigger in size and design.

The information I have received from Jim regarding the effectiveness of the crawfish fly was: "I know that pattern will take big fish, because the largest trout I ever brought to the net on a fly succumbed to a crayfish pattern. It was a beautiful brown of about 7 pounds taken from a deep run, which had an undercut bank - the perfect hiding place for a wise old trout. Not only was the cover perfect, but the undercut bank was riddled with crayfish burrows. It was a spot with a readily available food locker. She was a fine fish and she might just still be there, because I released her with nothing to show but the memories. On that day I had forgotten my camera."

Jim also suggests for readers who specialize on warm water species this pattern could also provide some exciting and satisfying days when other patterns are totally ignored.

Those of you that might have some crayfish in your area, give it a try, whether it be for trout or other species. You might be totally surprised with the results. We all have to thank Jim for his really effective crayfish pattern.

MATERIALS	Jim's Crayfish
THREAD:	Brown or black waxed monocord, brown buttonhole twist
HOOK:	Mustad 3665A, 79580
SIZES:	2-6
ANTENNAE:	Two stripped brown hackle stems
EYES:	30 lb mono burned at both ends
PINCERS:	Fox squirrel tail
BACK:	Fox squirrel tail
UNDERBODY:	Heavy lead wire
BODY:	Reddish brown dubbing
LEGS:	Brown saddle hackles

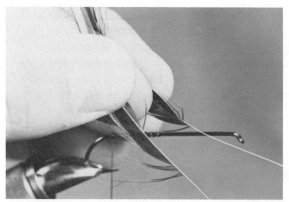

1. Take two brown hackles and strip the hackle fibers off for about 2".

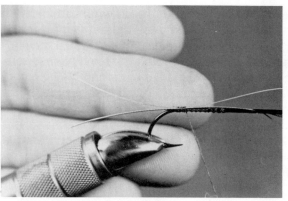

2. Tie these in just above the bend with curves facing out from each other.

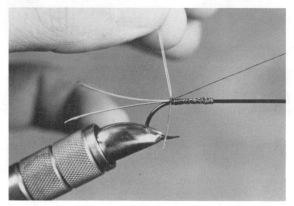

3. Tie in a piece of 30 pound monofilament for the eyes. Tie this across the hook.

4. Cut the monofilament off so that there is approximately ½" extending on each side. Light a match and burn each end forming the eyes.

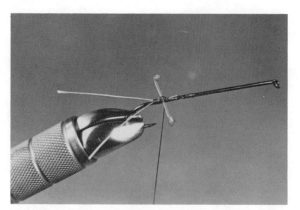

5. This is what the pair of eyes should look like.

6. With the thread approximately halfway down the shank tie in a small bunch of fox squirrel tail. Wrap over this thoroughly to the bend of the hook. Note above picture.

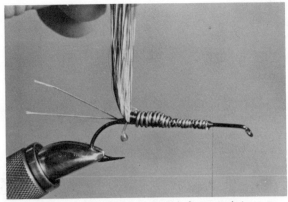

7. Wrap some heavy lead forward to one-third behind the eye. Wrap the tying thread back and forth through the lead securing it to the shank. It may be helpful here to add a drop of lacquer to the lead.

8. At about one-third back from the eye, tie in a small bunch of fox squirrel tail, approximately half the diameter of a pencil. Tie in another bunch of squirrel on the other side. These will form two pincers.

9. Make circular wraps around each separate bunch of squirrel hair, this will bunch the squirrel tail together.

10. With some buttonhole twist thread make a simple over-hand knot. Slip this over the squirrel tail end. It might be wise to place a little lacquer on the squirrel tail before slipping the knot over, so that the fibers stay together.

11. Pull the knot tight. Repeat with the other leg.

12. Coat both of the pincers thoroughly with lacquer.

13. Trim the fibers on the pincers. Notice the trimmed fibers as in Step #14.

14. Pick out two long, light brown saddle hackles, tie in just behind the eye.

15. Apply a generous amount of dubbing to the thread.

16. Bring the thread around the pincers and underneath the eye. It should come over the top of the squirrel tail bunch.

17. Pull back the squirrel tail bunch and make a wrap of dubbing in front of the pincers.

18. Dub forward forming one layer of dubbing. Wrap back over top of this with the thread. Apply more dubbing to the thread. Lift pincers, dub underneath pincers. Continue dubbing toward the eye of the hook, forming a second layer of dubbing.

19. Wrap the saddle hackles forward one at a time. These should end approximately halfway down the shank. Tie off and trim.

20. Trim the hackle fibers off the back.

21. Tie in another bobbin which has heavy buttonhole twist thread. Pull this bobbin back so it is out of the way.

22. Add another bunch of dubbing, and dub to the eye of the hook. Whip finish and trim the thread off.

23. Shows the rear part of the dubbed body.

24. Pull the bunch of squirrel backwards forming the back. Grab the heavy thread and make several tight turns.

25. Space these tight turns evenly to just behind the eye of the hook. Note the above pictures.

26. Make several turns of thread here.

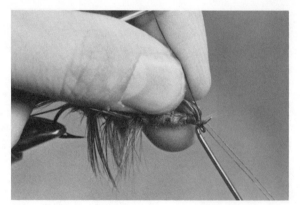

27. Pull back the tail and whip finish the heavy thread.

28. Apply a generous coat of lacquer to the back.

29. Trim the hackle fibers beneath the body.

30. Trim the tail into a fan-like shape. Note the above picture.

31. Pick out any fibers that are caught under.

32. This is the Crayfish from beneath.

33. This is Crayfish from the front.

34. Crayfish from the top.

35. The Finished Fly.

THE ROYAL HUMPY

We first introduced this fly to the fly fishing public back in 1972. Little did we know how important and well received this creation would be. Designed in collaboration with my friend, the late Charlie Ridenhauer, this fly has brought me hours of enjoyment and it has been my constant friend in many different fishing situations.

The need which led to the development of this fly underscores the key to its success and popularity. The famous Humpy fly had a problem with visibility. Its grey color combined with the glare of the water made it almost impossible to see in certain conditions. Adding white wings to the Humpy and changing the hackle color gave it greater visibility and an uncanny resemblence to certain insects in our area.

The appeal of the Royal Humpy has been world wide. I have received letters from anglers who have used this pattern in South Africa, New Zealand, Australia, South America, Alaska, and most recently we had a report that, tied in large sizes, the fly was an excellent Atlantic Salmon pattern, when used as an attractor pattern.

One of the most gratifying fishing experiences I had was on the Murray River in southeastern Australia at the end of a hot summer's day at a time when a person would swear there wasn't a fish in the river. With the setting of the bright orange sun, as evening came, the fish began to rise as if someone had summoned them with a bugle call. In that too short period of time before darkness engulfed us, I caught and released more than two dozen hard fighting Australian browns. The amazing thing is that all this action took place within 30 yards of a busy highway bridge. What is even more amazing is that I didn't move more than 20 feet the entire evening. While I hadn't seen a rise all morning and afternoon, in those fleeting minutes before dark, I had fun with fish that had probably never seen the Royal Humpy, my old friend which worked its magic 8,000 miles from where it originated.

What a memorable sight it was to see the small fly drift over a rising fish, and to watch it disappear in the swirl of a take. Almost every good cast would get a response. My Australian buddies threw everything they had in their boxes with no luck. After that evening, the Royal Humpy had gained many Australian converts, and you can bet they are now experiencing what I had discovered many years ago about the far flung success of this pattern.

The Royal Humpy has been my constant fishing companion for many years. I have used it on the Snake River in Wyoming with incredible success, as well as on numerous sloughs and spring creeks throughout the West. It makes an excellent attractor pattern, especially in fast water sections.

The variations that can be applied to this fly are numerous and allow it to be used as imitations for many different hatches. Using dark elk hair for the body gives the fly a grayish brown cast, making it a good imitation for the Brown Drake. If you like to fish light mayfly hatches, try tying it with cream hackle and a light elk hair hump. Different colors of monocord should be used to help match the body color.

Reflecting back, the day sticks in my mind when Charlie Ridenhauer almost knocked down the door. Full of enthusiasm, he bolted in and explained to me his new idea of a super Humpy. Charlie may you rest in peace, your fly is a success.

MATERIALS:	Royal Humpy
THREAD:	Red, yellow, or green monocord
HOOK:	Mustad 94840, 7948A, 7957B
SIZES:	8-18
TAIL:	Dark moose hair
BODY:	Light gray natural deer hair
WING:	White calf tail
HACKLE:	Blue dun, brown, badger, grizzly or cree neck hackles

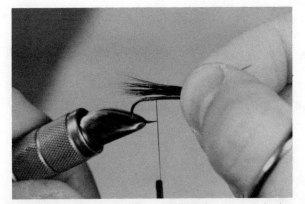

1. Cut out a small bunch of moose hair, stack until even and measure for length. The length should be the same as the hook shank.

2. Tie in the hair securely and cover it with thread. Select some fairly even white calf tail. Pull out any uneven fibers.

3. Tie of calf tail wing tightly with tips of the wing protruding over the eye. The length of the wing should be equal to the shank length.

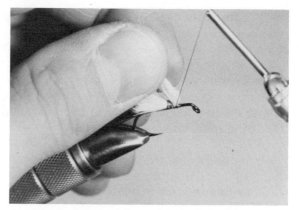

4. Tie in front of the wing using thumb and finger to pull back wing. This will keep the wing from sliding forward.

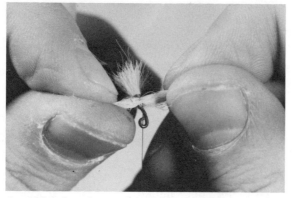

5. With forefinger and thumb, divide wing in half.

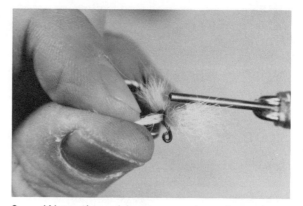

6. Wrap thread between wings from front to back.

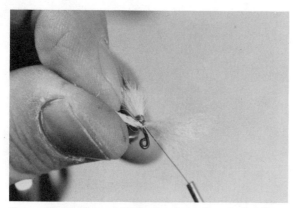

7. Wrap thread from back to front dividing wing. This method is repeated forming an "X". We call this method "X-ing".

8. Wrap a circle of thread clockwise around the wing, wrapping it up and around the wing, giving it a base of thread and tying it in tightly.

9. Repeat step #8 with the other wing.

10. Is a top view of the "X'd" wing.

11. With sharp pointed scissors, trim hair close to the wing, leaving as little a butt protruding as possible.

12. Cut out a small bunch of light deer hair. Remove the underfur and tie it in at the base of the wing.

13. Cover the deer hair from front to back with thread forming a smooth underbody.

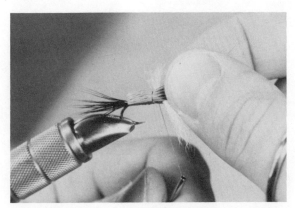

14. Pull the hair over forming a nice even hump. Tie down with several wraps of thread. The deer hair tips should protrude between the wings.

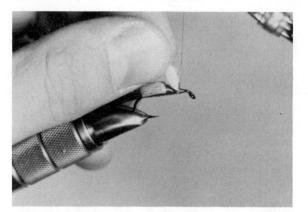

15. Pull the deer hair up and trim as close to the wing as possible. Leave as little deer hair showing as you can.

16. Cover the hair butts with thread. Pull back the wing then wrap just in front of it.

17. Tie in either saddle hackles or neck hackles, depending on the size of the hook. Hackle colors vary on the color of fly desired. Hackle size should be 1½ - 2 gaps.

18. Wrap the hackles forward both behind and in front of the wing. You should have a total of twelve wraps of hackle.

19. The Finished Fly

THE HUMPY TRUDE

A fly tying colleague of mine, Bill Tessman, brought this fly to my attention. One morning he rushed in and exclaimed "I've got a new fly for you that should be in your book." I thought to myself, "Oh brother. Everytime I turn around, somebody has a new fly that ought to be in my book!" If I put every one in, the books would contain between three and four thousand flies each, and one would need a wheelbarrow to carry them around. Being in a polite mood that particular morning I said, "Sure Bill, bring it in " figuring the fly was some abomination that no angler in his right mind would use. Bill, however, is an artful fly tyer and fine fisherman. His constant referral to this fly gave me the thought that maybe he really had something!

Later that morning he rushed to the door "I've got it. Here it is." Dropping back like a quarter-back to throw that touchdown pass, he looped through the air a dark black object. I reached up and caught it. "Bill, this is just a film container." "Well look inside" wailed Bill. So I popped open the top and as it contained what at first appeared to be a humpy, "So, what's so different about this?" I said, "Well look at it! Pull it out!" Bill retorted. I held it up to the light, the fly was a humpy with a white wing going over the back, tied Trude-style. Bill, with an excited look on his face, exclaimed "That's a Humpy Trude." I thought for a second, a Royal Trude is a great fly in our country. A simple fly to tie and an easy one to see. Why didn't I think of that!" Bill, how did you ever come up with it?" Bill began his story "Well you know your Royal Humpy, the fly that is so visible and floats so well. The only trouble I have is tying the darn wing in. This way, I just tie it Trude-style, because it's much easier to wrap the hackle. I essentially have the same thing as a Royal Humpy, a white wing with the Humpy body. It's a natural! It's a winner. That fly will catch fish! I know, I have used it."

Slightly flabbergasted, I was wrong, it was a good fly. The fly that never occured to me. In fact, I don't know if anybody had made this discovery. I showed the Trude to other people, and the comments were good. We think it's a fly that does have merit, and deserves to be in the book. So, we are showing it to you, in hopes that you fish it and let us know your comments, as we feel that it may have a place in the world of fly tying. It has application to western angling during caddis hatches, or as an effective imitator during the flying ant hatch. The fly can be varied by tying an elk hair body and by using elk hair instead of calf tail for the wing. You may have some ideas yourself, do not hesitate to experiment with any pattern. It is important that you change a pattern so that it will fit your area and your needs. Experiment, this is what makes fly fishing and fly tying so wonderful.

MATERIALS:	Humpy Trude
THREAD:	Red, yellow, green, brown monocord (can use various colors)
HOOK:	Mustad 94840, 7957B, 7948A
SIZES:	8-18
TAIL:	Dark moose, dark elk, deer hair
BODY:	Natural deer hair, light elk
WING:	Calf tail or kip tail
HACKLE:	Brown, badger, cree, or grizzly neck hackles

1.   Cut out a small bunch of either the moose hair or stiff elk hair. Stack the hair so that the points are all even. Tie in the hair halfway down the shank of the hook and bring the tying thread to the bend of the hook, covering the hair with wraps of thread.

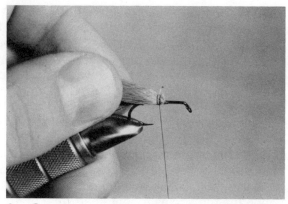

2.   Cut out a small bunch of deer hair approximately the diameter of a pencil. Remove the underfur and small hairs. Tie in halfway down the shank of the hook, as shown in the above picture.

3.   Advance tying thread backwards over the deer hair covering it to form an underbody. Bring the thread forward again to the point where the deer hair was tied in.

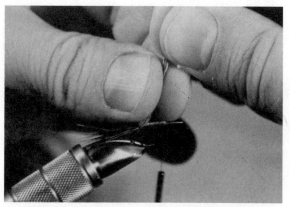

4.   Pull the deer hair over with the right hand forming a hump.

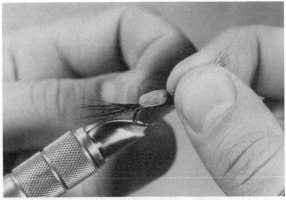

5. Holding the hair with the right hand and the bobbin with the left hand, make several loose wraps of thread around the deer hair. Pull tight on the third wrap of thread.

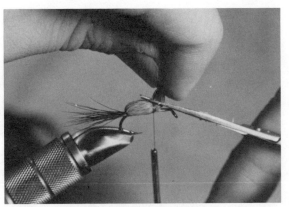

6. Trim the hair butts at an angle.

7. Cover the exposed hair butts with thread as shown in the picture.

8. Cut out a small bunch of calf tail and even the tips. Lay along the top of the hook and measure for length. The calf tail wing should extend beyond the bend of the hook approximately half the length of the body. Tie in the calf tail wing with several tight wraps, holding along the top of the hook.

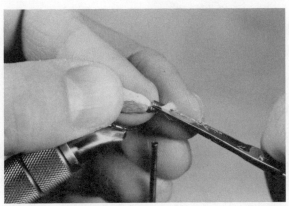

9. Trim the butts of the calf tail at an angle.

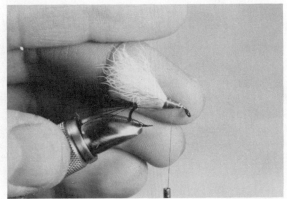

10. Cover the calf tail butts with thread, making a smooth base on which to wrap the hackles.

11. Select three hackles, remove the fibers from the butts and tie in at the base of the calf tail wing. The dull side of the hackles should be facing you.

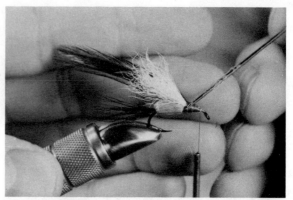

12. Place a drop of lacquer on top of where the hackle butts were tied in.

13. Wrap the hackles forward and tie off.

14. Whip finish the head, trim and lacquer.

15. The Finished Fly

WRIGHT'S ROYAL

Wright's Royal is an answer to the age old question of why a particular fly works. Perhaps it's the color or maybe the form that causes the strike. Most anglers haven't figured this out yet. There are, however, a number of flies which we tend to put into the category of "attractor patterns". One of these patterns is the famous Royal Wulff.

Late one cold winter night, Phillip Wright was pondering this same question. What makes the Royal Wulff work; is it the form, the color or a combination of both? The iridescence of the peacock herl gives the same sensation of color that many beetles do, and the two clumps of this look very much like the gasters of an ant. All this spells terrestrial.

However, there are a couple of things about the Royal Wulff that point to mayfly. The upright wings and the tail are definately components of a mayfly and not a terrestrial. It is possible that the trout takes this classic fly as a terrestrial despite its shortcomings? Who knows for sure?

Phillip Wright, however, decided to consider this hypothesis as true and worked with those components he thought were indicative of a terrestrial. He removed the tail altogether, and replaced the upright wings with a single wing slanted at a 45° angle. What he came up with was Wright's Royal.

This ingenious fly has been used for more than two years on the Big Hole River in Montana with considerable success. Some say that it works even better than the Royal Wulff.

We thank Phil for his impressive contribution to the world of fishing and fly tying. Please take a few minutes of your fishing time to try this effective pattern. I think you will be pleased with the results.

MATERIALS:	Wright's Royal
THREAD:	Black monocord
HOOK:	Mustad 94840, 7957B, 7948A
SIZES:	8-16
BODY:	Peacock herl and red floss

WING: Light elk

HACKLE: Brown

1. Select four to six bushy peacock herls. Tie in halfway down the shank; cover the herl butts with thread toward the bend of the hook.

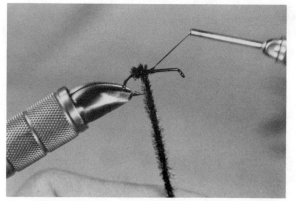

2. Advance the thread forward a few turns. Make several turns with the peacock herl forming a thick, bushy clump. Tie off and trim.

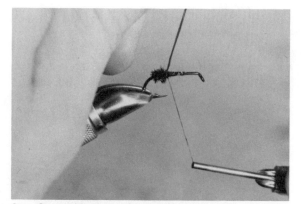

3. Over the top of the clipped ends tie in a piece of red floss approximately 2" long.

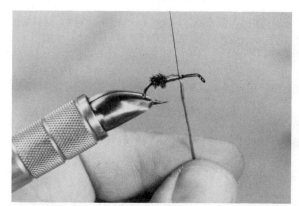

4. Wrap the red floss forward to approximately halfway down the shank of the hook. Tie off and trim.

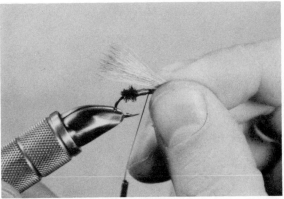

5. Cut out a small bunch of light elk. Stack until even. Measure for length as above.

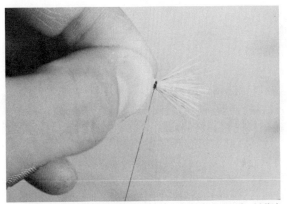

6. Transfer the wing to your left hand. With thumb and forefinger, hold wing directly on top of the hook and make several tight wraps. Continue forward with several more tight wraps.

7. Shows the tied-in wing.

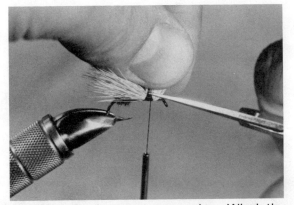

8. Trim the butts at an angle. Wind the thread over the trimmed butts forming a smooth base for the hackle.

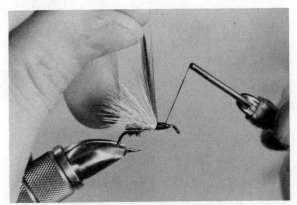

9. Prepare a badger hackle and tie in at the base of the wing.

10. Tie in a peacock herl at the base of the wing.

11. Lacquer a base for the hackle and peacock herl to be wrapped.

12. Wrap the peacock herl forward. Tie off and trim.

13. Wrap the hackle forward. Tie off and trim.

14. Whip finish and lacquer the head.

15. The Finished Fly

THE HAIR SPIDER

Whether it be the East or the West, the spider has always been known as an effective deceiver. During the past few years, emphasis on matching exact hatches, stream entomology, and Latin names have pushed some of the more traditional aspects of fly fishing to the sidelines. As a result, the once prominent spider patterns have been almost forgotten.

When one reads the early angling literature, the words of skating spiders across chalk streams in England bring back some nostalgic thoughts of cane rods and gut leaders. The problems that we have always had with spiders is finding one that would float properly in our heavy, fast western streams. Most spiders were tied with spade or large saddle hackles. Sometimes the saddles were not stiff, and when the fly caught one fish, it made for a fast sinking fly instead of a high riding dry.

This particular pattern, the hair spider, was shown to me by Al Troth, one of the West's most innovative fly tyers. Al's thoughts on the fly were to produce a spider that would float under all conditions, especially under heavy waters of some of the western rivers. When I first saw the fly I was struck by its stiffness and its simple design. Al was quick to point out that even though he had tied the first sample with a coarse, whitetail deer hair, tannish brown in color; other kinds of coarse dyed deer hair, and even elk hair could be used to create a variety of colors.

In Australia, they cast their moth or spider imitations out on a large lake, letting it settle on top of the water with about thirty feet of line out. With one quick motion, the Aussies lift their rod straight up as if to make another cast and without bringing any extra line, drag the fly across the surface. This method is used from late evening until early dawn in hopes of attracting any large cruising fish on the lookout for some type of dying terrestrial or fluttering moth. Aussie anglers tie their spiders extremely large, dark and bushy. They also craft Muddler Minnows with huge unclipped hair heads to imitate big moths. Adopting the Aussie method can be an effective way also of handling spiders in large heavy water. Cast the fly directly across the river or slightly upstream, then lift the rod high as if to make another back cast. With the fly just barely touching the water, pull it across the top of the ripple. Surprising results can be achieved and buoyancy of the hair spider assures a proper drift.

The traditional method on windy days of skating spiders can be productive. Try fishing it on a gusty, wind-swept day, in a good trout pond or a large deep pool. You can lift a long rod up in the wind and with the wind at your backside, let your fly float in the air like a kite!

Gradually lower the line until the fly touches the water. By raising and lowering the rod, skip it or pull it across the water letting the wind just barely lift the spider with the tips of the hackle just brushing the water. It is suggested the long rod, at least eight and a half foot in length be used. In merry olde England, they used fourteen foot rods to accomplish this method.

Whether you find this effective or not, also try fishing the fly the standard dry fly way, casting upstream and letting it drift through, or any other way you might find effective. One of the beautiful things about our sport is that you can vary from the rules and find your own thing! I do believe this spider offers a forgotten dimension in western fishing, and this is a time for a fly that brings back the good old olde days.

MATERIALS:	Hair Spider
THREAD:	Nymo "A" yellow, could use CSE flat waxed nylon
HOOK:	Mustad 94838 or 7948A
SIZES:	12
TAIL:	Natural deer flank hair
HACKLE:	Natural deer flank hair, same as tail

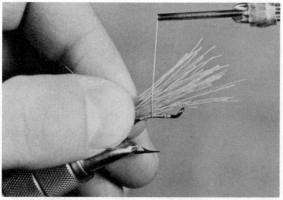

1. Cover the hook shank with tying thread, bring the thread back to a third of the shank length from the bend of the hook. Prepare some hair for the tail. Tie in at this point with several tight wraps. Wind the thread back towards the bend, making looser wraps towards the bend so that hair does not flare excessively.

2. Take thread back to just above the point of the hook, winding evenly as you go.

3. Cut a small bunch of deer hair, remove the fuzz and stack thoroughly.

4. Tie the bunch of hair in about one-third back from the hook eye, as shown above. Make about four or five turns to hold the hair in position. Do not pull tight to make a flare at this point.

5. Clip the butts short, no longer than 1/8".

6. Note the above picture for the clipped butts.

7. Now carefully unwind all but three turns. Pull tight on the thread as you spin the hair.

8. Spin and flare the hair around the hook shank.

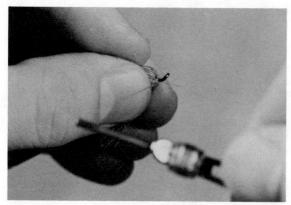

9.   Hold the hair back with your fingers and make a few turns in front of the flared hair to stand it up.

10.   Whip finish and lacquer. The fly should have about a one inch hair diameter for a number 12 hook.

11.   This is the fly from the front.

12.   The Finished Fly.

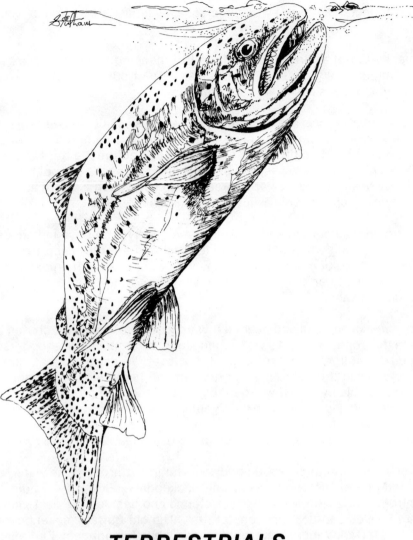

TERRESTRIALS

Today's fly fisherman has a growing interest in the use of terrestrials — grasshoppers, beetles, ants, crickets, spiders and other land-based creatures. Because of more new materials available to the tyer today, and more emphasis on realistic patterns, the challenge of matching these pesky little critters has become an exciting and interesting asset to fly fishing.

I recall my first exposure to fishing with terrestrials. I was only a boy of 11, spending a day along a particularly difficult spring creek that flows through the western part of Jackson Hole. This slow, clear stream was marked by long deep runs bordered by grassy banks. Although the stream meandered through private property, this occasion took place long before the on-slaught of the tourist fisherman and access was fairly easily obtained. One of my friends happened to be a local rancher boy whose relatives owned a considerable portion of this marvelous creek.

My favorite flies on the creek were usually the high floating Humpy or one of my all-time favorites, the Dark Variant. The fish, however, were extremely sensitive and fishing required the use of small tippets at least 5X or thinner. With limited fly fishing experience at this tender age, I had difficulty in keeping from breaking off everytime one of those big spring creek trout sipped in my offering. Whenever I would increase my leader size, the fish would simply refuse the fly.

At that time, I was not aware of the sinful art of plunking heavy Muddlers and other deadly streamers that might have tempted some of these larger trout out of the deep weed beds which covered the bottom of the slow moving stream.

My boyhood friend, Ken, was a child of basic needs. His $18.00 Shakespeare Wonderglass rod showed up like a sore thumb next to my Philipson Peerless cane rod, the one my grandfather had given to me on my tenth birthday. A big South Bend automatic fly reel was clamped on the seat of this 9-foot piece of fiberglass, and in the hand of a less than 5-foot boy, made him almost look comical. My beautiful Hardy Perfect reel which sang such a pretty tune when a large fish was on seemed no match for Ken's awful sounding coffeegrinder.

As always, there was a certain sort of rivalry when two young boys fished a stream together. It was almost like seeing who could hit the longest home run or keep from striking out first. There was always sense of competition to see who would catch the most, the biggest and the quickest. On this particular day, the city boy was about to learn a lesson, that would soon be called, "by country means."

We strolled across a hayfield and headed toward a piece of water which Ken assured me held several trout in the trophy class. As we tripped along, swarms of grasshoppers clattered before us, adding their counterpoint to the music of this lovely Wyoming summer day. As we neared the stream, we crawled through the sagebrush and slithered along the bank of a magnificent long run made possible by an old wooden foot bridge that had probably been built in the early 1900's. It had decayed and fallen apart with gentle flowing riffles on the backside of each of the naked pillars protruding through the surface. Ken immediately spoke of hugh dark shadows that broke water, devoured Humpies, and then snapped heavy leaders like they were thread.

A cold shiver went through my young body as a hugh cutthroat broke water, and then quickly vanished behind one of the bridge's swirling backeddies. Both of us almost wet our pants. Still shaking from excitement, we had a conference and decided the best plan would be to flip a coin to see who would attack the monster first. The old Buffalo nickel bounced in my favor, so I tied on a trusty Dark Variant and went to work, while the unhappy Ken retreated to the high willows on the side to watch the action. Cast after cast, different fly after different fly, nothing! No action!

Now, it was Ken's turn. The country boy with the 9-foot Shakespeare quickly snapped the silk line through the guides and a fly leaped on the water. I must admit, my friend did an admirable job even though he was using a clubby $18.00 rod. However, neither the large fish nor any of his friends gave either of us any encouragement.

After several minutes, Ken decided to give up and retreat to the willows for another strategy conference. Just as he started up the bank, the fish rose again with a loud slap of the water. This gesture brought out the ire that lies in every Scotman's temperment. Ken being a good Scotsman, proceeded to beat the ground and the willows with his 9-foot Wonderod in deep humiliation. The last I saw of him, he was stomping off under the weeds mumbling under his breath, "I'll get that fish."

Suddenly, like a moose tromping through the brush, Ken returned with cupped hands like he was trying to keep something from getting away. He sneaked behind the willow next to me and said, "Watch this." Suddenly he flipped his wrist and an object went flying through the air.

206

Fluttering and then dropping, it hit the water behind the bridge and twirled around. I looked down and squinting against the glare, I could see movement coming from the object. Before I could distinguish what it was, there was a big swirl and a familiar slap of the water.

Ken let out a yell that would make any self-respecting Indian very proud. He charged back into the field and minutes later returned again with cupped hands. He slid down the bank of the willows, and said, "Give me a fly that's torn apart — any fly, anything you don't want." I looked in my box and fished out a well-chewed Humpy that had nothing but a small bit of deer hair left on its back and a few wraps of thread. I handed the hook to Ken, who had already removed his previous fly. With his hands still cupped around this little treasure, he tied on the Humpy. Very carefully, he opened his hands and with a quick movement, hooked the Humpy into the object, turning his back so I couldn't see what he was doing. He then moved to the back of the run. With one great flip of the Wonderod, a line shot out and the object again landed in the same place, this time with Ken's hook and line attached.

Now that I had a better angle, I could see what the object was. It was a two-inch grasshopper, squirming and kicking on the water. About the time I said, "I'll be!", the water exploded and the line went taut. I saw the deep brown back and the golden side of a large cutthroat trout as he engulfed the squirming grasshopper. The old South Bend Reel smoked and the old stiff Wonderod bent in a perfect bow. All Ken could say was, "Get the net, get the net!" Just then, I realized the net had been left upstream.

As I ran back to retrieve it, falling in beaver holes, and tripping over furrow logs, I felt happy, yet a little preplexed about my reaction to the situation. My grandfather had always taught me that it was a sin to use bait with a fly rod. As I ran back downstream, I paused and for a few short seconds, my conscience tugged at me, but I figured that at least once in my life there was something worth being a sinner for. Feeling much better, I tromped, jumped and half swam into the water until I was beside Ken who had the fish hopelessly tangled in the middle of the stream around an old piece of log, barb-wire and moss. Yet, somehow, with some careful maneuvering, I slipped the net behind the monster's tail and scooped him up. Even though he was hopelessly tangled, I was able to break off the leader. We both made that triumphal wade back to the bank, and couldn't wait to take a close look at that fish. It was a hugh 7 or 8 pound trout — bigger than anything either of us had ever caught before. We sat there and stared at it, and then opened his mouth to remove the hook.

After the excitement was over, I promptly lectured Ken on the evils of his deed and how bad he should have felt. But, nothing was going to take away the excitement of that moment. He defended himself, saying, "I caught it on a fly rod, and caught it with a fly hook. I caught it with some of nature's own materials. You can't call that sacriligious."

I got the point, and at that young age, perceived there was more to fishing than limiting myself to classic dry flies. Not long afterward, I was shown a pattern called the Joe's Michigan Hopper, which I started tying that summer and have used many years to catch trout large and small.

Through the years of guiding and outfitting fishermen from all over the country, I have found the Joe's Hopper to be effective on large rivers and small creeks. This is an especially good fly for people who have trouble seeing some of the smaller dry flies. In that magic time of August, when all the grasshoppers are out, and large fish come to the surface to dine on such meaty fare, a good hopper pattern can provide a lot of action.

However, there is more to terrestrials than just grasshoppers. Ants, crickets, and beetles all have an important place. Even large moths provide the main ingredient for some exciting fishing experiences as I learned from a trip to some of the fine trout lakes of New Zealand and Tasmania. There is a whole new world in terrestrials, which is just being discovered throughout the land, and I hope you will find as interesting as it has been for me.

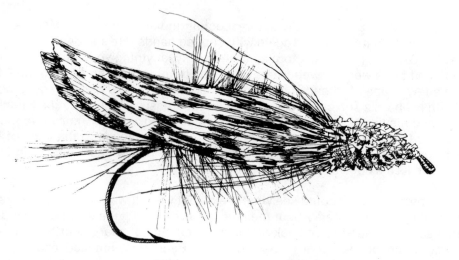

AUSSIE HOPPER

It was at a dinner table, overlooking the Cathedral Group of the Tetons at the Jenny Lake Lodge, when my new acquaintance, Bruce Whalen, tried to paint a picture of fly fishing in Australia. My impressions of Australia always ran along the lines of vast deserts, large sheep ranches and one over-powering thought ... DRY! Yet Bruce changed my mental picture with his talk of beautiful spring fed rivers flowing over western looking plains, with virtually no people fishing, and two to four pounders under every rock. The more he talked, the more excited I got. It has always been intriguing to me to find new and different trout fishing waters, especially in a country where one would never expect trout to be. And one of the most intriguing thoughts about Australia was the lack of fishing pressure in close proximity to large city populations, something that we find quite uncommon here in our country. Bruce had moved to Australia from the U.S. and had married an Australian girl. He was a pilot with Pan American Air Lines, and loved fly fishing about as much as anything. While first living in Australia, he had a chance to meet some of the fishing fraternity, and learned some of the choice waters. It took three years after our first meeting before I had my opportunity to go to the land of kangaroos and find out the truth.

The first teaser came in the form of a book called **Fly Fishing in Australia** by David Scholes. The book outlined the type of fishing that was available both in Australia and its island state of Tasmania, commonly referred to by the Australians as Tassie. From what the publication indicated, they had a very strong population of terrestrials in the form of beetles, moths and most important, grasshoppers. The book's pictures showed some very interesting hopper imitations, which had a striking similarity to our Muddler Minnows. After reading the book, I found that Joe Brooks, a well-known American fisherman, had visited Tasmania and introduced the Aussies to the Muddler Minnow. The Aussie tyers incorporated into some of their Hopper patterns the Muddler's deer hair head as we have done with many deer hair hoppers in this country. The book again increased my excitement as far away places to lure trout to net had been my life-long dream.

My chance came in 1978; as the Pam Am 747 drifted out of the clouds, and I had my first look at the brown Australian countryside. I had just left the isles of New Zealand, whose lush greenness had overwhelmed me, and its fabulous fishing had already made my trip. To me, Australia would be the icing on the cake. As I first looked at the Australian landscape, I saw a completely different setting than I had originally expected. The countryside looked dry and brown with splotches of light green trees sprinkled through low rolling hills. My thoughts were of disappointment; this is not what I had been told to expect. Where were spectacular rivers? Maybe somebody made a mistake. Everyone I talked to in New Zealand said that other than Tasmania, the mainland Australia had no fishing at all, or relatively little. Being a little uneasy, I would only have to wait to find out who was right.

Jovial Bruce and his lovely, pleasant wife Rosalee, met me at the airport and whisked me off to their home in the suburbs of Melbourne. When first walking into Bruce's house, it really did not seem much different than if it were somewhere in the United States. Everything seemed so right at home. Bruce showed me into his den which housed a fine collection of **The Fly Fisherman Magazine**. Before we hardly settled, he was showing me pictures of some of the waters we would be fishing, and making plans about all the different places we would be stopping. Before that evening was over, out came the Australian flies, the fly tying vises and the beer. A delightful evening of fishing chatter and ideas were expressed.

Reaching into a hidden fly box, Bruce pulled out his fly tying masterpiece called a "Latex Hopper", a different, intriguing deer hair hopper. My host explained that in Australia there are many different types of grasshoppers and a hopper season lasts from mid-January through mid-March, their middle summer to early fall. This is a period when the fish feed almost exclusively on grasshoppers and only intermittently touching insect hatches. "Thus", exclaimed Bruce, "we have had a chance to try almost every grasshopper imitation that modern man has devised, including many American hoppers." As he held up the fly, he pointed out the latex body, saying that it was a more natural silhouette that rode low in the water, and truly imitated a grasshopper's body. Underneath the latex he had wrapped different colors of floss that gave the body a transluscent colored appearance. The wings were tied by using golden pheasant tippets, spread out to look and imitate the fanning of the grasshopper's wings as they hit the water in attempt to become airborne again. Bruce noted that most grasshoppers light on the water with a tremendous amount of movement. The critters attempt to flee the foreign area and become landborne again with their legs kicking and their wings fluttering. Bruce felt that with the use of a fan down wing would match the grasshoppers natural movement as he lights on the water. By adding a clipped deer hair Muddler head similar to the Aussies' favorite Nobby Hopper, an Australian variation of the Muddler was designed as a grasshopper pattern. The Australian anglers had found the small Muddler Minnow was a very good imitation of the grasshoppers, as we have in the United States.

Our chance to find the truth about Australia came the next day as we headed to the Snowy Mountain range of New South Wales and the fabled streams that flow gently from the 6,000 foot mountains. The first day our fishing entourage cast several flies to smaller rivers, that actually would be called creeks in our country. The clear, pebble bottomed streams were only ten to fifteen feet in width with deep blue-green pools trimmed with dense vegetation. All had surprisingly good trout populations and were paralleled by paved highways.

My Aussie friend's plan was to visit the Murray River, which is Australia's longest river and the Swampy Plain, a beautiful lush spring creek about the size of Armstrong Spring Creek in Montana. The spot we headed for was the point where the Swampy Plain flowed into the Murray. Each river was so gin clear you could see every rock or twig on the sandy bottom as well as the cautious trout. The Swampy Plain was approximately twenty-five to thirty feet in width, and the Murray was over a hundred feet with many small side channels breaking off from the main river. There were lush plants and overhanging ferns that actually touched the water, forming trout holding pockets. The lofty green eucalyptus trees resembled our magnificent cottonwoods here in the West. This pristine setting included Hereford cattle that grazed on green carpeted hay meadows reminiscent of the Western Rockies. It almost felt like home, but the cries of the white cockatoos quickly underscored the fact that I was over seven thousand miles from my favorite fishing waters.

Bruce and I quietly sneaked along the banks peering for feeding fish. Quickly the Aussie raised his rod and pointed upstream underneath a steep undercut bank. Straining my eyes, I sighted the dark shadow of a fish rising to the surface and sucking an active insect that floated by. Anxiously, Bruce decided that this fish could be best approached from downstream. Slipping into the cold water, he stripped out some fly line, and the line zoomed through the guides. Being careful not to cast over the top of the fish, the expert caster laid a gentle curve to his orange line, and gently laid the fly three to four feet above the feeding trout. With a right curve in the fly line, the fly drifted over the dark motionless shadow as the line floated to the side. The shadow slowly rose from the bottom, holding for a second until the fly was right above his nose, and then with one big swirl devoured the morsel. The reel sang that familiar song as the fish screamed upstream charging toward a large brush pile. Bruce immediately turned the powerful trout and maneuvered the quivering leader away from the dangerous brush pile and back into the deep sanctuary of the pool. There were many other obstructions in the pool, ranging from large underwater logs to clumps of heavy vegetation. The fish continually made long, strong runs, until finally after about ten minutes he retreated to the deeper part of the hole. Bruce eventually got the upper hand, and with a quick flip of his wrist brought out the folding net, and scooped up at least what appeared to be a three to four pound trout. I rushed down with my camera, taking pictures all the way and screaming like a young kid who had just discovered fishing for the first time. The fish turned out to be a large German brown trout, with a bright golden body color; sprinkled along the back were rich red and black dots. The exhausted trout had fought admirably, better than most six pound trout, but the fish weighed just slightly over three pounds. Hooked inside the trout's jaw was Bruce's Latex Hopper, as he mumbled to himself, "It works everytime." Being the stubborn American, I continually tried Joe's Hoppers and Dave's Hoppers, all to no avail. I just was not ready at that time for the Latex Hopper.

We continued working our way up the Swampy Plain and discovered each placid pool to be different in character. Every occasion we spotted a rising fish, I would have my chance, then Bruce would step in with his Latex Hopper and pluck the trout out. By mid-afternoon, I was finally convinced that it was time for the Latex Hoppers. Bruce opened a near empty box and all three Hoppers were slightly used and had seem some better days. The Aussie angler smirked and said, "You better be careful, the only Hoppers left after these will have to be cut out of my hat." I glanced up and saw two Hoppers clinging to a wrinkled, Irish fisherman's hat.

We came to a fork in the river and Bruce journeyed up one channel while I ventured in a small, intimate side stream with a deep cut bank, five feet in height. Peering over the bank to the other side, so my silhouette would not be skylighted, I observed in the middle of the pool a large dead stump with a swirling back eddy directly behind it. The elevation of the bank made is possible to look straight down into the depths of the dark pool. Behind the brush pile, I could see one large black shadow. My heart started to beat a little bit faster, as this was so far the largest fish we had seen that day. In the dilemma of not being in the right place and feeling uncomfortable with the fishing situation, I again analyzed to see if there was any better place to approach this fish. There just didn't seem to be any better place to cast, but being downstream from the motionless shadow with his feeding window upstream I felt I still had a chance. Stripping out the line, I carefully checked my Latex Hopper. The bug was still intact and the leader was wind-knot free. Everything looked right, so I prepared myself, knowing that there is nothing worse than actually seeing a trophy trout feeding knowing you have a chance. It always seems to make one's backcast dip or tangle the line in some way, but this time it did not happen. The line shot through the guides and landed perfectly above the stump. The Latex Hopper drifted down and just about the time that it got in front of the shadow, the fly sank. The shadow rose and came over the drowned fly, but let it pass. Several more casts proved to be futile for the fly kept sinking; the shadow would quickly refuse it and retreat behind the stump. I retrieved the Hopper and tried to analyze it. The deer hair gave it bouyancy but the latex added enough weight to sink the fly. I thought there must be a way to improve it, but first, the important thing was to catch that fish. The fly tying experimentation would come later. Quickly I dried out the head of the fly and rubbed in more fly floatant. With several false casts, I dried the fly out even more, hoping this time it would stay dry and give me the chance I wanted. With a cast and a

prayer, the fly landed above the stump and floated down into the back eddy. This time it did not sink. The shadow rose up, followed the fly down for about six inches, then very gently raised his nose out of the water; the fly disappeared. Zing! I set the hook just as quickly as the strike had been. The fish then made a tremendous run straight up river. The reel screamed as I palmed its rim hoping to slow down the run of the large trout. I screamed back to Bruce that this time it was his turn to get the picture. The fish continued to run, getting the line towards the backing.

Bruce came running, tripping over sticks, and thrashing as best he could to get over the island and to the channel. Just as I heard that he was ready with the camera, the fish turned and with the same ferocity as in his first run, he screamed directly toward me. Madly reeling line, as the charging brown created slack, I started hand stripping the loose fly line. Running backwards in an attempt to tighten the line and regain control, I didn't see the log. From across the stream came, "Gee!! Look at the size of that fish!" With that sound, I tripped backwards over the hidden log landing on my rear end as the line wrapped around me. Madly getting up, quickly I grabbed the graphite, feeling that agonizing, empty, gut-hurting of defeat. Only a slack line and an empty Latex Hopper remained. The only thing that irritated me more than losing the fish was my friend's biting laughter. Thoroughly embarrassed and somewhat irritated, I gathered my things and trucked quickly upstream, hoping for another challenge of the Australian brown trout. After a few steps a shout rang from the bushes, "Big brown on!" This time the cagey trout lost, and Bruce netted a large, five pound brown that had been plucked from under a willowly overhanging fern. The grinning angler proudly exclaimed, "Now that's a decent trout, mate!" Nothing like a large fish to make you keep casting.

In the next couple of beautiful hidden pools I beached several nice trout in the two to three pound range. I had broken the ice. Thoroughly amazed at the strength of these underwater missiles, the Aussie trout had to be some of the finest fighting trout that I had experienced. Even the smaller one to two pounders fought like most four pound plus trophies and stripped off yards of line. The Aussies attribute this to the pure wild strain of trout that they have carefully nurtured throughout the last century.

That evening we had a chance to discuss the days happenings over a fire with a delightful bottle of Australian white wine. Our host had kept a couple of the fish to charcoal over a wood fire. The flesh of the Australian trout was a deep red, with a sweet salmon-like flavor. Exchanging tall fishing untruths, I recounted the tale of the monster trout to the relaxed crew and how the fly had not floated so well. Reflecting, Bruce spoke, "I have had trouble keeping the fly high floating, especially after catching several trout." The thought went through my mind that something needed to be put under the latex to help it float. Suddenly it came to me, "deer hair!" Rushing through my fly tying materials I discovered some green and yellow deer hair. Out came the Thompson A Vise and quickly some yellow deer hair. Tying it as one would do in tying a Humpy, I folded it over, crossing the hair with thread. In the light of a Coleman lantern, I wrapped latex over the deer hair and tied in the golden pheasant wings. Instead of making a Muddler clipped head, I added a bullet type head of folded over deer hair, in the manner shown to me by Montana tyer, Al Troth. In the dim rays a new hopper was crafted and quickly Bruce examined the creation. The excitement in his eyes was evident. Carefully studying the hopper, he softly exclaimed in his Texas Australian accent, "This might be the answer."

In the weeks coming up we had a chance to try the different types of flies using different colors. We definitely found that the deer hair added bouyancy to the fly, and bullet head made it a relatively faster fly to tie. It also had a more slender appearance, representative of the head of a natural grasshopper.

Thoughts then went toward the United States. Would this fly work here? I brought back some of the hooks that Bruce had used on his fly. The particular hook which had applications to our fly tying was called a Captain Hamilton Hook. It was invented by a New Zealand gent who had fished both Australia and New Zealand, and was looking for a hook that had a wider gap. They are manufactured in England and are available from several fly material houses both in Australia and soon in the U.S. The hook, besides having an extremely sharp point and a wide gap, is just the right length for tying Hopper flies. One of the bad things about the Hopper fly is that when you add all the materials you cut down the size of your gap, leaving an improper hooking angle. This particular hook solves that problem, and is extremely durable.

After experimenting more with the fly, I decided to tie some and try them in the United States.

In the summer of 1978, we tied several up and passed them around to friends. The reports came back, the fly was an extremely good pattern, and would definately take fish in the United States. Not only would it take fish, but it would take large fish. The reports came in, the fly worked and worked well. It floated with a low profile, which is a shortcoming of many grasshopper imitations. The Aussie Hopper appears natural and floats in the surface film. Besides being durable it was not hard to obtain materials, which is not the case with turkey quills, and was relatively easy to wrap. Its possibilites are far reaching.

When I considered what name to give the fly I thought it appropriate that it be called an Aussie Hopper and my fellow colleagues in our shop felt it was just a natural. We suggest that you try it, and be as pleasantly surprised as I was. When I look at the Hopper it still brings back many fine memories, distant rivers, colorful sunsets, great friends and a land seven thousand miles away.

MATERIALS:	Aussie Hopper
THREAD:	Yellow monocord
HOOK:	Mustad 3906, 9671
SIZES:	8-14
RIBBING:	Latex strip
BODY:	Yellow dyed deer hair
WING:	Golden pheasant tippet
TOPPING:	Natural deer hair
HEAD:	Natural deer hair in a bullet shape

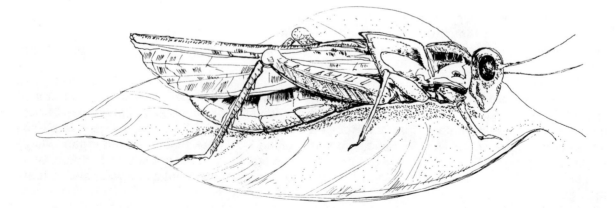

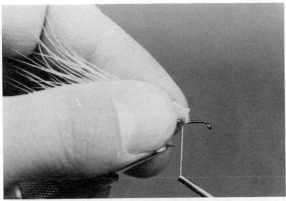

1. Cut out a small bunch of yellow dyed deer hair, remove the small fibers in the underfur. Trim the butts square. Tie down one-third behind the eye.

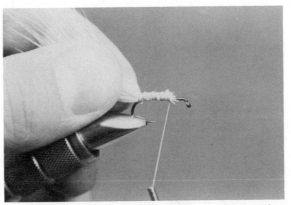

2. Advance the thread backwards to the bend, tying down the deer hair, then forward to where the hair was tied in.

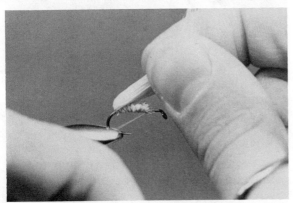

3. Pull the deer hair over as shown in the above picture.

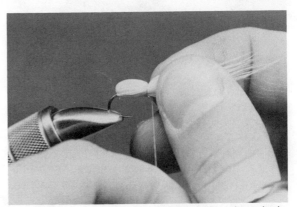

4. Make a loose wrap around the deer hair and then several tighter wraps.

5. Trim the hair butts.

6. Crisscross the deer hair making a smooth body. The thread should now be at the bend of the hook.

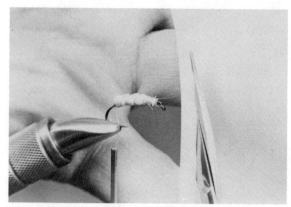

7. Cut out a piece of natural latex approximately ¼'' wide, trim to a point.

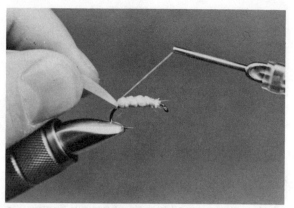

8. Tie in the latex directly behind the body, as shown in the above picture.

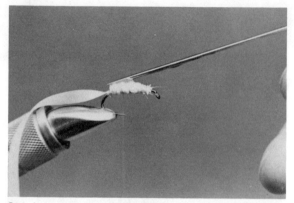

9. Lacquer the body and advance the thread forward with the same pressure as before.

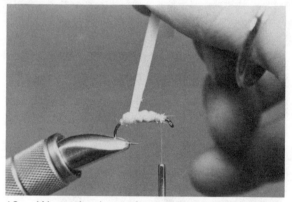

10. Wrap the latex forward overlapping the wraps and stretching as you bring it forward.

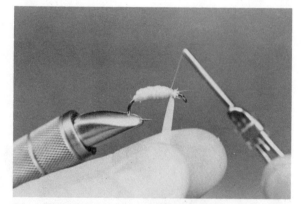

11. Tie off with several tight wraps and trim. Touch a drop of lacquer to keep the latex from slipping.

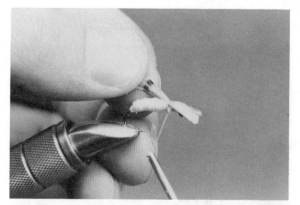

12. The thread should now be one-third back from the eye. Cut out a golden pheasant tippet. Hold it at a slight angle across the hook on the side farthest from you. Tie in with several tight wraps. Trim the butts.

13. Cut out another golden pheasant tippet. Hold it at a slight angle across the hook on the side nearest you. Tie in with several tight wraps.

14. With circular wraps encircle the wing farthest from you. This will keep the fibers together and lift the wing. Repeat the process with the wing nearest to you. Trim the butts and wrap over the top of them.

15. The fly should appear as in this picture.

16. Cut out a small bunch of deer hair approximately the diameter of a pencil.

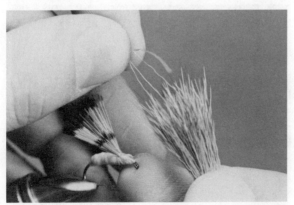

17. Remove the small hairs and underfur.

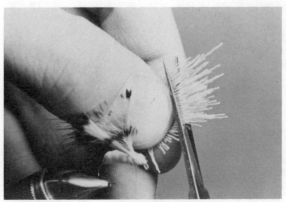

18. Measure the hair bunch to be approximately 1½ times the wing length, trim the butts.

19. Hold the hair between your thumb and forefinger of the right hand, directly over the top of where the wings are tied in. The thread should be just behind the eye.

20. With several loose wraps come over the top of the hair butts. Make the third wrap tight, which will flare the hair.

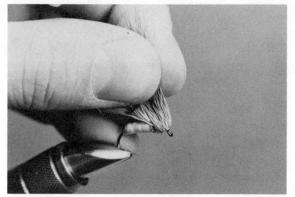

21. Trim the hair butts and wrap over top of them with thread, covering them over. Advance the thread to the base of the wing.

22. Pull the deer hair back with the left hand holding it up and keeping it from getting underneath the hook.

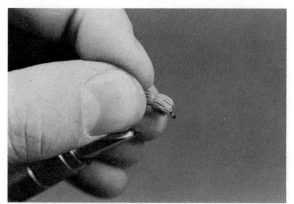

23. Make a loose wrap around the deer hair as shown in the above picture, then make several tighter wraps allowing the hair to flare out.

24. Pull the thread under the head. Make several wraps and whip finish. This is the completed fly.

AL'S HAIR HOPPER

This is another one of Al Troth's hair creations that really deserves special notice. Al has taken the traditional Letort Hopper, added hair for a body, and incorporated the down wing style of his elk hair caddis, crafting an especially good small grasshopper imitation.

The main purpose of the fly is to imitate the smaller grasshoppers that seem to hatch early in the season. I have found that early in the season when the hoppers first appear, many of them are of the miniscule variety. This can be the best time for catching large trout. Most of us have used either small Muddlers, the famous Letort Hopper or the standard Joe's Hopper in small sizes. A smaller hopper fly can have trouble floating in some of the heavier waters. This is where I feel that the Hair Hopper of Al's comes into its own.

One would be very surprised at how many fish could be caught in some of our gin-clear, wild, western spring creeks. I have fared well with hoppers at times when there was no hatch during the middle of the day. A long leader with light tippet should be used. A piece of advice on these crystal spring creeks is not to cast directly over or near visible fish, as heavy hoppers do not land as lightly as do your small wispy dries. Try to spot a cruising fish and figure out its feeding pattern. When a trout is in a feeding position he will have a window, or area of sight, where he can observe the fare passing over. If the area you are fishing has enough current, cast your hopper with plenty of distance ahead of the wily adversary, so your fly or leader enters his feeding window free of disturbances. When the fly floats near the intended victim, give it a slight twitch to imitate movement from the deceiving hopper. A couple of small jerks on your line is usually sufficient. Be ready! Don't be surprised when the large trophy you see comes charging from the bottom, crashes that fly, and makes your day complete. Clear spring creeks can be fun during those hot midday's.

It is important when tying this fly to put some vinyl cement over the body as the teeth of big trout will rip into the hair and soon destroy your beautiful creation.

I might also mention that Al's Hopper can be tied in different colors by simply switching the color of the deer hair. It could be an olive, green, pale yellow, a bright yellow, or different shades or deer hair to imitate the different colors of hoppers that might frequent your country. Don't hesitate to experiment! Without people who take the time and effort to innovate, we would not have some of these wonderful fly creations that are available today!

MATERIALS:	Al's Hair Hopper
THREAD:	Nymo "A" yellow shade 2780 or CSE flat waxed nylon
HOOK:	94840
SIZES:	10-16
BODY:	Either the long hair at the base of a yellow dyed buck tail or long cream elk rump dyed yellow
WING:	Bunch of natural whitetail deer flank hair
LEGS:	Short side of a red dyed goose quill

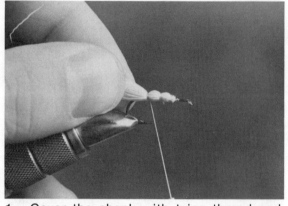

1. Cover the shank with tying thread and bring the thread back to a point one-quarter the shank length behind the hook eye. Select a bunch of hair for the body, a bunch about the size of a wooden match or if using elk hair, about 25 hairs for a number 12 fly. Remove the short hairs from the bundle and clip the ends square and tie down as shown in the picture above. Spiral the tying thread down the shank forming segments in the hair.

2. Make a couple of turns of thread at the end of the body.

3. Make a couple of half hitches at the end of the body.

4. Pull the hair forward.

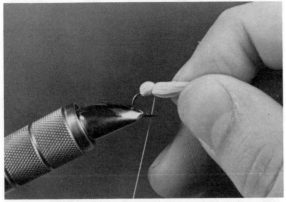

5. While holding the hair forward with the right hand, wind the tying thread toward the eye forming segments. Tie the hair down in front of the first initial tie in.

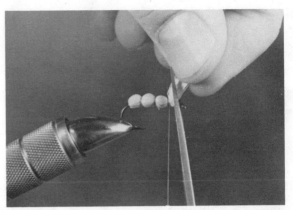

6. This will eliminate a bulky lump where the legs and wing will be tied in. Clip the hair as shown above. Touch a drop or two of lacquer to the body.

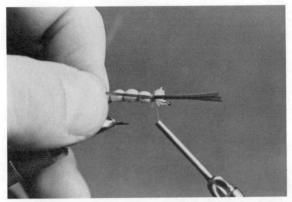

7. Tie in a piece of goose quill on each side of the body.

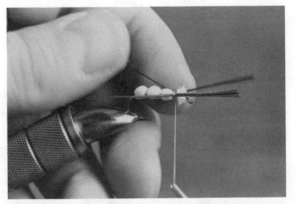

8. Fibers should have a natural curve away from the body.

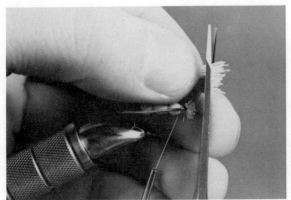

9. Cut a bunch of white-tailed deer flank hair for the wing. Place the hair in a stacker and stack until all points are even.

10. Measure the hair for length as in the above picture.

 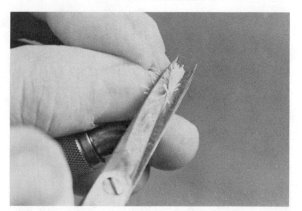

11. Tie in the hair at the same place where the legs are tied in. Make a couple of loose turns of thread first, then tighten with the third wrap. Be sure to keep the hair on top of the hook. Take a turn or two of tying thread through the flared ends toward the eye of the hook. Pull the hair back and make several wraps in front of the hair. Whip finish and varnish.

12. Clip the ends as shown in the above photograph.

13. The Finished Fly.

THE TEVORAVICH HOPPER

This is another one of the interesting Australian hopper patterns I discovered on a trip to that island-continent. Dan Tevoravich was a Yugoslavian army officer, who fled during the take-over by the Russian troops during World War II. Escaping the Communists, Dan was able to pursue his love of fly fishing on the many beautiful streams of Australia. His life long love for the sport and his love of freedom were apparant as I talked to him in Australia. One of Australia's most talented fly tyers, Dan has been known for producing many innovative patterns.

This Hopper is an offshoot of the Australian's famed Nobby Hopper (which is a variation of our dry style Muddler Minnow). Dan's enthusiasm for angling and his flare for fly tying impressed me so much that I felt this fly was a "must" for this book.

The Australians have great pride in their streams and a love for fly fishing that is unequaled. The Aussie way of fishing is unique to their part of the world. Their casual approach to life is reflected in their fishing. It is not uncommon to see an Australian carrying a bottle of brandy, a fly rod and a flash light, heading out to fish his favorite lake as the sun sets. He and his mates will fish until the sun rises in the morning. Many large browns are caught in the dead of night on large dry flies. A little sip of brandy, a little cast here and there and a lot of good fellowship are the important ingredients of some truly memorable occasions of the laid back Down Under style of fly fishing.

MATERIALS:	Tevoravich Hopper
THREAD:	Yellow monocord and yellow CSE flat waxed nylon
HOOK:	Mustad 79580, 9672
SIZES:	6-12
UNDERBODY:	Yellow art foam
BODY:	Chartreuse dubbing
WING:	Golden pheasant tippets and turkey quill sections

LEGS: Brown hackle stem trimmed and knotted

HEAD: Natural grey deer hair

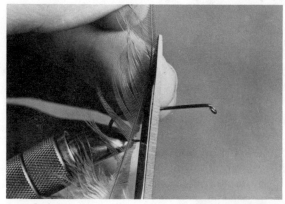

1. Select a medium length hackle with a large vein running through the hackle. With sharp scissors, trim approximately three-quarters of the hackle, leaving only a small stub along the hackle vein; trim on both sides.

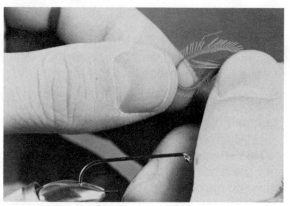

2. The hackle vein should appear as in the above picture.

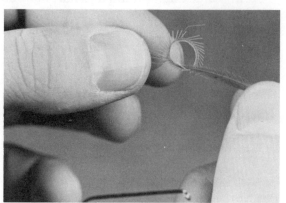

3. Take hackle and tie a slip knot approximately a third of the way down the hackle vein.

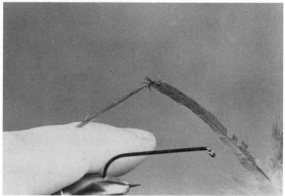

4. Tighten the knot forming a hopper leg, see the above picture. Repeat steps 2-4 with another hackle so that you have two legs for your hopper.

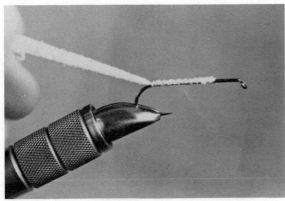

5. Tie in a strip of art foam and secure it to the shank of the hook.

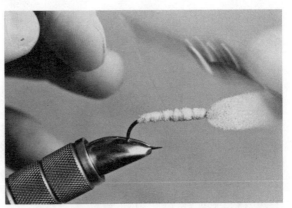

6. Wrap art foam forward and tie off approximately ¾ way down the shank of the hook. With your tying thread wrap back towards the bend.

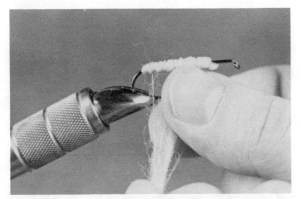

7. Select some polypropylene body material and dub onto the thread.

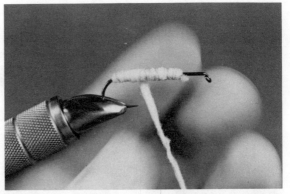

8. Wrap dubbed polypropylene forward covering the art foam.

9. The dubbed poly body should have a nice gentle taper and should follow the above proportions.

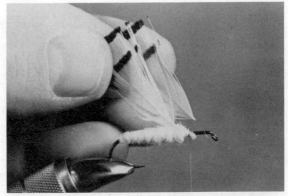

10. Select two golden pheasant tippets to represent wings. Place light side against light side so that both feathers form one large wing. Tie in just in front of the body.

11. The golden pheasant tippets should both be even and melded together to form one wing as above.

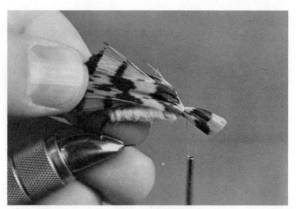

12. Tie in two mottled feather sections, one on each side of the golden pheasant tippet wing.

13. Trim mottled feather even with golden pheasant tippet.

14. Spray each trimmed hackle vein leg with clear spray lacquer.

15. Holding leg between thumb and fore-finger, place leg along side mottled wing and tie in.

16. Repeat step #15 on other side of fly forming a second leg. Trim butts of each hackle leg.

17. Tie in some very light gray, soft deer hair along side of the wing. Pull tight and flare hair.

18. On other side of the wing tie in another clump of deer hair, also flaring it.

19. Spin and securely tighten deer hair. Whip finish and lacquer thread.

20. With sharp scissors, trim deer hair head forming a small bullet head.

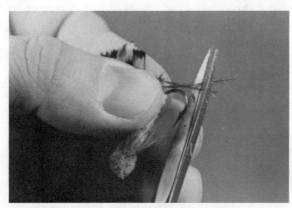

21. Trim hackle legs even with point of hook.

22. The Finished Fly

JIM'S HAIR HOPPER

Recently, I have found this creation of Jim Chestney, the talented mid-western fly tyer, to be an excellent meadow stream hopper. Tied sparse and small, it represents the small hoppers which are abundant in the spring creeks and meadow trout streams.

Flat Creek is one such stream which meanders through a section of the National Elk Refuge, just north of the town of Jackson, Wyoming. In one-half mile of land area, the stream must flow at least six miles as it snakes back and forth through a lush hay meadow like a long, flowing ribbon. At each bend, the current forces its way under the bank, carving some excellent cover for big cutthroat trout.

The banks of this beautiful meadow stream provide an excellent opportunity for the grass-hopper fisherman. The hoppers found at the Elk Refuge pasture are usually matched by a size 10 or 12 pattern which incorporates colors ranging from green to pale yellow. When these terrestrials jump, fly, or are blown into the stream, they are often swept under the cutbank where the hungry trout lie under the shelter of that protective roof.

Many people think that a large trout always make a large swirl or a lot of commotion when taking a fly. But, such is not the case — especially with the Flat Creek cutthroats, which use very little energy in taking a floating insect. Usually they just stick their noses barely out of the water, making a little round ring that gently detects their presence. Sometimes you have to blink twice as you try to convince yourself you actually saw it happen.

Here is one place where the angler's approach is important. Keep a low profile and stay back from the edge of the stream. The trout can spot the intruder at a great distance. Tread softly. The soft undercut banks set off vibrations which telegraph your presence to the sensitive fish.

Under these conditions, I have found Jim's Hair Hopper to be just the ticket to open the mouth of a hungry trout. One effective technique is to cast it to the grass of the opposite bank, and then gently pull it into the water. Give it an occasional twitch, but for the most part let it float on down stream in as natural a drift as possible. The fish in this sort of water are usually wary and will turn tail at the first false move from your offering.

Most fishermen use too heavy a leader when fishing with hoppers. A heavier leader will restrict the movement of a drifting fly and cause it to drag much more easily than with a lighter tippet.

Once a trout rises to your carefully presented hopper, don't fall to the temptation to set the hook too quickly. Many fish are lost because the person on the other end of the rod was too anxious.

Don't hesitate tying Jim's Hair Hopper is sizes as small as 14 and 16. As you walk through the meadow, take the time to observe the size and color of the hoppers jumping away from your footfall. You will be surprised how many small green and yellow hoppers you will see in size 16. (This is especially true early in the season before the hoppers have matured.) I am sure that once you use one of Jim's Hair Hoppers, you will find it to be a good addition to your meadow stream fly selection.

MATERIALS: Jim's Hair Hopper

THREAD: Yellow monocord and yellow CSE flat waxed nylon

HOOK: Mustad 9671, 9672

SIZES: 6-14

BODY: Chartreuse dubbing, or color of hoppers in your area

WING: Turkey quill section

HEAD: Natural light gray deer hair

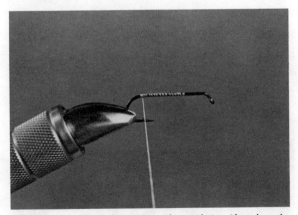

1. Begin by tying the thread to the hook.

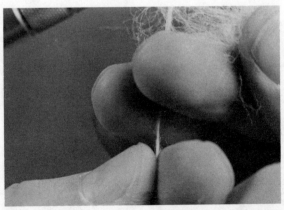

2. Apply a generous amount of dubbing to the thread, squeezing tightly between thumb and forefinger.

229

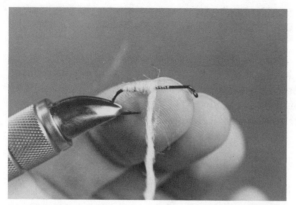

3. Begin dubbing a tapered body forward.

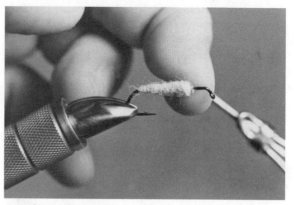

4. Continue dubbing forward until approximately ¼ back from the eye.

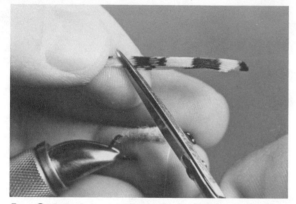

5. Cut out a section of mottled turkey for the wing. This should be approximately ⅓ of an inch across. Fold the section in half and trim at an angle. Note the above picture.

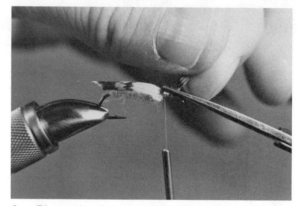

6. Place the folded quill over the top of the body, tie on and trim excess. Note the length of the quill.

7. Cut out a small bunch of deer hair, remove the underfur and small hairs, stack in stacker until even. Measure for length.

8. Hold the deer hair bunch between thumb and forefinger on top of the hook.

9. Make a couple of fairly loose wraps around the deer hair bunch and then pull tightly with the third wrap. Keep the deer hair bunch on top of the hook, not allowing it to spin underneath.

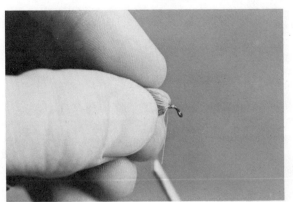

10. Pull back the deer hair bunch and make several wraps just in front of it.

11. Cut out another bunch of deer hair, remove the underfur and small hairs, and trim both ends.

12. Hold the deer hair bunch in front of the second bunch and on top of the hook.

13. Make a fairly loose wrap of thread around the deer hair bunch.

14. Pull tighter with the second wrap.

15. Pull tightest with the third wrap and spin the hair. Make a couple of wraps through the hair, bringing the thread to the eye of the hook.

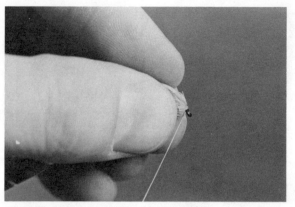

16. Pull back the hair and make a couple of wraps just in front of it.

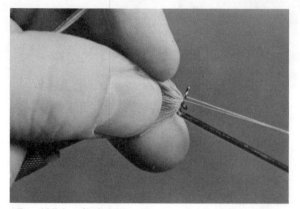

17. Whip finish in front of the deer hair.

18. Trim the deer hair head flat on the bottom.

19. Begin trimming around the sides.

20. Form a nice rounded head, around the side. Notice that no collar is left on the bottom or the sides.

21. Continue trimming the deer hair around the side forming a rounded head.

22. Trim excess deer hair on the top allowing a small collar.

23. Shows the fly from the bottom.

24. Shows the fly from the top.

25. Shows the completed fly.

THE GARTSIDE PHEASANT HOPPER

This fly was first shown to me by Bud Lilly of West Yellowstone, Montana. Bud suggested that this fly should definitely be a part of this book. It was developed by Jack Gartside, a very talented fly tyer and angler who frequents the West Yellowstone area during the summer months. The story on the development of this fly had been often told, but let me recount it once more.

While fishing the fabled Firehole and Madison Rivers of the West Yellowstone area, Jack was having a wonderful time fishing for trout which were real grasshopper freaks. After a period of heavy fishing, Jack ran out of the hopper imitations he had wrapped during the winter months. Hurriedly, he set up his fly tying equipment along a roadside parking area in order to tie up some new imitations and get back to fishing as soon as possible.

After looking through his materials, the frustrated angler could not find a single mottled turkey wing. There on the bottom of his tying box was an old pheasant skin he had acquired some time ago thinking that there might come a time when the beautiful feathers would be useful. The skin was virtually intact as only a few feathers had been used for tailing mayfly nymphs and an occasional rump feather had been wrapped on an exotic Carey Special.

Looking at the multicolor pheasant skin, he saw a feather that resembled the turkey wing. He plucked the feather, stripped the fluff off, dipped it in head cement and stroked it into shape and let it dry. The shape was surprisingly natural, and the even taper to a notched end suggested a grasshopper's legs and wings. Using the available materials, he crafted what is now known as the Gartside Pheasant Hopper.

This fly was a consistent producer, and the trout attacked it viciously. The pheasant wing proved to be as effective and even more durable than the mottled turkey. Since the feather had a center stem, it retained its shape and did not break up when cast or attacked by trout. With further experimentation at home, Jack settled on a standard pattern which we are demonstrating.

It is a pattern which has proved to be more effective than older hoppers using scarce, mottled turkey quill material. It proves once again that many flies are invented by accident, necessity, or panic rather than by design. Give the Gartside Hopper a float. We have, and we like the way it works.

MATERIALS:	The Gartside Pheasant Hopper
THREAD:	Yellow CSE or Danvilles Flat waxed nylon
HOOK:	Mustad 94831 or 9671
SIZES:	8-14
TAIL:	Dark moose hair
RIBBING:	Stiff badger or furnace hackle
BODY:	Light gray, olive, tan, or yellow polypro yarn, tapering front to back
WING:	Mottled pheasant feather from back of bird (see pictures)
UNDERWING:	Deer hair to blend with body color
HACKLE:	Deer hair
HEAD:	Deer body hair trimmed to shape

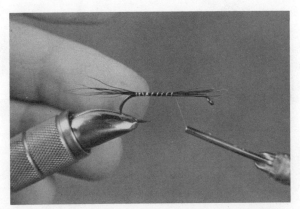

1. Tie in a small clump of moose hair at the bend of the hook and advance the thread forward to approximately one third back from the eye.

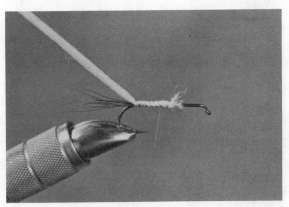

2. At the same place, tie in a strand of yellow polypro yarn. Wrap the thread back over this to the bend of the hook.

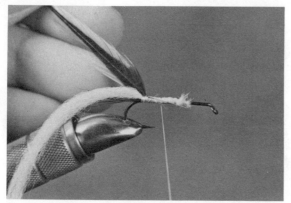

3. Pick out a stiff badger or furnace hackle. Tie in at the bend of the hook.

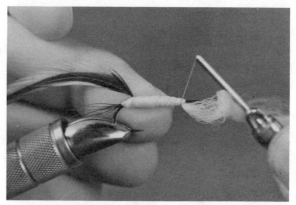

4. Wind the polypro yarn forward forming a smooth body. Be sure to make one wind behind the saddle hackle before advancing it forward.

5. Palmer the saddle hackle forward.

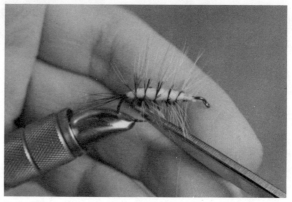

6. Trim the saddle at an angle towards the tail.

7. Cut out a small bunch of yellow dyed deer hair, remove fuzz and small hairs, measure against the hook. Note the above proportions.

8. Tie in the deer hair underwing in front of the body. Be sure to cover all the butts to form a smooth base for the wing.

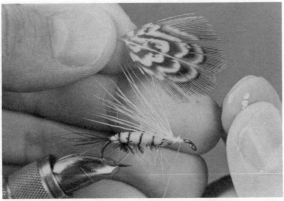

9. Pull out a church window feather from a cock pheasant skin. Remove the fuzz from the base. Put a drop of lacquer between thumb and forefinger.

10. Pull the feather through your thumb and forefinger, cementing the fibers together.

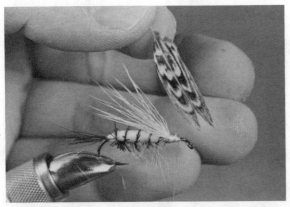

11. The completed wing.

12. Tie in the wing on top of the underwing as shown above. Notice the length of the wing.

13. Cut out a small clump of deer hair. Remove the fuzz and short fibers. Hold the deer hair clump on the side nearest you. Make two loose wraps around the clump and pull tight with a third wrap flaring the hair.

14. Repeat the same procedure on the opposite side of the hook. Advance the tying thread through the hair pulling tight with each turn. Pull the deer hair back and make several wraps of thread just in front of it. Whip finish the head.

15. Trim a rounded head as shown above. Trimming first on the bottom and then around. Leave only a small amount of deer hair collar on the sides to imitate the legs.

16. Shows the completed fly from the top.

17. Shows the completed fly from the side.

HENRY'S FORK HOPPER

By Mike Lawson

*This unique hopper pattern was introduced to me by Mike
Lawson, the talented Idaho fly tyer and proprietor of Henry's
Fork Anglers. I asked Mike to write a story for me on how he
developed this most effective pattern and I thank him for the
following story.*

About six years ago, Rene Harrop and I were fishing the Railroad Ranch stretch of the Henry's
Fork in Idaho. As usual, the wind came up in the afternoon, which made fishing with small dry
flies very difficult. The wind was blowing a lot of hoppers on the water, so we cut back our tippets
and started working hopper patterns along the bank. We'd always done well in the past with low
riding patterns such as Dave's Hopper and the Letort Hopper, but not today. There were so many
naturals blowing in that the fish could accept them at their leisure and then paid no attention to
our artificials. We experienced the same problems the next few trips into the ranch with hoppers.

After our last unsuccessful hopper trip, I caught a couple and brought them home for observation. When viewing the natural from below, I realized that not only must the artificial ride very
low, almost flush with the surface film, but the pale body of the insect is most distinctive. The
answer to this was to develop a pattern with a very low riding natural silhouette, as well as a
smooth well segmented body. I felt the only way to keep the fly afloat and also have it float low
enough in the surface film, was to tie the fly entirely of deer or elk hair. To accomplished the slick,
smooth, segmented body I decided to use elk hair tied back past the bend of the hook and then
pulled forward; this was ribbed tightly with thread forming a segmented body. In fact, the initial
patterns were tied with a very complicated extended body which several years later I decided
was unneccessary. Adding pale yellow deer hair for the underwing and mottled turkey quill
for the wing, I crafted what I felt to be a very effective hopper pattern. Since then I have discovered
more suitable wing materials which are very durable and more readily available. The head is
gray elk hair tied forward and then pulled back into a bullet head allowing the tips to form a collar.
These elk hair tips are left about ½ the body length giving the appearance of legs. For a more
realistic appearance, you can also add large kicker legs of turkey or pheasant tail segments.
These are knotted and lacquered, or just lacquered.

The next time Rene and I finished the ranch I was armed with some of my new hopper patterns;
the extended body type. The success was unbelievable. Every fish we cast to that was feeding
on hoppers accepted our imitations without one refusal. Even when the wind blew entire rafts
of hoppers on the water, the trout still took the new pattern.

In the past few years, I have done very little to improve on the original pattern. I have found the method used by Jack Gartside of lacquering a pheasant rump feather with flexible vinyl cement to be a better wing than the mottled turkey quill segment. You can also use grouse feathers and hen saddle feathers, anything with a mottled effect.

It is important to realize that this hopper pattern was developed for spring creek type fishing. It floats so low that it is very difficult to see. It has been used successfully on Henry's Fork, Silver Creek, the Madison, Firehole, Montana spring creeks, the Letort and most other spring creek waters across the country.

EDITOR'S NOTE:

The Henry's Fork Hopper that we have tied here is the extended body version. To tie the regular version, leave out the monofilament and don't wrap back over the elk hair past the beginning of the bend of the hook. I thank Mike for this most effective pattern and hope you will give it a try.

MATERIALS	Henry's Fork Hopper
THREAD:	Yellow monocord
HOOK:	Mustad 94831, 9671, 94840
SIZES:	8-12
BODY:	Cream Elk Hair (Elk rump patch)
UNDERWING:	Pale yellow deer hair
OVERWING:	Pheasant rump feather or brown mottled hen back feather lacquered with flexible vinyl cement
KICKER LEGS:	Pheasant tail fibers knotted and lacquered with vinyl cement
HEAD:	Light gray elk or light gray deer hair
RIBBING:	Yellow "B" monocord or yellow embroidery yarn
EXTENDED BODY:	30 lb monofilament

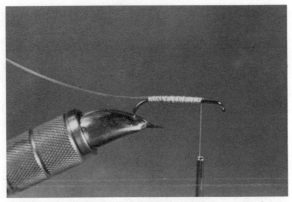

1. Beginning ¼" behind the eye, tie in a piece of 30 pound monofilament, cover thoroughly with thread.

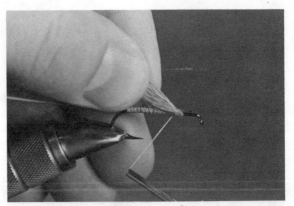

2. Cut out a small bunch of very long cream elk hair, tie this in ¼ behind the eye by the tips. The length of this hair should be twice the shank length.

3. Cover the elk hair completely with thread.

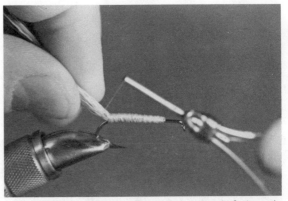

4. With the elk hair bunch in the left hand, slightly lift it and begin making circular wraps around the hair.

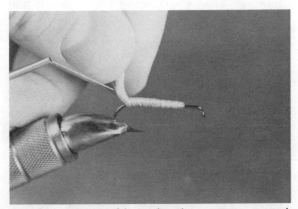

5. Continue making circular wraps around the elk hair bunch until ½ the shank length past the bend of the hook. The bobbin should come over the top of the vise. Make several tight wraps at the end of the body.

6. Tie in a piece of yellow embroidery yarn or heavy yellow monocord, such as "B" monocord.

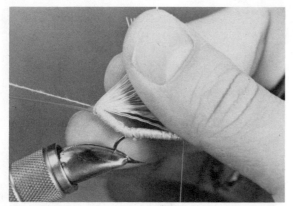

7. Holding the ribbing material and monofilament in your left hand, pull the elk hair over with your right hand.

8. Tie off the elk hair bunch where it was tied in at the front. Your body should now appear as in the above picture.

9. Begin ribbing forward with firm pressure; make two wraps of ribbing behind the bend of the hook.

10. Continue ribbing forward in even spacings. The stray fibers will be bound down by the ribbing. Tie off at the front of the elk hair bunch. Trim the ribbing and the elk hair.

11. Cut the 30 pound mono close to the end of the body.

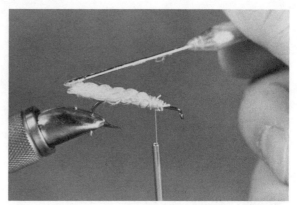

12. Coat the body liberally with lacquer; this will make a very durable body.

13. Cut a small bunch of yellow dyed deer hair. Measure for length. Hold between thumb and forefinger of left hand and tie in. Trim the butts and cover with thread.

14. Select out a church-window feather from the rump of a pheasant, place a drop of lacquer between thumb and forefinger and pull the feather through the drop of lacquer. This will make a nice lacquered wing.

15. Notice the prepared wing in the above picture.

16. Tie on the wing on top of the deer hair bunch.

17. Select out a church-window feather, place a drop of lacquer between thumb and forefinger, roll the feather in your fingers forming a leg. Notice the above picture.

18. Tie in the leg on the side nearest you. Prepare another leg for the other side and tie in. Trim butts and cover with thread.

19. Cut out a small bunch of light gray elk or deer hair; remove the small fibers and underfur. Measure for length; this should be the same as the shank length. Hold between thumb and forefinger of left hand on top of the hook just behind the eye; tie in with several moderately tight wraps.

20. Make several tighter wraps and then trim off the butts. Cover the butts with thread back to where the wing was tied in. Notice the above picture for the proportions of the elk hair and wing.

21. Pull the elk hair bunch back over the body forming a bullet head.

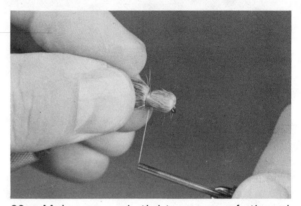

22. Make several tight wraps of thread around the bunch. Firmly secure the head. If any stray fibers have come up, these may now be trimmed out. Pull the thread beneath the eye and whip finish.

23. Trim the wing at an angle, as shown in the above picture.

24. The completed fly.

BING'S HOPPER

By Paul M. Bruun

Paul Bruun is a man of many talents. He's politically active, a professional writer, and an excellent fishing guide. When not writing colorful articles for Fly Fisherman Magazine or other publications, he's busy with the Jackson Hole Daily News, in which he is part owner.

Bing Lempke is so convinced that his extended body fly patterns are the best way to fool big trout, that it should come as no surprise that he even ties his hoppers this way. Today the term "innovative" and "creative" aren't unusual in their application to many contemporary tyers, but Bing lends new meaning to both these phrases.

Anyone viewing Bing for the first time, on the waters near his Idaho Falls home, is usually intrigued by the enigma created by this genuine character. He's always in a hurry, usually hustling after a big rising rainbow, yet he's never too wrapped up in his own fishing to investigate a floundering angler and see if he can help out. "Here, try one of these flies," is normally how most of Bing's acquaintances begin. He then sets about finding his new pal a fish to fool. That's how we met nearly six years ago. His friendly routine doesn't vary much, even to the present day.

Although Bing is adamant about fishing only dry flies, he admits to trying a few nymphs and streamers "for experimental purposes only, you understand." For years, I never believed Bing tied anything but these "experimental" flies. He was forever handing me a "new caddis", a "better green drake", or some "improved" tiny stonefly. In fact, I always carry a small plastic tube of Bing's creations around with me to display to my friends. Then they, too, can marvel at this man's self-honed talent.

Bing Lempke's hands and fingers look like redwood trunks beside the extra small flies he so dearly loves to fish. He is famous for his tiny, matchstick-mounted displays of five perfectly-tied number 28 extended body mayflies set around a size 32 hook. "The smaller the fly is, the easier I can fool a trout with it," he exclaims enthusiastically. "I like to fish small to hook 'em, but I never hold 'em," he sighs, concluding, "But it's sure fun to fool 'em anyway!"

The last time we chatted, Bing explained he was working on a new acid dye to impart a purple (rainbow) cast to his feather spinner wings. While not an Escoffier of fly tying materials and tools, Bing is perfectly content to use such sophisticated parts as paint brush bristles (for stonefly antennae), alligator clips (for holding materials), and his favorite, the Key Caddy for almost everything.

The unique extended body tying attachment for his vise features the Key Caddy and is truly something to see in action. It works on everything from his handsome green drakes to his tiny slate wing olives and naturally his hoppers, too.

When Bing began tying some 35 years ago, he was content simply to create a useable fly. The serious entomological bug bit him nine years ago while he was running a sporting goods department in Salmon, Idaho. Now Bing is acutely aware of the Latin names and the tiny, subtle insect differences that Eastern Idaho rainbows seem to require in their diets. Learning and perfectly imitating the proper bugs are his constant challenges. Recently he asked me to be on the lookout for a good microscope to add to his already crowded tying room.

Tying delicate and tiny insect patterns perhaps isn't the ordinary recreation of a professional pipefitter whose paws are nearly the size of Island Park. But Bing is eagerly anticipating his upcoming retirement from the Department of Energy's AEC site outside of Idaho Falls so he can devote more time to custom tying for his friends and a few customers. He's got dozens of "experimentals" left to construct.

MATERIALS: Bing's Hopper

THREAD: Yellow Monocord

HOOK: Mustad 9672

SIZES: 6-12

RIBBING: Yellow floss

UNDERBODY: Yellow art foam, 30 lb mono

BODY: Yellow art foam or tan art foam

WING: Mottled turkey quill or bleached barred turkey

UNDERWING: Yellow or brown dyed deer hair

HACKLE: Ginger

HEAD: Yellow or chartreuse dyed deer hair

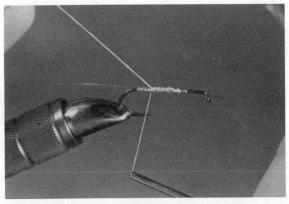

1. Tie in a piece of 30 pound monofilament one-third behind the eye. After this tie in a piece of yellow embroidery thread.

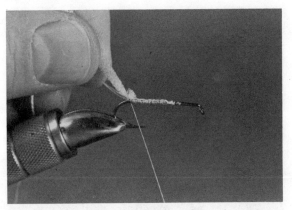

2. Tie in a piece of yellow art foam just above the bend of the hook. This piece should be approximately ¼" wide and 3" long.

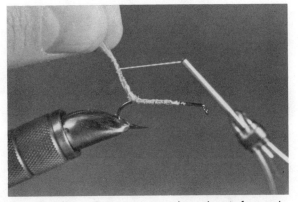

3. Holding the monocord and art foam in your left hand spiral the monocord approximately half the shank length past the bend. Then bring the thread back down to the bend of the hook.

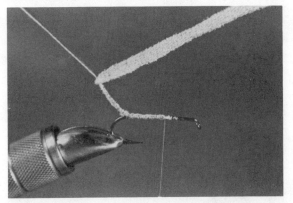

4. Holding the monocord and ribbing in your left hand, begin wrapping the art foam around to form the extended body.

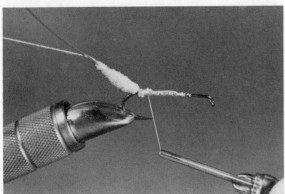

5. Continue wrapping around to form a nice fat body until you reach the bend of the hook. Tie off and trim.

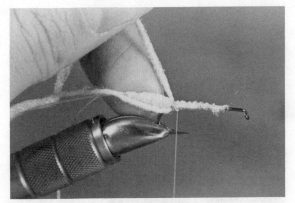

6. Cut out another piece of art foam approximately 4" long. Tie in just above the barb. Tie in a piece of yellow polypro yarn, also just above the barb.

7. Wrap the polypro yarn forward to one-third behind the eye to form a nice fat underbody, tie off and trim.

8. Cover the body with the art foam wrapping forward to the front of the body.

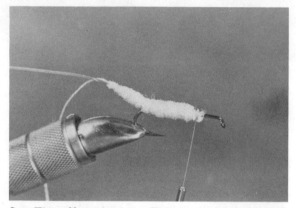

9. Tie off and trim. This is how the body should look before ribbing is advanced.

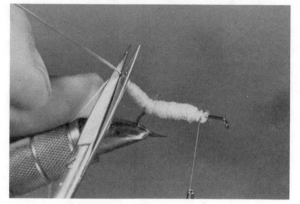

10. Trim the monofilament.

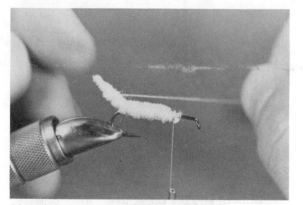

11. Advance the ribbing forward in even spacings.

12. Cut out a small bunch of yellow-dyed deer hair. Measure for length, tie in, trim the butts and cover them with thread.

13. Cut out a section of turkey quill that has been sprayed. This should be approximately ¼" across. Measure for length.

14. Holding between thumb and forefinger, tie in the wing on the side of the hook.

15. Cut out another turkey quill, measure for length and tie in on opposite side.

16. Select two light ginger hackles, tie in at the base of wing.

17. Cut out a small bunch of yellow-dyed deer hair, remove all underfur and small fibers. Hold between thumb and forefinger of left hand, spin hair on the hook.

18. Pull the hair bunch back, make several wraps in front of it. Put a couple of half-hitches in the monocord and trim.

19. Trim the deer hair into a rounded shape.

20. This is the trimmed deer hair head. Attach the monocord to the hook again.

21. Wrap the hackles forward, tie off and trim.

22. This is the completed fly from the side, notice the curve to the body.

23. This is the finished fly.

JIM'S CRICKET

Many of the West's most effective patterns had their origin in the eastern part of the United States and were modified for western use.

This particular cricket pattern came to me by way of Jim Chestney, a well known mid-western fly tyer, who also happens to be a consultant on new products for the Thompson Vise Company. Jim is a very creative fly tyer, and when I questioned him about originating patterns, he made a very interesting point: "I have always been reluctant to say that I originated any particular pattern or tying style. Most of them have turned up in my vise as a result of evolution. In other words, they are the end result of putting together materials and tying procedures picked up from other tyers. Quite frankly, I believe this is the manner in which most patterns are developed, regardless of what some tyers would like to have you believe." I believe this statement reflects the views of many tyers today.

Jim showed me this cricket pattern which offers a very good imitation of an insect which is prevalent in most areas of the United States. This pattern, of course, reflects the eastern influence which emphasizes small, low-floating terrestrials. According to Jim, these are take-offs on the great Letort Hopper pattern developed by Ed Shenk. However, this imitation contains much more deer hair than the traditional patterns and this helps it to float better in an upright position. Jim's Cricket has a good silhouette, and it hits the water with a juicy "splat" which often proves to be irresistible to large fish.

Floatibility is the key to the success of this fly in rough water. However, it can be tied in very small sizes and can be extremely effective on wee spring creeks when the very tiny patterns fail to produce. These terrestrials are especially good during the middle of the day, when the larger insect hatches are not occurring. Try them in the pocket water of small streams.

In fishing smaller waters, tie this cricket on a smaller hook and use a sparser hank of hair. For larger streams and heavier water, go with a larger hook and more hair.

MATERIALS: Jim's Cricket

THREAD: Black monocord

HOOK: Mustad 9671

SIZES: 8-12

BODY: Black deer hair

LEGS: Two fibers from the short side of a goose quill

WING: Black goose quill

HEAD AND COLLAR: Black deer hair

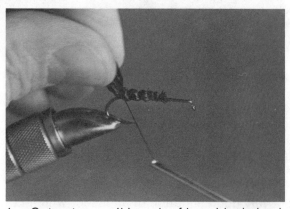

1.   Cut out a small bunch of long black dyed deer hair, tie in ⅓ behind the eye, spiral the thread backwards forming a segmented body as shown in the above picture. This hair should be twice the shank length.

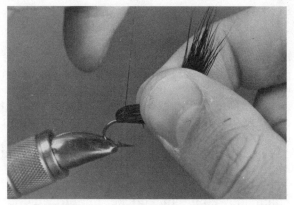

2.   Pull the deer hair over, note the above picture. Begin spiraling the thread forward.

3.   Wrap thread forward forming a segmented body. Stop the body just above where it was tied in. Do not cut off deer hair.

4.   Cut out a black goose quill fiber approximately 1/8'' across. Tie in along the side of the hook. Note the length of the goose quill.

5. Tie in another goose quill fiber on the opposite side of the hook. See above picture for proportions.

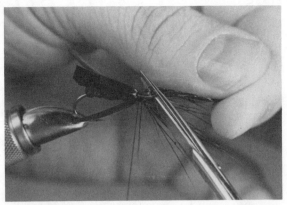

6. Cut a piece of Swiss Straw several inches in length. Tie this in on top of the hook with several tight wraps. Trim butts just behind the eye.

7. Grasp the deer hair with left hand and pull over the top of Swiss Straw butts.

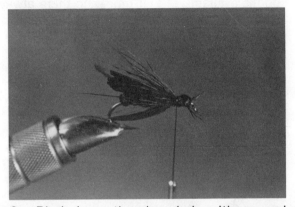

8. Bind down the deer hair with several tight wraps, forming a smooth head.

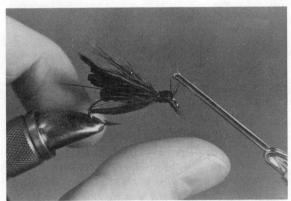

9. Bring the thread underneath the deer hair head; make several wraps and whip finish. Lacquer the small fibers protruding from the eye, these will form antennae.

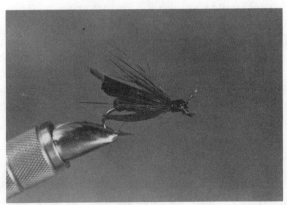

10. The Finished Fly.

THE CARPENTER ANT

When I was a much younger lad, I recall looking through the various fly catalogs and fly tying books available at that time, and there always seemed to be several fly patterns which never seemed to work for me. One of these was the Black Ant. I remember tying hundreds of dozens of Black Ants for several of my wholesale accounts, but I had never tried them with success.

I suppose part of the problem was the poor floatability. Most of them were tied with thread or floss bodies and didn't seem to float properly. I didn't know much about fishing them either. I thought most of them were either fished as a nymph or used as a wet fly. In fact, I couldn't see why a trout would ever want to eat an ant, as I thought they stuck to ant hills.

One day I was thumbing through an Orvis catalog and saw a fly called the Fur Ant. Aha! I thought. This might be better, especially with a buoyant fur that could be dressed to float high and dry. I tried it and this time the fly floated. I knew about a small high mountain stream which was filled with small brook trout running from six to twelve inches. When dropped in a dutch oven filled with butter and seasoning, they were just about the best eating a man could ever have.

I drifted the fuzzy jewel over these brookies and, to my surprise, caught several. But then, I remembered that almost every fly that I used that day caught a few of these little brook trout, so it really didn't make the fly that special. Consequently, I filed it in compartment 13 in the farthest corner of my desk.

One evening while sitting by the fire on a cold winter day, I was thumbing through an interesting little fly tying book I had picked up in Australia. One section of the book detailed the tying of a fly called the "Carpenter Ant." The tyer had used dark deer hair to form an ant body and black hackle and deer hair to form legs. It sounded interesting and I thought this might be something really worth fooling around with.

The following spring I set out to fish a favorite lake of mine which has a good population of mackinaw trout (lake trout). During the early part of June one could catch cruising mackinaws coming up from the deep waters where they had been holding up all winter long. I had good luck casting feathered streamers to the lake trout running in the two to three pound class, for these macks were cruising the surface in search of small minnows. It was fun watching the silvery shadows as they followed and took the slowly stripped streamers.

Suddenly I felt a twinge of pain in the back of my neck. I reached up expecting to swat a deer fly, but instead felt a wiggle under my finger and looked down to find a big black flying ant that had just stung me.

I threw the ant in the water and proceeded with my fishing. About ten seconds later, out of the corner of my eye, I saw a large swirl in the direction where I had thrown the ant. I quickly looked over to see a shadow descending deep into the water disappearing under some logs. Very interesting! I had seen this happen before, when somebody had thrown out either a stonefly or a grasshopper which had seemed to catch the attention of a trout who was lying nearby. Suddenly in the distance I saw several rises, and then a large swirl. Then closer to the bank there were several more rises — all within a period of a couple of minutes. I looked down on my arm and there was another one of those pesky black ants. I brushed him off and started to look in the air. It was filled with flying ants! They were dropping to the water and the fish were taking them with wild abandon. I knew there was a fairly good population of cutthroat trout there, so I quickly tied on one of my new deer hair ants, within a short period of time I pulled in several nice two-pound cutthroats. The action continued for the rest of the afternoon.

I told several people about my experience and found that several other anglers had also run into the flying ant hatch during the late summer along several western rivers. At that time, it was common to see flying **red** ants fill the air.

Through my years of selling flies to folks all over the world, I have had the chance to talk to people who have told me that often find their trout gorged with ants — especially the trout of smaller streams. With careful thought, I considered that some of the darker dry flys such as Wulffs and humpies may have been mistaken by trout for ants that either fly and drop to the surface, or are brushed off the banks. But there must be something better. After a great deal of research I have become convinced that this pattern is one of the best—East or West.

It can be tied with several different colors of dyed deer hair, allowing you to imitate a number of the common ants in your area.

Terrestrials such as beetles, hoppers, and especially the ants have really become more widely used by fishermen in recent years, as well they should be. Don't be caught without a selection of these in your vest.

MATERIALS:	The Carpenter Ant
THREAD:	Black monocord
HOOK:	Mustad 3906, 7957B, 7948A, 94840
SIZES:	12-16
BODY:	Black deer hair
LEGS:	Black deer hair

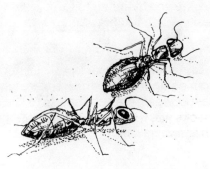

1. Cut out a small bunch of deer hair and remove the under fur and small hairs. The batch of hair should be approximately the size of a pencil for a large fly and half the size for a small fly.

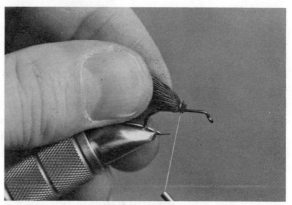

2. With the butts trimmed, tie in the hair on top of the hook half-way down the shank. Be sure to tie in firmly.

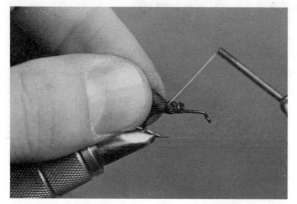

3. Advance the tying thread back towards the bend of the hook not making your wraps too close together, as shown above in the picture.

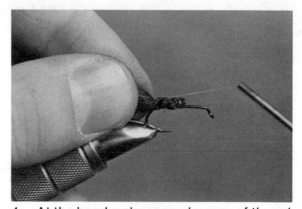

4. At the bend make several wraps of thread to secure the deer hair to the bend of the hook, then advance the thread forward making three or four wraps towards the middle of the shank.

5. Shows the deer hair tied in and the thread advanced forward.

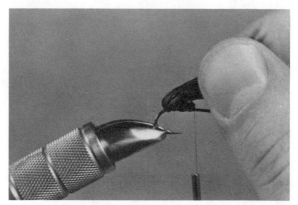

6. Pull the deer hair over with thumb and forefinger of right hand.

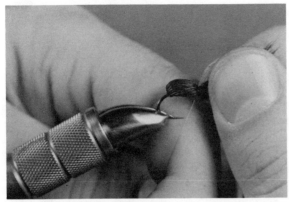

7. With several wraps of thread tie the deer hair down.

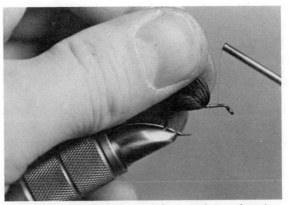

8. Advance the thread forward to about a quarter of the length of the shank behind the eye.

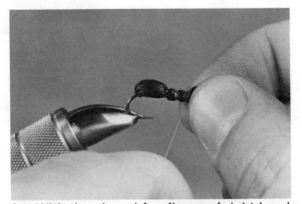

9. With thumb and forefinger of right hand pull the deer hair forward make several tight wraps at this point, pull the deer hair back again and advance thread toward the eye of the hook. With thumb and forefinger of right hand repeat the same process as before making a second bump.

10. Shows the completed body before pulling back the legs.

11. Select several fibers of deer hair off of each side bunch of deer hair standing up.

12. Hold back these fibers of deer hair and clip the excess.

13. Cover the deer hair butts with thread and advance the thread slightly backwards to hold the legs back, as shown in the above picture. Whip finish and lacquer.

14. Shows the Carpenter Ant from the top. Notice that the gaster of the ant is considerably thinner than the rear of the ant.

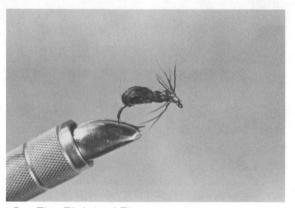

15. The Finished Fly

THE BEETLE

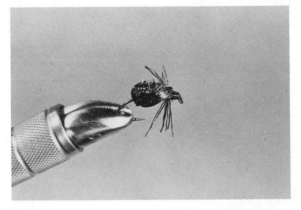

These insects seem to be overlooked in much of our angling literature. Fishermen who examine the contents of a trout's stomach (either through dissection or using a stomach pump on a live trout) will usually find a beetle. Yet, how many patterns do you know that effectively imitate the beetle? Though fly fishers have largely neglected the beetle, it is a very important part of the diet of most trout.

Until the use of deer hair became more widespread in the art of fly tying, it was very difficult to get an effective beetle imitation to float properly. This particular pattern had its origins in the East on the great limestone meadow streams which had a plentiful supply of Japanese beetles.

On many of the brush-lined western waters you will notice the presence of beetles in the streamside growth. These crawly critters are brushed or blown into the water and are soon snapped up by the trout. In many areas they have become a staple trout fare at certain times of the year. Some streams, (especially those in the Gallatin River valley in Montana), have a pine bark beetle which will fall into the river in the mid-summer months. This can provide some explosive fishing.

The common patterns originally developed to imitate the beetle were crafted with lacquered feathers tied horizontally on the top of the hook. Even though the patterns proved to be somewhat of a success, they still did not produce a lifelike appearance or drift when cast upon the water. The lightweight material did not produce the noticeable splat so characteristic of beetles when they hit the water. The use of twisted deer hair solved that problem in that they have proved to be successful and representative as well.

There are several different ways of creating the back of the beetle. You can experiment with paint or latex to create different effects. The particular pattern that we are tying for you is another creation from the mid-western vise of Jim Chestney. Our thanks to Jim for another interesting terrestrial.

MATERIALS: The Beetle

THREAD: Black monocord

HOOK: Mustad 94840, 7948A, 7957B

SIZES: 12-16

BODY: Black deer hair

WING: Black goose quill, coat with bronze powder or paint

LEGS: Black deer hair

1. Cut out two black goose quill sections, approximately ¼" wide. With the thread in the middle of the hook tie in one section, with the tip pointing inward.

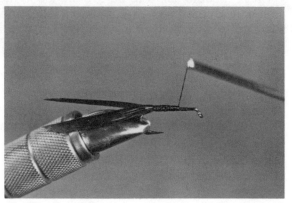

2. Tie in the other section of goose quill with tip pointing inward; notice the above picture. Advance the thread to approximately ⅓ back from the eye.

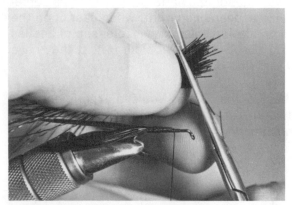

3. Cut out a small bunch of black dyed deer hair, remove all the underfur and small hairs. Trim ends even.

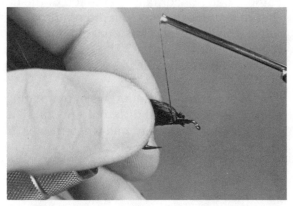

4. Tightly tie in the deer hair bunch and begin to advance the thread backwards.

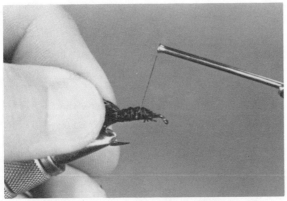

5. Make several tight wraps backwards to the bend of the hook. At that point make several more tight wraps, binding down the deer hair bunch to the hook bend. Advance the thread forward to just behind the eye.

6. Separate the deer hair bunch in half. With thumb and forefinger twist the bunch.

7. Pull the deer hair bunch over and tie off. Do not trim. Twist the second bunch between thumb and forefinger.

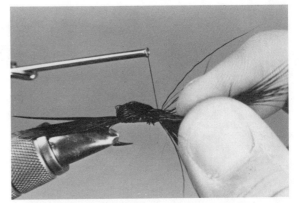

8. Pull the bunch over and tie off.

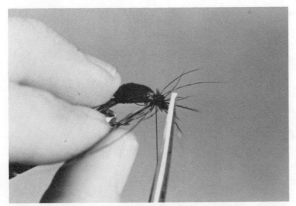

9. Cut off surplus deer hair except for a few strands which should be pulled back, bound out and back to form the legs. Touch a drop of lacquer to the deer hair hump.

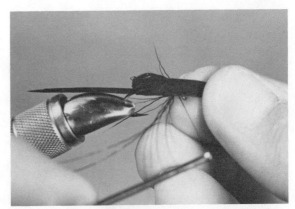

10. Pull a goose quill section forward over the deer hair base and tie off.

11. Pull the other section forward over the deer hair base criss-crossing slightly and tie off, trim the excess quill.

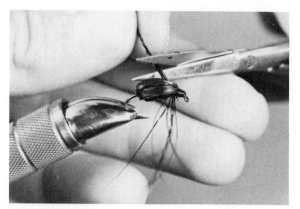

12. Trim legs to about one hook gap in length.

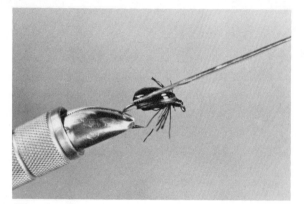

13. Apply a large drop of lacquer to the goose quill back.

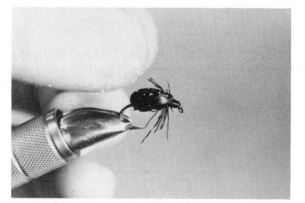

14. While the lacquer is still wet, sprinkle on a little bronze powder. This should be allowed to dry and then coated with another coat of vinyl cement.

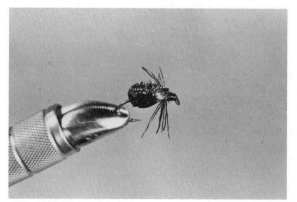

15. The Finished Fly.

THE MOUSE

This is another one of Jack Gartside's patterns that was developed in the West Yellowstone, Montana area, where he spends much of his time in the summer fishing and testing out new flies. Jack Gartside is a practical fly tyer whose approach to fly tying is making wise use of the common materials that many fly tyers overlook.

On this particular occasion Jack was sitting at a picnic table on the Madison River, Montana, tying some of his fabled Pheasant Hoppers (shown on 238). In the tying process he plucked quite a few feathers from the pheasant skin and discovered a long dun gray down plume attached to the base of each. Since boredom from tying the hoppers had set in, he tied one of these plumes to the base of the hook and wound it on. It was surprisingly easy to work with and after winding several of the plumes on, the entire hook shank was covered. Without much effort he had tied what looked and felt like a gray mouse.

Whether the trout actually take this pattern as a mouse is of no consequence. It has a fat buggy appearance that, if weighted, could be used to imitate a dragon fly nymph. The next time you're tying some of Jack's Pheasant Hoppers or his Pheasant Muddlers don't forget to save the plumes.

MATERIALS: Mouse

THREAD: Black monocord

HOOK: Mustad 9671

SIZES: 6-12

BODY: Pheasant filo plumes

COLLAR: Pheasant or partridge

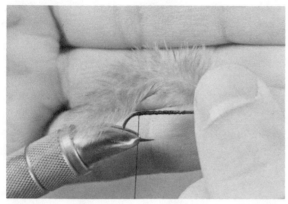

1. Select an under plume from a pheasant skin to the dimensions that are pictured above. Wrap your thread to the rear of your hook and prepare to start from there.

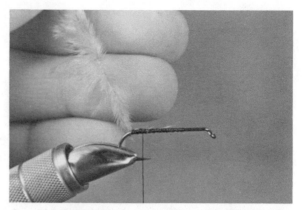

2. Tie the smaller end of the plume in at the far end of the shank at the bend of the hook.

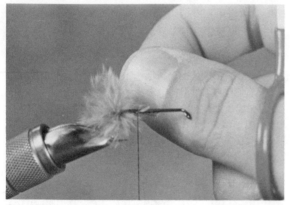

3. Wrap plume gently forward as if you were tying hackle. Tie off the first plume at the base and advance thread forward.

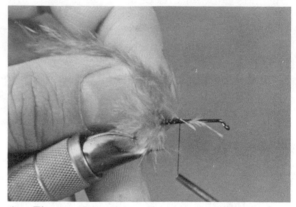

4. Tie another plume in at the base.

5. Pull back on the first fluff that was first created by wrapping the first plume and wrap the second one right next to it advancing forward towards the eye. Continue this process until the hook is completely covered.

6. Tie on a piece of partridge hackle at the front of the hook.

7. Wrap the partridge hackle forward creating a soft hackle front of the furry mouse.

8. With the point of your scissors trim off any excess plumes that might be longer than the rest of the body.

9. This is what the completed mouse should look like.

MINNOWS, SCULPINS, SMALL FISH, OTHER CREATURES AND THEIR IMITATIONS

I am one fly fisherman who enjoys all phases of the sport — nymphs and dry flies, the big stuff and the minute — but, I am particularly fond of streamer fishing. However, it wasn't always that way. It took awhile for me to develop into a streamer fisherman. Not being from streamer country, it was difficult for me to learn about streamers and their use. It took a little while for me to recognize that sculpins and small fish make up a large portion of the trout's diet.

Some of the most commonly imitated baitfish are the sculpins, or bullheads, as they are locally called. These bottom-hugging, strange-looking creatures scoot along the bottom, darting through the mud and rocks in search of food. Most western streams from spring creeks to large rivers have significant populations of these sculpins.

For many years, the bullhead was one of the most popular live baits for fishing the West. Many large trout have met their doom because they fell to a well-presented sculpin. Sculpins are still popular in many areas where the use of live bait has not been restricted, and their use is ranked as one of the most effective ways of catching large trout. We, as fly fishermen, have developed some realistic sculpin imitations which you will find in the chapter to follow.

Another one of the small fish that fly tyers imitate is the minnow or shiner as represented by our traditional streamers such as: the Mickey Finn, Black-Nose Dace, Royal Coachman Streamer and others. Today, they are joined by some new and sometimes more effective streamers such as the Muddler Minnow, Marabou Muddler, and the revival of an old New Zealand favorite, the Matuka.

For a while there was a popular fly series called the Little Trout series. This series of streamers imitated the little rainbow, brook and brown trout by using different colors of bucktail. Although the use of these patterns is somewhat limited today, they are still effective in many different areas of the country during low water conditions when the fish are wary. In the following chapter, we will also offer you many new streamer patterns to help put some zest into your streamer fishing.

To help you understand streamer fishing, let me first clear up a couple of fallacies. A number of fishermen believe that streamer fishing is always best accomplished by using a fast-sinking line to take your fly straight to the bottom and then stripped back in a short, jerky retrieve. This couldn't be further from the truth. Streamer fishing involves a large variety of methods, as you will see in some of the following stories.

Another popular misconception is that streamer fishing is only for lakes. At times, these patterns can be your ticket to fast action in any kind of water. Depending upon the stream and conditions, the streamer is an excellent choice whether one goes for a large trout or a large number of fish. My favorite place for a streamer is a bushy, pocket-laden stream with a lot of boulders and hiding spots for lunkers.

I clearly recall the bright October morning in 1967 when I became a streamer addict. I was fishing with my good friend and fellow fly flinger, Bob Senior. Bob had been urging me to fish the Wind River from the time he read a tantalizing article on fishing on that underrated stream. The only problem with the Wind is that it is seldom clear. Its tributaries start as snowmelt from the rugged peaks of the majestic Wind River Mountains near the little town of Dubois, Wyoming. The river changes from a high mountain stream to a fast water river as it plunges through the red, yellow and gold colored sand hill canyons of Fremont County. Bordered by lush green cottonwoods and brightly colored bushes, the Wind twists its way through many small ranches and wooded groves as it swiftly flows toward the Wind River Indian Reservation. This is where Bob had talked of fishing. We had heard reports of large rainbows, browns and occasional cutthroats that fill the waters.

Because of the long runoff season and the summer showers which quickly discolor the water, this stream carries a murky flow during much of June, July and even part of August. But, my, how things changed when autumn rolled around! The stream ran low and clear, and the weather had a sunnier disposition.

Bob and I drove on through Dubois and arrived at the Wind River Indian Reservation, where we purchased the special permit required by the tribal council for non-Indian fishing on the reservation, and then headed towards this intriguing river. Several people in town had told us that the fishing had been quite good that year and the river had been running clear for the previous two weeks. However, they had very little information about our particular fishing location because few people had fished there. Since we didn't know the private land situation, we brought along a boat so that we could float fish the water.

Soon, we were at the river and found a spot from which we could launch the boat. After enticing a local with a five dollar bill, he agreed to move our car down to the end of our journey. At noon, we started out on what was to be one of the best fishing adventures I have ever had in my life.

I started off fishing a large Humpy. My friend, Bob, tied on a succulent Wooly Worm which has always been one of his favorite flies. From several years of guiding, I have found that when floating in a boat, it was better to cast a wet fly upstream somewhat behind the craft and then work it back towards you, letting the pull of the drifting boat help swing the fly underneath the deep banks and rocks. Bob had been fishing with me for several years and knew my method of fishing. He skillfully cast his Wooly Worm back upstream, allowing the current to bring his trout-fooling morsel underneath the deep bank, luring out the big fish which held in that cover. After a couple or three hits, we had boated several nice cutthroats in the two-pound class. I continued to watch Bob expertly work his weighted wooly and soon thought of a brilliant idea. Why not work a big streamer in this same way, just below the surface?

We pushed the boat up on a gravel bar and proceeded to work a long glassy run. The water was so clear you could see the outline of almost every pebble on the bottom. In the middle of the run lay a large, golden boulder that stood out like a gem. I pulled out a large, White Marabou Muddler and decided this might be gaudy enough to attract one of the monsters I had heard about from my father and others who knew the Wind better than I. Carefully tying on the fly, I looked up to watch Bob drift his Wooly Worm through the lower end of the run. He connected with a glistening three-pound rainbow. As it shot through the water, tail overhead, Bob kept yelling, "These rainbows have to be wild the way they are fighting. These aren't hatchery trout!"

The Marabou Muddler flew like a wounded duck as I slopped it in the water, and landed with the delicacy of a bull moose in a quiet pond. Every trout in northwest Wyoming must have heard the splash. I started pumping the fly across in slow jerks as though I was fishing the fly on the bottom using my trusty old sinking line. It just didn't look quite right. I picked it up and started to experiment, letting the current swim the streamer across as I pumped it up and down using a little bit faster strokes than I would use if I was using a heavy sinking line. As I worked down toward the golden boulder, I continued to experiment with the way I worked that fly. I usually cast it slightly upstream since there was a heavy current down the middle of the pool with slow swirling water on both sides. As the fly sank in the swirling water and then darted back out as the current swung the line around, I kept thinking in my mind, something ought to like that.

One cast plopped in behind an exposed rock, and as my streamer swung past it, it was followed by a dark fishy shadow. It followed the streamer across the current into the rough water, but there was no strike. I started slowly stripping it back, looking the water over to see if the fish had returned to its original location. Just as I was ready to pick up the fly, the fish struck and I very daintily jerked it completely out of its mouth — quite by accident of course. I was startled and surprised that the fish had followed the fly all the way across the river, which at some point stretched 75 feet wide. The fly must have looked enticing, but why he didn't strike it on the swing. I wasn't quite sure.

On the next cast, I tried to duplicate that drift and sure enough, another trout began to pursue the fly. I tried to entice him as I jiggled my Marabou Muddler just like a minnow which knew it was in a heap of trouble. All of a sudden, whack! He took a swing at it. The heavy force of the current made me miss him, but the fish came back, and kept hitting it. Finally, on the third strike, I connected, and I pulled in a nice pound and a half rainbow. I was surprised. This rainbow did not come out of the water and give me the typical rainbow aerobatics. He decided to keep towards the bottom of the run and continue to bulldog his way around like a brown trout would. After getting him in, I quickly released him and got back to fishing.

By now, I had worked my way down towards the golden boulder I mentioned earlier. A stiff breeze had risen, making casting very difficult, and I was having a tough time getting the streamer out as far as I wanted. During a couple of swings, the fly had gone over the top of the boulder. The golden color of the boulder illuminated the fly from below. But while it looked very pretty, alas, nothing showed any interest in it. I needed to get over to the other side of the boulder and let it pull across the top in order to give it that enticing swing.

Finally, after five or six casts, I was able to put it exactly where I wanted it. I quickly picked up the slack and prepared to pump the fly. As the large Marabou drifted over the top of the boulder, I gave it a couple of quick jerks. Suddenly, there it was — one of the most beautiful sights I have ever witnessed in my fishing career. A huge rainbow materialized out of the depths and he was clearly outlined against the golden background of the boulder. It was almost like the experience of watching a slow-motion movie as this big fish deliberately opened his huge mouth and my fly disappeared inside. I felt my heart pounding and a surge of excitement pulsed through every nerve of my body. I had to set the hook and somehow my arm shot into the air tightening the line. I screamed at the top of my lungs, "Bob! Bring the net, bring the net!" I started downstream as the fish slowly moved towards the center of the stream. I don't think he quite understood what had happened to him. I don't think that he knew that he had me hooked to the end of his line.

For the next hour, many different emotions went through me — excitement, joy, fear, worry — all the range of human emotions over a seemingly silly situation. It was just a fish, yet somehow it was my life, my life of fishing.

Bob quickly analyzed the situation and gave some fatherly advice. "Don't pull him too tight, let him go when he wants to go." He told me all of the things I was supposed to tell him as a guide. Bob reassured me when I began to get a little ragged around the edges of my emotions. But all his efforts to calm me were lost when he observed, "I've seen fish and caught fish over twelve pounds in New Zealand. I know a big fish when I see one. That fish has to be at least fifteen pounds!"

I continued to work the big trout closer to the bank, but he managed to stay just out of reach of the net. There was a steep drop-off, so I couldn't move toward the bank without going in over my head. Downstream, there were logs blocking the water. Upstream, was a fast raging torrent. The battle had to be fought right here and nowhere else.

I was exhausted. The rod trembled in my hand, and I begged Bob to take the rod and let me rest. "No, it's your fish, it might be a record. I can't touch it" he yelled back. Slowly, an inch at a time, I finessed the fish closer to the bank. The monster's tail slowly moved. It had been over an hour since hook-up and the fish had to be getting tired. Finally, it started to tilt slightly on his side and now one fin was out of the water. Bob carefully and slowly edged the net under the fish. Suddenly, as if someone had shot new life into the lunker, he started to move. He pointed his head upstream and made one final run, and you guessed it — the line just went slack and I felt that familiar agonizing feeling of disappointment. I was crushed; the fish was gone. The fly floated to the surface. It had just pulled out. Bob tried to console me, but nothing would work.

I was dejected, sad, angry — all the human emotions that are partners with failure. It took a while for me to thoroughly assess what had really happened.

Over many years I've had numerous occasions to reflect on that situation, and it finally dawned on me that although I failed to land the biggest trout I had ever hooked, the experience wasn't a loss by any means. I had learned something that day. I learned a lot about fishing streamers with a floating line, and that opened a whole new avenue of fishing.

I've gone back to that pool many times, but I've never again had a strike in that run. However, it holds a special memory in an important time of my life. There was another time, years later, when I would win, when I would catch the big fish, but it was that experience on the Wind which provided the schooling to make it possible.

Since then, I have had chances to compare notes with other guides who often fish streamers with a floating line. This offers the chance to manipulate a streamer in many different ways. Whether it be the Beaverhead, the Yellowstone, the Madison or other rivers, casting a streamer up against a bushy bank and bringing it out in an enticing way rivals dry fly fishing in my book. You see the streamer, you see the fish, and you see the hit. And that is what I call your basic fun, my friend.

There is a time and a place for streamers on a sinking line as you rake your big patterns across the bottom of the stream, but for those of you who haven't tried it, a shallow swimming Muddler or Marabou on a floating line offers a world of excitement hard to duplicate with any other method of fly fishing.

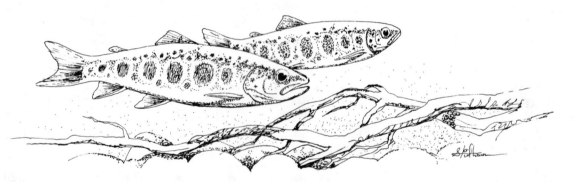

THE KIWI MUDDLER

The Muddler Minnow throughout the years has become probably the most versatile fly of the many patterns one may choose. I was searching for a good variation of this fly, that would be different from the sculpins, Spuddlers, and various types of Marabou Muddlers. Some patterns had not met the criteria I was looking for: simplicity in design, easy to tie, yet extremely effective.

In 1968, a New Zealand friend gave me a streamer from New Zealand. The Kiwis call it the Rabbit, which is actually a strip of rabbit hair tied on the top of the streamer, Matuka style. The hide was coarse, heavy and had not been tanned. I gave the Rabbit to a fishing friend of mine, who tried it in several of the deep clear holes of the Snake River. He liked the pulsating action of the Rabbit as it was pumped through the water. It seemed to entice several of the trout in the hole and my friend had a fairly decent day of catching twelve to fourteen inch cutthroats out of an extremely productive hole. I got to thinking that maybe this application of rabbit hair could be modified and put into a more effective fly. I was not at first happy with the original New Zealand streamer, as I felt the hair lacked action. The hide that the hair was attached to stayed stiff in the water and performed like a Daredevil spinning lure. After carefully examining the fly, I realized that the hair was not tanned and was very stiff, besides being tied to the top of the fly, Matuka style. I felt that maybe something much more fluid might be more appropriate. I liked, however, the pulsating action of the guard hairs and the underfur of the rabbit skin. I experimented around, trimming off various sections of tan rabbit skins and wrapping them to hooks and observing their movement through the water.

The tanned multi-colored rabbit fur soaked up water like a chamois skin, and had an amazing fluid, lifelike movement through the water. The rabbit hair matched the swimming action of either a small fish or minnow.

The original New Zealand Rabbit streamer left a little bit to be desired in design, as it failed to match our sculpin or our small rough fish that frequent our wild, western rivers. Incorporating the old proven Muddler Minnow design, I crafted a pattern which had some definite possibilities.

The important aspect was the proper trimming of the hair, wide in the proper places, yet narrower towards the tail of the fly, to imitate the outline of the small minnows or sculpins.

After working with various designs, we were very anxious to try the fly in natural stream conditions. We worked on different types of heads, conventional or unusual underbodies and changed lengths of the rabbit fur. The wing needed a standardized length that would not roll under the hook, as often happens with streamer flies that have too long a wing. One of the most important things we discovered was, that if the rabbit fur was trimmed too wide, the soaking up of the skin caused the wing to shear off. Using a penetrating cement to cover the whole wing, in hopes of making it more durable, we found that it inhibited the action of the fly, even though it made the wing indestructable. The most essential aspect was to keep the natural absorbing qualities of the rabbit skin, and yet keep it from tearing an eighth of an inch from where the skin was tied to the head. At this point we applied a small portion of cement, just enough to add durability to the skin and keep the wing from pulling apart, yet still keeping its natural action. When completed, the fly in the water had an almost unbelievable action that resembled a swimming minnow. Even when the fly was not jerked or retrieved through the water, the natural current of the stream would move the wing, and resemble a small fish that was holding its position in the water. The gentle movement of the fly's tail was incredibly life-like. We found one of the biggest problems with the Muddler and other streamers was that they were not being retrieved properly through the current and floated dead through a productive hole. However, a streamer such as the Marabou would flow and move through the water, but needed retrieving to simulate body motion. The New Zealand Muddler did this and more! Besides showing the fluid movement of the wing, the fur pulsated like the Marabou, but simulated body motion without being moved through the water. A great alternate to the ever increasing problem of finding good brown turkey wings, it would be a simple pattern to wrap.

In the past summers we had a chance to experiment on several of the western rivers with this pattern. Many situations did not require the fly to go deep, so some flies were weighted, others were left natural. We found that the absorbing quality of the wing added a lot of weight to the fly, and it sank without the use of lead. In fast flowing rivers, such as the Provo River in Utah, we have talked to several anglers who have tried the fly extremely weighted, and have actually swum it down through the rocks in a boulder strewn river. Results have been nothing short of spectacular. The pattern also seems to be successful on larger brown trout, especially in areas where streamer fishing is prevalent.

One of the important things about tying this fly is that a great variety of rabbit skins are available. The fly can be tied in a multitude of colors, different shades of blue gray to dark brown to white. Since the rabbit population has so many different colors, almost any minnow or sculpin color can be achieved.

One of the best sources of finding good rabbit skins is to look in some of the many trinket and tourist gift stores in the Rocky Mountain area, as they are sold at a very reasonable price as momentos of the West. One can go through many stacks of rabbit skins in places like Yellowstone Park and usually find the color he is searching out.

I have found that many different body materials can be used, and that one's imagination or desire to imitate different bodies can be achieved by the uses of dubbed fur, tinsels, floss or whatever for the desired effect.

One of the first times that we actually had a direct comparison was on a particular afternoon while floating Beaverhead River in southwestern Montana. It was a clear bright day in mid-September, the kind of day that made you wish that fall would never end. The trees had turned in the beautiful shades of golds, reds, browns and yellows. We were floating that day with our fellow friend and tyer, Al Troth. We tried early that morning a selection of Girdle Bugs and nymphs with poor results. Al found our pattern intriguing the night before and had offered some suggestions on how to improve it. By mid morning we had tried several major Muddler patterns and still raised very little from the bushes. Al contributed the slow fishing to the bright sunlight and extremely low water. This was the bleak fall of '77 when the drought had taken a devastating effect on the fishing in the Rocky Mountain area. Our trusty friend mentioned that the river level was the lowest that he had ever seen. We had cut our usually heavy thick leaders down to fairly light, wispy sizes, in hopes that possibly our leader size was too large.

We were floating into some enticing looking overhanging bushes and deep undercut banks, when Al suggested to me "Why don't you throw out that God awful looking Muddler Rabbit, squirrely looking thing, and see what happens." I only had two in my box, but I reached in and brought out the furry looking monster. We were using light tippets, 5X to be exact, and at that size one must be very careful not to land too many casts in the fly-grabbing bushes. On the very first cast the fly hit under an overhanging branch and out shot a darting beaverhead brown, crashing down on my Kiwi Muddler. A couple of aerobatic jumps and a very powerful upstream run and I boated a nice hefty three pound brown. This, of course, was enough to get our attention. We drifted around several other bends and the results became obvious. The fish were crazy after the furry Muddler, as on almost every cast we would get a follow or a strike. However, after several bends of the river, and some not so expert casting on my part, my trusty variation Muddler and I parted company, and so did the fishing. As soon as we lost the two lucky Kiwi Muddlers the fishing again died back down. Of course, one can contribute this to a fluke of luck, which fishing sometimes is, but nobody can convince me any differently.

During the following summer more comparisons proved that the Kiwi Muddler was definitely as good a pattern as a Muddler, and at times produced better than the Muddler. The only way to truly judge this is over a long period of time. We feel it has its advantages because of its design, and the unique character of its motion in the water. The best way of proving it to yourself is tying some up and giving them a try. You too may become "rabid" about our Kiwi Muddler as I have these past few summers.

MATERIALS:	Kiwi Muddler
THREAD:	Tan monocord or tan nymo
HOOK:	Mustad 79580, 9672
SIZES:	4-8
TAIL:	Dark grey deer or elk hair or squirrel tail
RIBBING:	Gold mylar tinsel or gold embossed tinsel
UNDERBODY:	Lead wire (optional)
BODY:	Tan or cream dubbing
WING:	Rabbit fur on hide trimmed to triangular shape
HEAD AND COLLAR:	Light grey deer hair

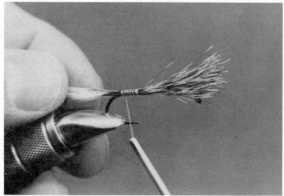

1. Cut out a small bunch of squirrel tail and remove the underfur. With the thread at the bend of the hook, tie in the squirrel tail and advance the thread over it to approximately one quarter of the way back from the eye of the hook. Trim the squirrel tail here.

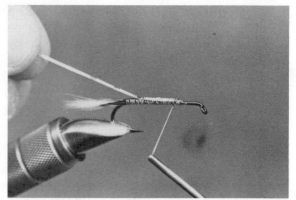

2. At the point where the squirrel tail was cut, tie in a piece of gold embossed tinsel and wrap the thread backwards over it.

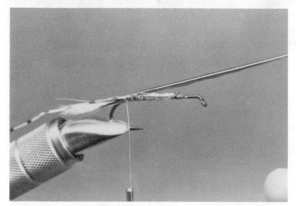

3. Place a drop of lacquer over the top of the tinsel, to secure it in place.

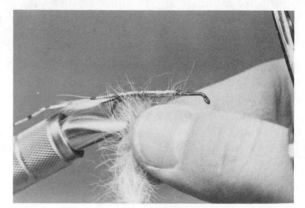

4. Apply some tan dubbing to the thread.

5. Begin dubbing a tapered body.

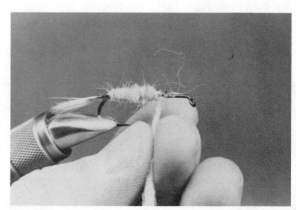

6. Continue dubbing forward to one third of the way behind the eye.

7. Rib the dubbed body with even spacings, as shown above.

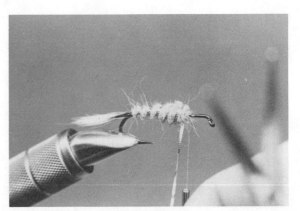

8. Shows the ribbed body.

9. Cut out a piece of rabbit fur, note the shape of the rabbit fur wing. The rabbit hide must be soft and pliable.

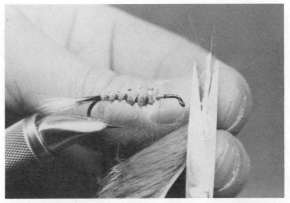

10. Trim the rabbit fur wing into an elongated diamond.

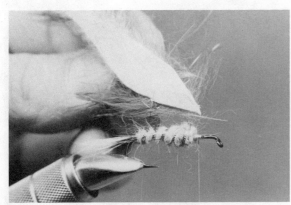

11. Note the shape of the wing.

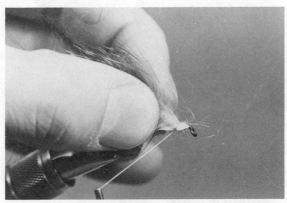

12. Tie in the rabbit fur wing approximately one quarter the length of the shank behind the eye.

13. Shows the length of the wing tied in.

14. Lacquer where the wing is tied in.

15. Cut out a bunch of natural deer hair. Remove the underfur and small fibers.

16. Holding the bunch of fur on the side facing you, make several loose wraps of thread around it.

17. On the third wrap of thread, hold tightly and flare the hair.

18. Shows the flared hair. Notice that the hair points have not gone past the point of the hook.

19. Prepare another deer hair bunch as before.

20. Hold the bunch of deer hair on the opposite side of the hook and make several loose wraps with the thread.

21. On the third wrap, pull tightly flaring out the deer hair.

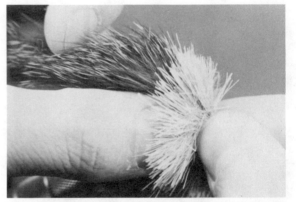

22. Advance the tying thread forward through the hair, pulling tightly with each wrap.

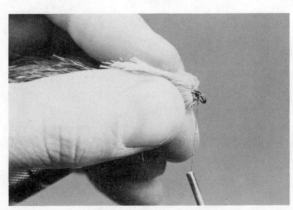

23. Pull the deer hair back and make several wraps of thread right in front of it. Whip finish and remove the hook from the vise.

24. Clip the bottom of the deer hair flat, beneath the eye of the hook.

25. Clip the sides of the deer hair at an angle as shown above.

26. Clip the top of the deer hair flat as shown above.

27. Shows the completed fly. Note the shape of the head and the length of the wing.

28. Shows the fly from the front.

29. The Finished Fly

278

THE SPRUCE MUDDLER

The idea for a Spruce Muddler first came to me while fishing the Yellowstone River. It was a typical cold, dark, gray afternoon in late autumn. This was an ideal day for fishing the Yellowstone brown trout. My friend, John Bailey, was working the oars and I was about to have my first real experience in fishing the immense, clear Yellowstone.

It was a slow day, but we occasionally picked up a cutthroat on a Joe's Hopper. John said fishing would be better if we went below the surface with larger flies. He pulled out one which he feels to be as effective a streamer as there is on the Yellowstone River — the Spruce Fly. I was familiar with the Spruce, but had not used it very often. Since we weren't taking many fish on anything else, we went with the Spruce. The action of this streamer intrigued me, and we started to catch fish!

Several years later, we spent a blistering hot August day on the Green River. When nothing seemed to move the trout, I remembered that cold day on the Yellowstone and fished a Spruce fly from my streamer box. By the time we'd stopped for lunch I had caught and released nine good sized "brownies".

That afternoon the idea came to mind that maybe a dressed up version of the Spruce might be even more effective. A collar tied of dark moose hair to create a turbulence in the water, similar to that of a swimming or dying sculpin seemed to be a good idea. The coloration and materials of the traditional Spruce Fly body married to the sculpin-like head of the Muddler seemed to make sense to me, too. But the question was, would it take fish? In this day and age of so many variations of flies that never seem to work better than the original, a unique challenge was presented.

We have used it for nearly 2 years and found it more effective than the original Spruce Fly, in certain situations. With the Muddler head, (which has always been a winner), it seemed to have consistently taken large trout in areas where we felt that the regular Muddler and Spruce were not as effective. Only time will tell how great this pattern will be. We have also tied it Matuka style with great results.

Try the Spruce Muddler in your area and let us know how it produces. We want to find out whether the Spruce Muddler marriage will work out or end up in just another divorce.

MATERIALS:	Spruce Muddler
THREAD:	Black monocord and Black "A" Monocord
HOOK:	Mustad 9672, 79580
SIZES:	4-10
TAIL:	Peacock sword fibers
RIBBING:	Embossed gold tinsel
UNDERBODY:	Lead wire if desired
BODY:	Red floss and several peacock herls
WING:	4 badger hackles
UNDERWING:	Gray squirrel tail
COLLAR:	Dark moose hair
HEAD:	Natural deer hair

1. With the thread in the middle of the hook tie in a small bunch of fibers from peacock sword feather.

2. In the same place tie in a piece of gold embossed tinsel and four-strand red floss.

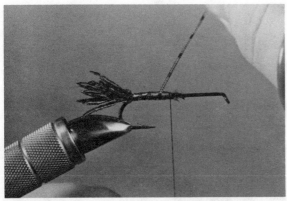

3. Wrap the red floss forward forming a smooth body to halfway down the shank. Rib in even spacings with the gold embossed tinsel.

4. In front of the body, tie in a piece of gold wire.

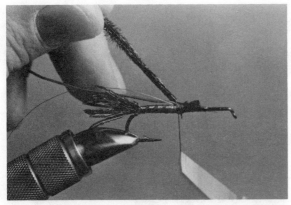

5. Tie in a piece of heavy lead and several strands of peacock herl.

6. Wrap the lead forward to ¼ of the way behind the eye; touch a drop of lacquer to it.

7. Wrap the peacock herls forward, tie off and trim.

8. Wind the gold wire through the peacock herl, tie off and trim.

9. Cut out a small bunch of gray squirrel tail. Measure for length as shown above.

10. Tie in the gray squirrel tail. Spread the fibers part of the way around the hook.

11. Select four large badger saddle hackles. Meld each pair together, light side to dark side.

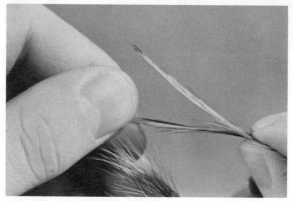

12. Place the melded wings together with dark sides facing each other as shown in the above picture.

13. With the wings placed together hold on top of the hook and measure for length.

14. Tie in the wing. The wings should look as shown in the above picture.

15. Cut out a small bunch of dark moose hair. Remove the underfur and small hairs. Hold on the side nearest you and make one loose wrap. The next wrap should be tighter and the next tighter yet.

16. Repeat Step #15 with another bunch of hair on the opposite side of the hook.

17. Pull the moose hair back and make several wraps just in front of it.

18. Cut out a small bunch of white, very coarse deer hair. Remove all underfur and small fibers. Clip the tapered ends.

19. Place the bunch of deer hair on top of the hook.

20. Make one loose wrap around the deer hair and a second slightly tighter wrap. Let go of the deer hair on the third wrap and spin around the hook. Advance the thread forward through the deer hair pulling tightly with each wrap.

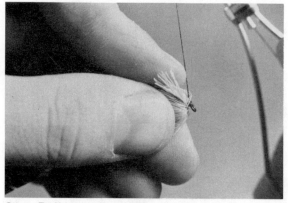 

21. Pull back the deer hair and make several wraps in front of it. Whip finish and lacquer the head.

22. Remove the hook from the vise. Trim the bottom of the deer hair flat.

23. Trim the sides of the deer hair at an angle as shown in the above picture.

24. Trim the top of the deer hair flat. Trim the moose hair collar longer than the deer hair.

25. The completed fly. Note that the moose hair collar is slightly larger than the deer hair head. Also note that there are moose hair fibers trimmed all around the hook.

THE GARTSIDE PHEASANT MUDDLER

The Pheasant Muddler was born out of desire by Jack Gartside for a minnow type streamer with a full, rather broad silhouette which could be viewed from the sides and beneath. A fly that would more effectively imitate some of the broader backed baitfish than some of the traditional patterns and perhaps do double duty as a hopper pattern, like the Muddler does. With this development of the Pheasant Hopper, it was natural for him to look towards the pheasant skin for feathers to tie this fly. He had thought of the popular eastern pattern, the Hornberg, and the way the wings are tied along the sides of the shank. Jack was looking for a feather that would have some of the markings of the brown trout or other bait fish common to the Yellowstone waters. The inventor had settled on the feathers of the lower back of the male ringneck pheasant. With gold braided mylar for the body, the wings were tied on Hornberg style and a deer hair head was shaped.

Jack's fly was definately a success. The guides and friends of the West Yellowstone area found out that it was a viable pattern that could take the place, in certain situations, of the Muddler Minnow. With the mottled turkey wing used in the Muddler being almost nonexistent, Muddler imitations are becoming more important.

According to Bud Lilly, it is one of the most effective patterns that he has in his West Yellowstone shop, and it will have a place in the annals of the fly fishing business.

Jack notes in a recent issue of **The Fly Tyer** magazine, a fine publication out of North Conway, New Hampshire, that the fly is a top notch pattern to use for browns that come up from the lake to spawn. Effective methods of fishing the Pheasant Muddler are stripping it fast under the surface or dead drifting the fly, either on the top or on the bottom.

MATERIALS: The Gartside Pheasant Muddler

THREAD: Yellow monocord

HOOK: Mustad 9672

SIZES: 6-10

TAIL: A short clump of rusty cock pheasant back or tail feathers

BODY:	Gold braided mylar (mylar tubing)
WING:	Matched pheasant back or rump feathers tied Hornberg style
UNDERWING:	Yellow-dyed deer body hair
HEAD:	Clipped deer hair with tips flared back as a collar

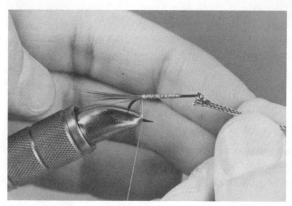

1. Tie on a short clump of rusty cock-pheasant back or tail fibers. Trim a piece of tubular mylar, either gold or silver, and slip over the eye.

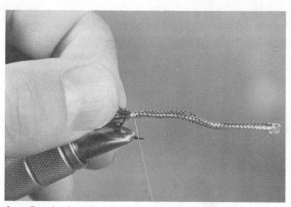

2. Push the tinsel to the rear of the hook. Tie down the tinsel tightly to the shank of the hook.

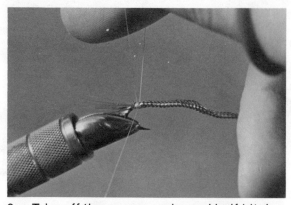

3. Trim off the excess mylar and half-hitch a knot at the end. Lacquer the tie off area.

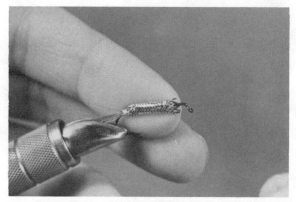

4. Push back on the mylar to make it bulge. Trim just behind the eye.

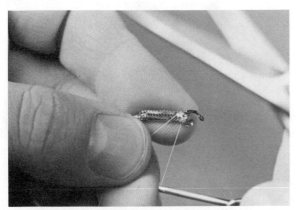

5.　Tie on the tying thread again.

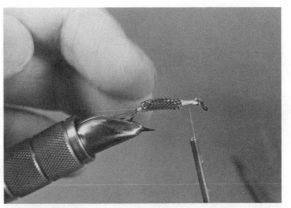

6.　Cover the mylar with thread forming a smooth base. Touch a drop of lacquer to secure the thread and mylar.

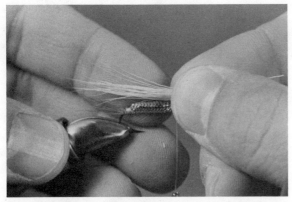

7.　Cut out a small bunch of yellow dyed deer hair. Measure for length.

8.　Tie hair on tightly, trim the butts and cover them with thread.

9.　Pull out a church-window feather from the rump of a cock pheasant.

10.　Measure for length and trim.

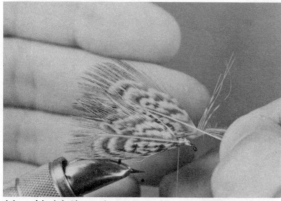

11. Hold the pheasant feather on the side of the hook and tie in tightly. Prepare another pheasant feather for the other side.

12. Tie in the feather on the other side of the fly. Cover the feather butts with thread and put a couple of half-hitches in.

13. Tie in some heavy black tying thread. Lacquer the wraps to secure in place.

14. Cut out a small bunch of light gray deer hair. Remove the small hairs and underfur.

15. Hold the deer hair bunch on the side nearest you. Make a loose wrap of thread around the bunch.

16. Pull tighter on the second wrap and tightest on the third wrap.

17. Cut out another bunch of deer hair and prepare as before.

18. Hold the hair bunch on the other side of the hook and repeat steps 15-16. Work the thread to the eye, whip finish a head and lacquer.

19. Trim a tight, Muddler style head. The bottom of the head should be trimmed flat.

20. This is the finished fly ready for a swim. Notice the shape of the head.

THE GREEN WEENY MATUKA

The Matuka is as exotic as its name indicates. The fly seems to have taken this country by storm, and there probably isn't a fly tyer left in the United States who hasn't heard this word. To the surprise of many tyers this is not a new pattern, but was developed many years ago on New Zealand's North Island.

Probably the first Matuka was tied by a Maori, an aboriginal New Zealander of Polynesian descent. The original fly was tied with two feathers from the brown bittern, a large member of the rail family that lives in swamps and marshes. The Matuka simulated the kokopu and the bully that were the two main forage fish in the vicinity of Rotorua Lake.

Today there are a large variety of Matukas. However, an olive green pattern seems to be the most effective of those used in the Wyoming area. Let me tell you how I first learned about the Matuka.

Several years ago I had an opportunity to take two noted fly fishermen, Doug Swisher and Dave Whitlock, on a float trip down the New Fork River in Northwestern Wyoming. That day we split up, Doug going with me and one of my fishing guides, and Dave going with the good Reverend Dan Abrams, in another raft. The sky was deep blue and cloudless, true to the phrase in the song, "And the sky was not cloudy all day." It was one of those Wyoming mornings that seemed to stay in one's mind forever, but not what you would consider to be a great day for brown trout.

As we looked around, we shook our heads and said, "It's too bright. It could be a rainbow day, but the browns are going to be too deep into the bank."

We suggested to Doug that he might try some dries, because at that particular time of the year the rainbows were on the surface looking for caddis and the large drakes which began to hatch around 10:00 A.M. Doug looked through his box, selected a #12 Royal Wulff, tied it on and started to work from the front of the boat, casting the fly downstream and letting it drift underneath the bank. I had tied on my trusty favorite, a white Marabou Muddler. We drifted by 4 or 5 good looking banks before the first fish was taken. The Reverend Dan had plucked a nice 16 inch brown from under one of the grassy banks with a slender #8 Muddler Minnow. The fish gave a nice aerial display, but he was quickly netted and released. Dan, of course, shouted the news to everyone that he had taken it on a streamer.

I turned to Doug and suggested he might want to try a streamer. With a shake of his head Doug indicated he was happy where he was. He seemed to be enjoying himself, so I continued to concentrate on casting my Marabou as close to the bank as possible, and working it back with short gentle strokes, stripping in enough line to keep the line tight, and allowing the movement of the boat to swing the fly along the undercut banks.

About 10 minutes and a couple of bends of the river later, I suddenly heard a large splash and I looked up to see a large rainbow dancing on top of the water. Doug was using a very light 7 ft. graphite rod, which was straining as the rainbow jumped a couple of more times and attempted to entangle his line with a deep submerged log. With great skill Doug maneuvered the fish away from the obstructions and guided it into the shallows. The beautiful deep dark green color of the rainbow reflected against the copper-colored rocks in a beautiful picture.

I thought to myself, "Golly, that's a heck of a fish to be taken on dry," (since we hadn't seen any hatches so far that morning). I readied my camera as Doug lifted the rainbow and held it high — a beautiful four pound native rainbow. Quickly he unhooked the fly and released the fish back into the water. Not wanting to be outfished on my home river I immediately started fishing harder, getting the fly underneath the bank and working it out time and time again. But the fish showed no interest in my white Marabou. On the next bend Doug hung another fish, another rainbow , slightly bigger than the first one. This time the fish jumped once and headed for the middle of the river. Excited and enjoying every minute of it, Doug looked back to see my reaction. Quite frankly I was dumbfounded; two fish on a Royal Wulff and my Marabou hadn't attracted any interest at all. I immediately looked through my box to pick out one of my nice, sparsely-tied Royal Wulffs, and proceeded to tie it on. Again I continued to concentrate on working from the back of the boat as Doug continued to cast from the front.

After a while, I began to wonder how he was fishing the fly, because I still had not received any action. From the back of the boat it was difficult to see what fly Doug was using. As I started to edge to the front for a closer look, another rainbow came careening out of the bank doing a tap dance across the top of the water. The fish was smaller than the first two, but definately a good 2 pounder. This time I was going to see what the story was.

Our guide said, "Be sure to get the fish in, because coming up on the next stretch of river is a particularly good run of overhanging willows." Doug hurried the fighting rainbow close to the net and with one fell swoop, the guide brought it in.

This time I immediately rushed up to the front before Doug could quickly put the fish back in the water, and there hanging from the fish's mouth was one of the strangest looking flies I had ever seen. It was olive green in color and looked like a streamer. I looked at Doug and said, "That's no Royal Wulff, you have been sand-bagging me, you 'No Hackle Humpy'."

He started to laugh, "Haven't you heard of the Green Weeny before?"

"Green Weeny!" I exclaimed. "What in the world is that?"

"Seriously," Doug said. "This is a Matuka, a pattern I call the Green Weeny, tied with olive dyed soft grizzly hackle. The secret of the fly is incorporating the body and wing together along the top of the hook giving the fly a very interesting minnow-like shape."

I had never seen anything like it. As I sat there looking at the fly in my hand, a very durable life-like fly that has definite possibilities, I thought to myself. We had all been taught a lesson; sometimes when one gets too familiar with a river he tends to fish only the flies that he knows work well and does not experiment. When the fishing isn't good, he sometimes passes it off to conditions, and doesn't think of changing his fly or his method of fishing to try and improve his success.

I learned a valuable lesson from Doug; not to be so stereotyped.

MATERIALS:	The Green Weeny Matuka
THREAD:	Black monocord
HOOK:	Mustad 79589, 9672
SIZES:	4-10
TAIL AND WING:	Olive dyed grizzly
BODY:	Green mohlon yarn or green dubbing
RIBBING:	Fine oval tinsel
COLLAR:	Olive dyed grizzly

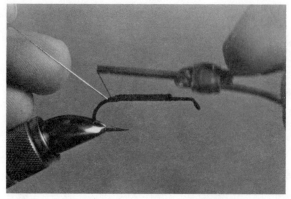

1. Tie in a 3-4" piece of oval gold tinsel securely ¼ back from the eye.

2. Tie in a 5 or 6 inch piece of mohlon yarn.

3. Secure this with thread wrapping back and forth over it.

4. Form a tapered body. Tie off and trim.

5. Select four to six dyed grizzly hackles. These hackles should have as much web as possible. Separate hackles into two bunches of two or three hackles each.

6. Place 2 or 3 hackles together, light side to dark side.

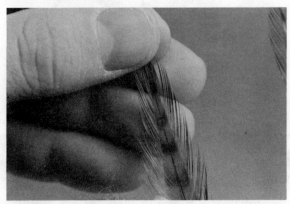

7. Even them up so that the tips match, forming a single wing. Repeat the same procedure with another hackle pair.

8. Place the two wings together with dull or concave sides together. Make sure that the tips match.

9. The completed wing. This will also form the tail of the streamer.

10. Measure the length of the wing and tail. Note the proportions above.

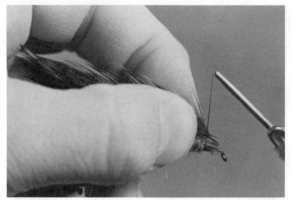

11. Remove the fibers from the butts of the hackles and tie in with several strong wraps of thread.

12. Trim the excess hackle butts. Pull the fibers off the bottom of the hackles on that portion which will be tied onto the body.

13. Hold the wing up as you make one complete wrap of tinsel around the body.

14. Make two wraps of tinsel at the end of the body separating the tail and tying it down firmly.

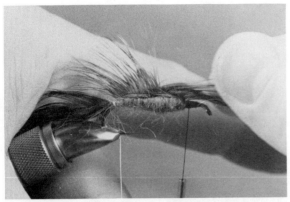

15. Begin wrapping the tinsel forward in even spacings. This is how you pull back the hackle fibers to wrap in between them.

16. Rib the body and wing with tinsel to the front, keeping a firm pressure on the tinsel. Tie off and trim.

17. With dubbing needle pull out any hackle fibers that have been tied down by the tinsel.

18. Select two olive dyed grizzly hackles of the proper size—about two hook gaps. Tie in just in front of the body and make several wraps with each. Tie off and trim.

19. The Finished Fly

MALLARD SPIDER

Hidden back in the antique fly boxes of some of the great old time fly fishermen, you will occasionally find a long-forgotten pattern whose day may have come again.

In the early 1960's many of the old time streamer patterns were neglected when the famous Muddler Minnow streamer fly appeared. Some eventually disappeared from the tackle boxes and the minds of most anglers. One such fly was the Mallard Spider, an old-time Jackson Hole - Yellowstone favorite. The fly was first popularized by Bob Carmichael, a well know fishing guide of the early days of Jackson Hole, along with the help of his good friend, Roy Donnelly, the noted west coast steelhead fly tyer.

This effective streamer pattern was first trolled behind a boat of the guides in the early days on many of the crystal clear lakes which dot the maps of the Jackson Hole - Yellowstone area. One such lake is Lewis, the jewel of Yellowstone and the place I first learned to cast a fly. Lewis Lake is filled with large, finicky brown trout, sprinkled with brookies, and an occasional Mackinaw Lake trout thrown in for some excitement. It can best be described in Bob Carmichael's own words as "gin clear". In thirty feet of icy water, a person could spot dark brown shadows cruising for food, and distinguish almost every small colorful pebble as if you were floating over a giant aquarium. This lake has always been considered one of the most productive brown trout fisheries in the northwest Wyoming, southern Montana, Idaho triangle.

Many of my fondest memories as a child were spent fishing with my grandfather, John Mears. My grandfather was a truly dedicated fly fisherman, and one of his favorite ways to fish was to troll a fly behind a small Penyan wooden boat in Lewis Lake. He liked the relaxed of sitting in the back of the boat with his feet propped up, holding his favorite long willowy split cane Philipson rod as a guide throttled down the motor to a snail's speed. Thus, they would weave in and out of the small intimate coves that dot the ten mile shoreline, and all the while they hoped for a slight breeze to alter the mirror like conditions which made fishing very difficult.

Trolling is a near-forgotten part of fly fishing in our part of the world. Spinning tackle and the deep trolling rigs have completely changed the style of lake fishing in the mountain West. But in the old days, trolling a fly was one of the most effective ways to fish our larger lakes. The skill of an angler was measured in terms of how well he could maneuver a boat, how intimately he knew the lake and how sensitively he was attuned to the feeding cycles of the fish.

My grandfather was an expert in the art of fly trolling. He would direct his guide to swing the boat through a small bay, in a slow circle while the trailing line made a big swing on the shoreward side of the boat. His uncanny ability to control both his line and the boat produced amazing results. Sometimes he would stop and just let the wind push the boat along as the fly gently drifted over the rocks abundantly sprinkled throughout Lewis Lake.

The Mallard Spider was one of my grandfather's favorite trolling flies. He also enjoyed casting this pattern, along the shallow golden pebble bars from the shore of this lake. The Mallard wing feather has an amazing minnow-like appearance, when submerged and has a tendency to "breathe" like a marabou plume. Its unique coloration and its spidery wings had a powerful magic over the will power of cruising fish.

While many fishermen have forgotten the challenge of fly fishing the lakes, we live in a day when crowded rivers and streams will restore the appeal of these deep clear rocky lakes in the wilderness areas where the pressure is almost nonexistent.

If you find yourself attracted to this style of angling in solitude, be sure to include a good supply of Mallard Spiders in your streamer wallet.

MATERIALS:	Mallard Spider
THREAD:	Black monocord.
HOOK:	Mustad 9671, 9672, 3906B
SIZES:	2-10.
TAIL:	Red hackle fibers
BODY:	Yellow floss
RIBBING:	Gold embossed tinsel
UNDERWING:	White or light yellow marabou
HACKLE:	Mallard breast feather pulled back

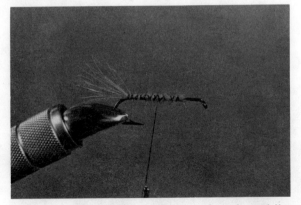

1. Pull out a small clump of red saddle hackle fibers, tie these in approximately one third of the way back from the eye and wrap over the top of the fibers to the bend.

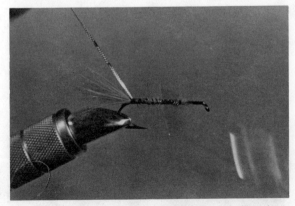

2. Tie in a piece of gold embossed tinsel at the same place and wrap thread over top of it to the bend.

297

3. Tie in a piece of yellow floss.

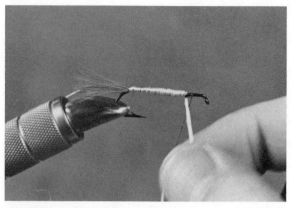

4. Wrap the yellow floss forward. Tie off and trim.

5. Rib the body with close, even spacings.

6. Tie off and trim. Shows the completed body.

7. Pick out a small bunch of dyed marabou, measure for length as in the picture above.

8. Tie in marabou just in front of the body.

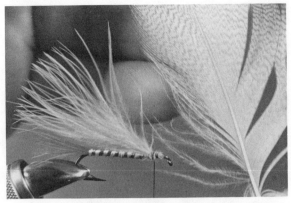

9. Select a mallard breast feather with fibers long enough to extend slightly past the tail.

10. Pull the fibers off the base of the feather and tie in by the base.

11. Trim the excess feather base.

12. Wind the feather around the hook, pulling the fibers back as you wind.

13. Wind forward all the way until there is no more feather left. Tie off and trim.

14. Shows the feather wound forward.

15. Pulling feather fibers backwards, wrap back over them and then forward again. Whip finish and lacquer the head. This is the completed fly.

16. Shows the fly when wet.

THE PLATTE RIVER SPECIAL

This streamer pattern has been around for a long time. It is considered one of the Colorado and Wyoming fishermen's favorites. First developed for the Platte River back in the early 1900's, its origins I am not quite certain, but one thing is for sure, the fly has taken more than its share of large trout. A simple, feathered streamer with the uncanny ability to take large trout in areas where Muddlers, Spuddlers and other streamers have failed to produce.

A particular place that has always been a Platte River streamer favorite spot, is the "Miracle Mile;" a stretch of the Platte River, near Casper Wyoming, which has probably yielded more large trout than any other place in the state of Wyoming. Hard hit these days by hordes of bait fishermen and spin fishermen, the pressure has certainly taken its toll on this stretch of river. Still, the fly fisherman who diligently fishes it with many varieties of the Platte River specials can take large fish. The Platte is rated one of the quality waters of Wyoming. Yet the feather streamer isn't just a Platte River fly. Robbie Garrett of Pinedale, Wyoming, rates it as one of the most effective streamer flies on the slow, tempermental Green River, especially in the fall when the lighter dressed streamers seem to work better. This streamer in the darker patterns is more effective for brown trout. Tied in cream, red, or yellow it has taken its share of rainbows below Boysen Dam in the Wind River Canyon around Thermopolis, Wyoming. This stretch of the tumbling, boulder-strewn river flows through the Wind River Indian Reservation and accounts for large trout and pike every year. It's water conditions change throughout the summer, due to weather and dam fluctuations. The Wind, below Boysen Dam, can get a heavy moss growth, which can make fly fishing very difficult. When water conditions are clear and low, it is still as fine a river as flows through the state. Accessability is terrific as the highway parallels the river in its swing through the canyon. The Platte River Special is best fished upstream, and swung down between the rocks, using either split shot or twiston lead to bring the fly down very quickly along the big boulders of the canyon. Then, swim it or strip it very slowly downstream with the current, looking, of course, for that moment when out of the rocks will come one of the six to eight pound rainbows that do frequent the area.

One gentleman had me tie the Platte River Special in yellow and red with a flourescent orange body. He claimed that it represented chunks of perch that were ground up in the turbines of the Boysen Dam. He fished slightly below the dam in the fast rushing water, and continually took huge glistening rainbows, where most anglers had failed to take even so much as a 6 inch trout.

This Platte River Special also has been an effective streamer in many other areas. You can vary the bodies and feather colors to match your certain area. Many anglers use the Platte as a night fly, tying it in black and orange colors. Realize this streamer is not just a Wyoming pattern, but an effective feathered low water streamer used everywhere. Give it a whirl!

MATERIALS: Platte River Special

THREAD: Black monocord

HOOK: 79580

SIZES: 2-8

RIBBING: Embossed gold tinsel

UNDERBODY: Lead wire

BODY: Brown chenille

WING: Bright yellow cock neck hackle with ginger cock neck hackle

HACKLE: Bright yellow and ginger brown mixed, tied back collar style

1. Tie in end of chenille approximately two-thirds of the way from the bend of the hook to the front. Wrap thread towards the end of the hook then secure in gold-embossed tinsel, tying it down towards the end of the hook.

2. Wrap chenille forward, tapering as shown above. Tapering can be best accomplished by increasing and tightening the wrap as you proceed forward.

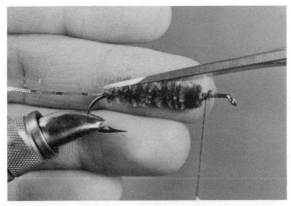

3. With sharp, fine pointed scissors, trim the chenille to accentuate tapering.

4. Wrap the gold embossed tinsel forward ribbing the body as shown above.

5. Select one light and one darker colored feather, melding them together, dark side to light side to form a single wing. If you desire a fuller fly, four feathers can be melded together.

6. The completed wing should appear as above, with the dark side facing you.

7. Repeat the same process to form another wing. Place the wings together with curves facing outward; this will form a v-shaped wing.

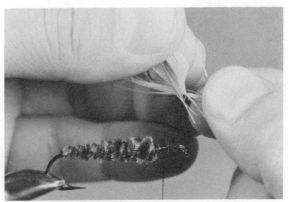

8. Strip the softer hackle away from the vein so that it may be exposed.

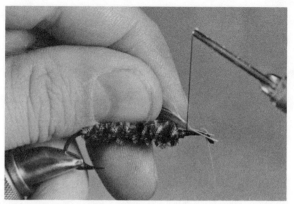

9. Lay the feathered wing on top of the hook and tie down with thread, securing the wing on top of the hook.

10. Wrap forward with thread and touch a drop of lacquer over it securing the wing.

11. Select a soft, dark and light feather, melding together, dark to light, with light side on the inside. Tie in behind the wing and wrap the hackle forward. Three wraps is usually sufficient; then tie the hackle off and whip finish the fly.

12. Completed fly, with V-shaped wing.

13. The Finished Fly.

304

THE MORMON GIRL STREAMER

This particular streamer has always been a favorite of mine. It's a fun pattern which has grown up with the tradition of old Jackson Hole. Well known steelhead tyer Roy Donnelly, with his old friend Bob Carmichael, changed the traditional wet fly pattern to the squirrel tailed popular fly that terrorized the cutthroats of the Jackson Hole country. It resembled the wild honey bees and several other flying critters that frequented the rocky banks of the mighty Snake River.

I will never forget the picture of my grandfather as he used to fish Granny's Bar above Moose, Wyoming. He would drift his Mormon Girl down through deep, blue riffles and slowly inch it back up. Cast after cast. Never moving from the same spot. Hour upon hour, he worked that fly, and never failed to bring home a limit of trout in those days.

The Mormon Girl is one forgotten streamer which could stand some resurrecting. With so much attention being given many of the new sculpin and minnow imitations, one should not forget some of the old, traditional streamer patterns. They are still very effective in many situations. For instance, the Mormon Girl has proved to be a rousing success on some of the more productive lakes.

We offer this fly as something a little bit different...a return to basics. Besides being a fun fly to wrap, we think you might find this fly effective in many areas around the nation. Give it a try. We would like to hear about your experiences with it. This is one pattern which always brings back the memories of the old days of covered wagons, old Winchester rifles, and old cane rods. It too, has earned its place as a part of the old West.

MATERIALS:	Mormon Girl Streamer
THREAD:	Black monocord
HOOK:	Mustad 9672, 79580
SIZES:	4-10
TAIL:	Golden pheasant tippet
RIBBING:	Gold embossed tinsel

BODY: Red floss and yellow chenille

WING: Badger guard hairs

COLLAR: Soft grizzly

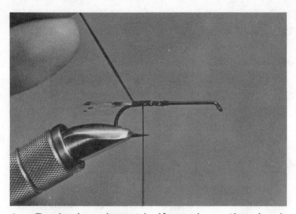

1. Beginning almost halfway down the shank of hook, tie in a small bunch of golden pheasant tippet fibers for a tail. Advance thread forward to where the tail is tied in and tie in red floss for the body.

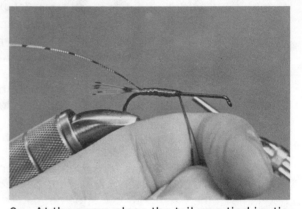

2. At the same place the tail was tied in, tie in embossed gold tinsel for the ribbing, advance thread backwards over the tinsel to the base of the tail and forward again. Wrap the floss forward and tie off.

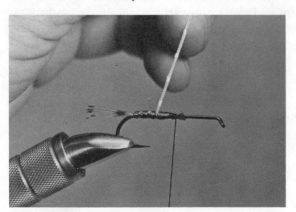

3. Advance the ribbing forward in even spacings, tie off and trim.

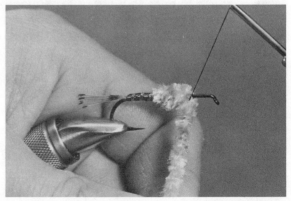

4. Tie in a piece of chenille about 2" long. Wind chenille forward to about one quarter back from the eye of the hook, tie off and trim.

5. Tie in a grizzly hackle a quarter of the way back from the eye of the hook. Advance the thread forward part of the way over the hackle stem. Trim the excess hackle stem.

6. Wrap the grizzly hackle forward four or five wraps, tie off and trim.

7. Shows the grizzly hackle wrapped and trimmed. Notice the proportions here.

8. Clip out a bunch of badger fur. Remove the fur leaving only the guard hairs for a wing.

9. Hold the hair bunch on top of the shank of the hook and tie in. Be sure to make several tight wraps.

10. Trim the hair butts at an angle.

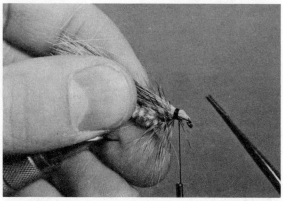

11. Shows the hair butts, trimmed at an angle.

12. Lacquer the hair butts.

13. Wrap the thread evenly forward covering the hair butts and forming a head. Whip finish and lacquer the head.

14. The Finished Fly

THE MATUKA SCULPIN

With a sudden interest in the Matuka Fly in the United States, there have been several new streamer patterns utilizing this style of tie. One of these, of course, is the Matuka Sculpin.

The particular pattern we describe was shown to us by Al Troth of Dillon, Montana. We feel that this new pattern deserves mention as a streamer with excellent potential throughout western waters. A variety of color combinations can be used in order to represent any of the sculpins in your area.

Al considers this fly extremely effective on the Missouri River, one of his favorite rivers during the autumn months. We had a chance to try some smaller, sparsely tied Matuka Sculpins on some of the clear and slower flowing rivers in Northern Wyoming, and there were times when they seemed to be more effective than the standard Muddler pattern.

Al emphasizes that this pattern must be properly weighted in order for it to imitate a sculpin minnow in a natural manner. Sculpins are bottom-huggers and they like to forage in the areas of spring seeps and large pools.

MATERIALS:	Matuka Sculpin
THREAD:	Black monocord
HOOK:	Mustad 9672
SIZES:	2-4
TAIL:	Same as wing
RIBBING:	.008"Gold wire
UNDERBODY:	Tan art foam
BODY:	Cream angora yarn
WING:	4-6 grizzly feathers dyed olive green, then blue dun

COLLAR: Dark deer flank hair dyed dark olive

HEAD: 1 amp lead wire covered with olive art foam then dubbing of dark olive
                   dyed hare's ear spun in a loop

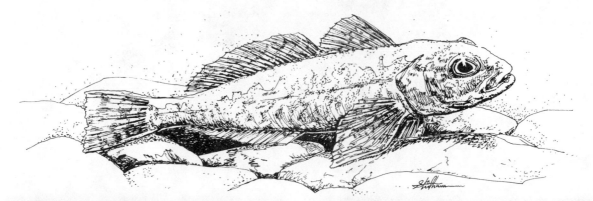

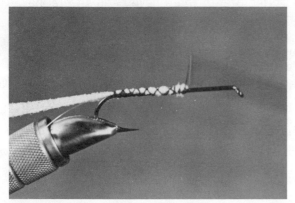

1. Cover hook shank with tying thread, tie in gold wire and art foam for body material.

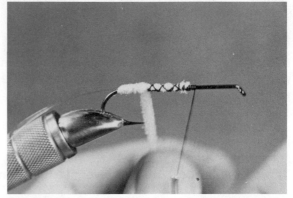

2. Begin wrapping art foam forward.

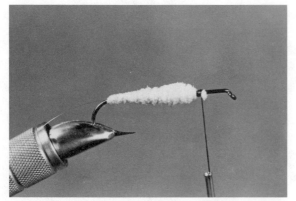

3. Form a tapered underbody with art foam as shown above. Note that the body ends ⅓ back from the eye.

4. Tie in yarn halfway down the shank. Wrap the thread over the yarn to the bend then back to the front.

5. Form a tapered body with angora yarn.

6. Select 4-6 dyed grizzly hackles. These should be webby.

7. Match the feathers up, concave sides together, forming two wings. Then put the two wings together with light sides facing each other.

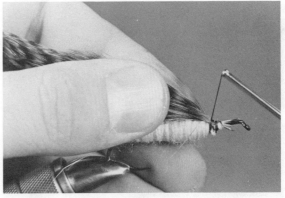

8. Tie in wing feathers.

9. Begin winding gold wire forward. Make three turns at the end to separate the tail.

10. Wind the wire through the hackle wing toward the front, tie off and trim.

11. Make four or five wraps of heavy lead wire to weight the head.

12. Tie in art foam, the strip should be approximately ¼" wide.

13. Wrap the art foam to make a base for the head.

14. Cut a bunch of dyed deer hair for the collar, remove the fuzz and short hairs from the butts.

15. Hold the deer hair on the side of the hook nearest you. Make several loose wraps of thread around the hair.

16. Pull tighter on the third wrap flaring the hair.

17. Trim the flared ends. Repeat the same procedure with another hair bunch on the opposite side.

18. Trim the hair butts. Notice that the tips don't come past the point of the hook.

19. Lacquer the thread and form a dubbing loop, move the thread forward towards the eye of the hook.

20. Place the dubbing into the loop and spin several times to form a thread with dubbing in it.

21. Wrap the dubbing loop forward to the eye.

22. Tie off and trim.

23. Shows the dubbed head.

24. Clip dubbing flat on the bottom.

25. Clip excess dubbing from the top, making a nice tapered head. This head should be flat on the bottom and tapered on the top, with much wider on the sides. See the following figures.

26. Fly from the bottom.

27. Fly from the top.

28. Finished Fly.

PARTRIDGE SCULPIN

Montana seems to be blessed with an abundance of excellent fly tyers and fishing entrepreneurs. Among these, from the thriving town of Missoula, is Frank Johnston. He and Rich Anderson, have formed one of the most complete fly fishing shops in the West, "Streamside Anglers". When not tied down to the store, Frank keeps busy crafting some very ingenious flies. One of these is the Partridge Sculpin.

Frank first tied this fly while fishing in Alaska. Here he ran out of flies and didn't have the materials to tie them. Luckily he came upon a Ptarmigan which had apparently been killed by a fox. He used these beautiful feathers to invent an extremely effective sculpin pattern.

Upon returning to Montana, Frank was so impressed with the pattern that he located some partridge tail feathers which worked very well for the wings and fins. Because these feathers are now nearly impossible to find, hen chicken saddle hackle is being used.

I highly recommend that you add the Partridge Sculpin to your fly box.

MATERIALS:	Partridge Sculpin
THREAD:	Black monocord
HOOK:	79580
SIZES:	2/0-6
RIBBING:	Oval gold tinsel
UNDERBODY:	Lead wire
BODY:	Coarse wool yarn (Lopi)
WING & TAIL:	Partridge (speckled) tail feathers or hen chicken saddle hackle
FINS:	Hen pheasant shoulders, hen saddle tips or grouse shoulder or body feathers
HEAD:	Chocolate brown dyed deer hair

1. Wrap some heavy lead on the rear ⅔ of the hook. Cover this with thread to secure it.

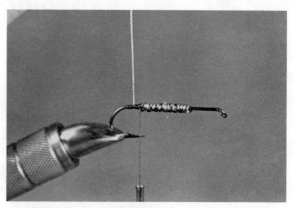

2. Tie off the lead and tie in some gold wire or gold braided oval tinsel at the end of the lead.

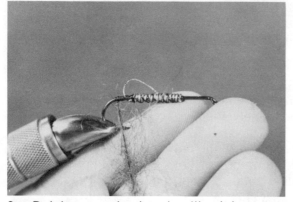

3. Dub in some dyed seal, rolling it between your fingers until it sticks to the thread. An application of tacky wax is recommended for coarser furs such as this.

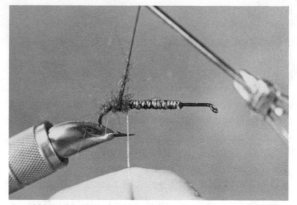

4. Wrap a small amount of seal behind the oval tinsel, as shown above.

5. Continue to dub on more seal and taper the body building it up gradually towards the front of the hook, approximately two-thirds down the hook.

6. Select two to four hen chicken saddle hackles. These should be very webby. Hen chicken saddles are available in a variety of natural colors.

7. Match up the feathers so that the tips are even.

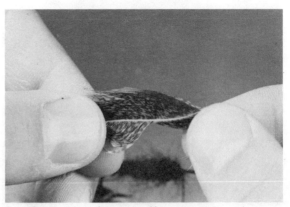

8. Strip the fibers off one side of both feathers starting at the butt for a distance of ¾ of the hook shank length.

9. Tie in the feather wing by the butt. The stripped vein should be along the body.

10. With the point of your scissors, separate the hen pheasant feather at the point where the tinsel protrudes from the body. Notice the position of the left hand.

11. With your right hand wrap the oval tinsel over the feather securing it to the top of the body.

12. Continue evenly wrapping the tinsel forward dividing the wing from back to front. Tie off the tinsel and trim.

13. Tie in a smaller hen chicken saddle hackle or breast feather for a pectoral fin. The length of this should be half the body length and it should curve outward.

14. Repeat the same process on the other side.

15. With the fins firmly in place, lacquer the thread.

16. Cut out a bunch of brown-dyed deer hair. Remove the underfur and small hairs. Measure for length.

17. Hold the deer hair bunch on the side and make several tight wraps to flare the hair.

18. Cut out another bunch of deer hair and prepare as before.

19. Tie this bunch on the other side of the hook with several tight wraps.

20. Bring the tying thread through the hair bunch. Push back with thumb and forefinger to make it compact. Pull back on the hair and whip finish a head.

21. This is the fly before trimming.

22. With your thumb on the bottom and finger on top, compress the hair bunch to the side.

23. With a sharp pair of scissors, trim flat beneath the fly.

24. Trim the top of the fly completely flat also.

25. Trim the sides at an angle. The fly should appear as above.

26. Shows a side view of the Partridge Sculpin.

27. Top view of the Partridge Sculpin.

28. Completed fly in a side view.